Jamaica and the
Sugar Worker Cooperatives

Westview Replica Editions

The concept of Westview Replica Editions is a response to the continuing crisis in academic and informational publishing. Library budgets for books have been severely curtailed. Ever larger portions of general library budgets are being diverted from the purchase of books and used for data banks, computers, micromedia, and other methods of information retrieval. Interlibrary loan structures further reduce the edition sizes required to satisfy the needs of the scholarly community. Economic pressures on the university presses and the few private scholarly publishing companies have severely limited the capacity of the industry to properly serve the academic and research communities. As a result, many manuscripts dealing with important subjects, often representing the highest level of scholarship, are no longer economically viable publishing projects--or, if accepted for publication, are typically subject to lead times ranging from one to three years.

Westview Replica Editions are our practical solution to the problem. We accept a manuscript in camera-ready form, typed according to our specifications, and move it immediately into the production process. As always, the selection criteria include the importance of the subject, the work's contribution to scholarship, and its insight, originality of thought, and excellence of exposition. The responsibility for editing and proofreading lies with the author or sponsoring institution. We prepare chapter headings and display pages, file for copyright, and obtain Library of Congress Cataloging in Publication Data. A detailed manual contains simple instructions for preparing the final typescript, and our editorial staff is always available to answer questions.

The end result is a book printed on acid-free paper and bound in sturdy library-quality soft covers. We manufacture these books ourselves using equipment that does not require a lengthy make-ready process and that allows us to publish first editions of 300 to 600 copies and to reprint even smaller quantities as needed. Thus, we can produce Replica Editions quickly and can keep even very specialized books in print as long as there is a demand for them.

About the Book and Author

Jamaica and the Sugar Worker Cooperatives:
The Politics of Reform
Carl Henry Feuer

Between 1974 and 1977, as part of a wider attempt by Prime Minister Michael Manley's regime to carry out a democratic reformist strategy of development, the three largest sugar estates in Jamaica were converted into worker-managed farms. Within a few years, however, the cooperative program was in disarray as the farms faced economic setbacks and as political conflicts developed among the sugar workers, local authorities, and the government.

Drawing on his extensive field research in Jamaica, Dr. Feuer traces the development and decline of the cooperative system and discusses the implications for the possibility of democratic reform. In his view, the logic of the cooperativization process conflicted with the priorities of the middle class, which continued to dominate the Jamaican economy. As a result, the reforms were never firmly rooted in a political coalition with the resources to carry them out. In light of the Jamaican experience, Dr. Feuer considers such questions as: What are the obstacles a nonrevolutionary regime is likely to face in an effort to help the poor? How feasible is it to mobilize the requisite political and administrative resources and neutralize the inherent constraints to reform?

Carl Henry Feuer is assistant professor of political science at Cortland College, State University of New York.

Jamaica and the
Sugar Worker Cooperatives
The Politics of Reform

Carl Henry Feuer

Westview Press / Boulder and London

To My Parents,
Leo Feuer and Fay E. Feuer

 The paper used in this publication meets the minimum requirements of the American National Standard for Permanence of Paper for Printed Library Materials Z30.48-1984.

A Westview Replica Edition

Published in 1984 in the United States of America by
    Westview Press, Inc.
    5500 Central Avenue
    Boulder, Colorado 80301
    Frederick A. Praeger, Publisher

Library of Congress Cataloging in Publication Data
Feuer, Carl Henry
    Jamaica and the sugar worker cooperatives.
    (A Westview replica edition)
    1. Agriculture, Cooperative--Jamaica. 2. Sugar
workers--Jamaica. 3. Sugar trade--Jamaica. I. Title.
HD1486.J25F48 1984   334'.683'097292   84-15202
ISBN 0-86531-897-2

Printed and bound in the United States of America

10 9 8 7 6 5 4 3 2

Contents

Tables and Figures

Currency Conversion

Until 1969, Jamaica's unit of currency was the Jamaican pound. Subsequently it was the dollar. In the text all currency figures pertaining to Jamaica are given in Jamaican dollars, except for the pre-independence period when I follow Jamaican usage and quote figures in pounds, shillings and pence. The Jamaican dollar depreciated greatly in the 1970s, falling from U.S. $1.20 in 1969 to U.S. $1.10 in 1976 and then to a rate of exchange in 1979 of Ja. $1.00 = U.S. $0.57.

Acknowledgments

Many people contributed to this book. Robin Lee Whittlesey has lived with it as long as I have. Without her emotional support, it would have remained just a good thought. Many of the ideas and perspectives embodied here also owe their origin to her. And what if she had never interested me in Jamaica in the first place and done much of the initial spade work?

Norman Thomas Uphoff also deserves an award for his staying power. His influence occurs throughout. His constant encouragement and positive reinforcement were essential in getting the neophyte field worker over the inevitable humps of working in a strange country. Both Norman and Robin contributed an immense amount of time and effort toward making me a writer and this work readable.

Though less intensive, the contributions of many Jamaicans were essential. First and foremost were the sugar workers and others I encountered in Vere, particularly those at Morelands and Springfield cooperative farms. With unfailing courtesy and good humor, they put up with much over long months of field work. It is not exactly usual to have to confront a peripatetic, bearded, white American wherever you turn. There was no privacy for them, not even in the midst of the cane fields during the harvest; nor at meetings of the management committees, which were unfailingly open to my inspection. I will not try to list individually all the members of the sugar worker cooperatives or their staffs who were particularly informative and helpful. There were many. A special word of thanks, however, must be extended to Trevor Coleman, education officer with the cooperatives, and the staff of the Social Action Centre, in particular, Horace Levy, Joe Owens and Jim Schecher. Without their friendship and assistance it is unlikely this research could have ever been started, much less completed.

And then there were the Maxwell, Murray, Parchment, Rigbye and Plunkett families, among others--friends as

well as "informants" about Jamaican society (even if
they weren't always aware they were "informants"). John
Maxwell, Myrtle Murray and George Murray were particularly supportive. My thanks also to Ralph Robinson who
provided detailed information about his own cane farm,
making possible the comparative information contained in
Chapter 9.

The Organization of American States provided much
needed funding. More than that, and over and above the
call of duty, Pat Healy and his staff in Jamaica were
tremendous. During the period when I was first embarking
on this voyage in Jamaica, the Institute of Social and
Economic Research and, in particular, Eddie Greene, also
assisted by naming me a visiting research fellow. The
staffs of many libraries in Jamaica were always cour-
teous and helpful. There were very few libraries I did
not explore for their "buried treasures."

Bud Kenworthy's friendship and incisive comments
have been valuable throughout this project. My thanks
also to Don Freebairn and Ted Lowi for their support
and intellectual nourishment, and to Evelyne Huber
Stephens and John Stephens for their comments.

Gert Fitzpatrick has been wonderful, not only because she is an extraordinary typist, but also for her
unfailing patience and efforts above and beyond the call
of duty. The book is also much improved because of her
assistance with editing.

None of the above mentioned individuals or organizations are responsible for any errors, misjudgments
or faulty analysis in what follows.

Carl Henry Feuer

1
Underdevelopment and Reform: The Case of Jamaica

The year 1962 was a momentous one for the small
island-state of Jamaica. After over three centuries of
colonial control, Jamaica finally achieved its political independence. The following ten years, however, did
not fulfill the needs, expectations or dreams of most
Jamaicans. By 1972, ten years after decolonization, it
was clear that the development process was moving in
reverse. Ten years of independence had contributed to a
deepening of the contradictions associated with underdevelopment. As a result, Jamaica was in crisis.

Fundamental to this crisis were the extremes of
poverty and prosperity that existed, often side by side.
In 1972 over half the labor force was either unemployed
or earning less than $10 per week.[1] The thousands more
who had dropped out of the labor force because of frus-
tration and alienation were not even recorded. Not
surprisingly, income in Jamaica was grossly maldistributed. The upper 10 percent of households received almost half of all income, while the bottom two-thirds
were left with only 19 percent of the total.[2]

In rural Jamaica over three-quarters of all farms
were under five acres. Worse, their cultivated area was
often of marginal quality, most commonly mountainous
and badly eroded; and each farm was frequently composed
of widely separated parcels. At the other extreme, less
than three hundred farms, 0.2 percent of the total, controlled almost 50 percent of the total farm land, over
600,000 acres of the best agricultural land in Jamaica.[3]

This extreme poverty and inequality in the early
1970s was all the more outrageous because it had been
preceded by twenty years of economic growth. The growth
in real production between 1950 and 1971 was 6.8 percent per annum and there was a 4 percent annual increase
in per capita incomes. But this growth benefited only
the few.[4] Rather than development, it was associated
with a heightening of socioeconomic problems.

For one thing, agriculture continued to stagnate.
This resulted in high levels of food imports, high

1

rates of rural to urban migration and a pattern of low
rural productivity.[5] Second, the growth was linked to
capital-intensive, consumption-oriented and import-
dependent patterns in industry. Both here and in agriculture, technological dualism was reinforced, with en-
claves of high technology existing side by side with
traditional methods. Partly as a result, unemployment
rose rapidly, from an estimated 14 percent in the early
1960s to 23 percent in 1972.[6] Finally, Jamaica's economy became more vulnerable and financially unsound in
the decade after independence. There were increasing
deficits on current account, chronic trade deficits and
increasing external dependence.

The rapid accumulation of power in Jamaica by
foreign corporations contributed to the country's political and economic difficulties. Bauxite-alumina, the
major industry in terms of capital investment, production, the generation of foreign exchange, and government revenues, was totally foreign-owned in 1972. The
sugar industry, the largest employer and second leading
exporter, was two-thirds foreign-owned, a twentieth
century legacy of three hundred years of plantation economics.[7] Tourism, rapidly overtaking sugar as a foreign
exchange earner, was also foreign dominated. Over 50
percent of hotel capacity was in the hands of overseas
investors by the late 1960s.[8] In addition, in the early
1970s, majority shares in about one-quarter of the
major corporations listed on the local securities exchange were foreign-owned; many of the others utilized
significant inputs of foreign capital and technology,
as well as expatriate top and middle managers.[9]

Jamaica's racist and elitist social structure
added to social tensions. The elite was composed primarily of a racially exclusive, European-oriented,
heavily intermarried group of families. Twenty-one family groups--all Jewish, Syrian, Chinese or Jamaica
white--controlled forty-one, or most, of the largest
companies, in a maze of interlocking directorates.[10]
Holding over half the directorships and almost three-
quarters of the chairperson positions in these forty-
one companies, these family groups thus dominated almost every sector of the economy not already under foreign control. Only six of the 219 directors of these
forty-one major companies were black, although this
racial grouping incorporated 75 percent of the Jamaican
population.[11]

The socioeconomic problems afflicting Jamaica were
perhaps borne most heavily by the young. Eighty-five
percent of those under 15 years of age were no longer
in school or youth camps.[12] With jobs scarce, it was
not surprising that 85,000 youths between 14 and 24
years old were officially classified as unemployed,
with an unemployment rate among them of 40 percent.[13]
The social problems associated with this were immense

and growing. Over 50 percent of all those convicted of
crimes and sent to prison were under 25.[14] Furthermore,
the young were largely excluded from the political system. While the minimum voting age was 21, in fact no one
under 23 voted in the 1972 election since the electoral
lists were closed in 1969.

Young people were active participants in the series
of riots and militant demonstrations that rocked Jamaica
in the late 1960s. They were increasingly attracted,
moreover, to the rebellious religion of Rastafarianism
and to the black power, revolutionary-nationalist militance of people like Walter Rodney. This represented a
particularly dangerous threat to the established
order. [15]

MICHAEL MANLEY AND REFORM

Elected prime minister in 1972, Michael Manley
moved to respond to the economic, social and political
crisis gripping Jamaica. Within a few years, his govern-
ment:purchased control of the bus, utility and tele-
phone monopolies from their foreign owners; sharply increased taxes on the bauxite-alumina industry; expanded
the state role in sugar manufacturing, tourism and banking; established a state company to take over importa-
tion of grains and other basic food products; set up a
National Housing Trust which became the main source of
housing finance and development; initiated a national
program to eliminate illiteracy; adopted a land reform
program to provide short-term, supplemental tenancies
for small farmers on government-leased or owned land;
abolished all secondary school tuition fees and made
tertiary education free; established a minimum wage;
legislated maternity leave with pay; and initiated a
number of measures to increase the availability of
basic foods for the masses. It was an extensive program
of reform carried out within the context of Jamaica's
democratic political order.

One of the most significant reforms of the Manley
period was the establishment, between 1974 and 1976, of
twenty-three sugar worker cooperatives. Where once the
cane cutters, irrigation workers, laborers and others
were chattel and then wage slaves on foreign-owned estates, they were now to be collectively in control of
their own cane farms.

The sugar cooperativization program epitomized the
reformist ideals of the Manley regime. It aimed at providing direct and palpable benefits to dispossessed
members of the society; exemplified clearly the government's claims to be moving toward a more just and egal-
itarian order; focused on agriculture and, in particular, on that aspect of the rural economy that was most
closely identified with colonialism and foreign exploi-

tation; and aimed at structural changes, not just redistribution. As Michael Manley himself remarked in one
speech to sugar workers: "When I go to every corner of
Jamaica I hold you up as my chief example of what we
are trying to do."[16]

Within a short time, however, the sugar worker cooperatives were in disarray. Real incomes were declining. Production levels and trends were poor. The cooperatives were deeply in debt. Labor indiscipline was
growing. The general membership was losing interest and
no longer attending general meetings. And there was
substantial conflict concerning the nature and role of
the cooperatives, both among the workers themselves and
between the workers and other local strata.

The disarray extended beyond the government's
sugar policy. The growth in unemployment during the
1960s had been one of Manley's key issues, but by the
late 1970s it had risen even further, to over 30 percent. A high rate of inflation, reaching 50 percent in
1978, and a chronic scarcity of basic products were
other burdens on grass-roots supporters of reform.
Working-class disenchantment increased as real incomes
started to decline after a number of annual increases.

Macroeconomic indicators also provided evidence of
the disarray in the government's program. Declines in
the gross national product helped erode the legitimacy
of the reform process, while budget deficits of over
$700 million in the late 1970s (40 percent of expendi-
ture) further destabilized the economy. The country's
foreign debt and external accounts deteriorated sharply.
Between 1972 and 1979, gross external debt increased
fivefold, and by the end of 1979 net foreign reserves
totaled minus $759 million.

Disarray also characterized the society and politics. In the 1977-1979 period, the government seemed to
backpedal on its reformist program. Shortly after con-
demning attempts by the IMF to impose its will on
Jamaica, Manley agreed to one of its stringent austerity programs. Soon thereafter leftists were forced from
high posts in Manley's own party, the People's National
Party (PNP). Polls meanwhile showed a steady increase
in public support for the opposition party, the conservative Jamaica Labour Party (JLP). Between October 1976
and September 1979, PNP support declined from 48 percent to 37 percent, while support for the JLP among the
populace increased by the same amount.[17] The general
elections held in 1980 confirmed this trend, with the
JLP sweeping 58 percent of the vote and 51 of 60
parliamentary seats.

ISSUES RAISED BY THE JAMAICAN CASE

The issues raised by the Jamaican case are of fun-

damental importance. The need for social and economic
change has been and continues to be essential to the
process of development. The democratic reform model,
many have said, offers a more pragmatic, less conflictual, more open and more feasible route to such change
than the revolutionary approach. At the grass roots,
reformist policies of land distribution, cooperativization, expanded education and health services, and the
like seem manifestly beneficial to those people affected by them. They provide increased resources and increased access to resources, or so it seems. At the
same time, constitutional mechanisms and democratic
forms are enhanced.

Yet the historical record has not been favorable.
Has there been, in most cases, any great mobilization
for development on the basis of such policies? Is reform a false ideal, providing only hopes and limited
benefits for the poor majority? In some cases there
have even been detrimental results, with the reforms
failing or the reformers being replaced by authoritarian regimes.[18]

The fundamental issue, one that is central to the
Jamaican case, as well as others like it, is whether a
middle-class party of reform can carry out the political
and administrative tasks essential to the implementation of radical change at the grass roots. Can it mobilize the requisite resources at the international,
national and local levels? Can it neutralize the inherent constraints to reform? Does it have "staying power":
a commitment and realistic capability to allocate resources and support to the reform process during the
sometimes lengthy transition period? These are the questions posed in this case study of the Jamaican experience between 1972 and 1980, in particular its attempt
to radically restructure social and economic relations
in the cane belt.

This is a study of the reform process as it was
reflected in the attempt to establish sugar worker cooperatives. Its focus is at the grass roots. Major field
work was conducted at one of the estates which was
transformed into worker cooperatives. What happened
there, however, is described and analyzed, as it must
be, in the context of national and international dynamics. The study seeks to ascertain the factors that
contribute to the success or failure of such a process
of reform.

What is most striking about the reform process in
Jamaica was the failure of the regime to understand the
nature of the radical changes upon which it had embarked. The political leadership neither allocated nor
mobilized the requisite political and administrative
resources to implement this reform. Political momentum
and mobilization more or less halted just at the time
when the cooperatives were starting and needing con-

siderable support. As a result, fundamental economic difficulties were systematically ignored; grass-roots mobilization was repressed; social relations within the cooperatives were allowed to deteriorate; education was ignored. And then, within two years, the government all but certified the cooperatives as a failure.

How is this possible? How is it possible that a regime could mobilize the will and power to adopt a significant land reform, yet systematically restrict the allocation of political and administrative resources to carry it out? How is it possible that the most successful rural worker mobilization in almost forty years, if not the most successful in all of Jamaican history, could so easily be bureaucratized and depoliticized?

The answer lies primarily in the nature of the regime--its political ties, commitments and resource base. These to a large degree helped to determine how this regime responded to the forces set in motion by its own program of reform.

This study analyzes the political and administrative forces that constrain the reform process, when carried out under the auspices of middle-class parties. The cooperativization process in Jamaica was indeed complex, encompassing a political-economic-social dynamic which no regime could completely predict or control. What any regime can control, however, are its political commitments and the way it responds to the inevitable twists and turns, ups and downs, of a process of grass-roots change. This study raises questions about the political-economic capacity of the middle strata, encapsulated within a reformist coalition, to respond to those "twists and turns" in ways that carry forward the process of reform.

In the Jamaican case, the logic of the cooperativization process, and the process of grass-roots reform in general, conflicted with the priorities of the middle strata which attempted to carry it out. The reforms were not firmly rooted in a political coalition with the resources to carry them forward. Good intentions and liberal ideals could not substitute for political will and political capacity. Too much political power was in the hands of those who were unwilling to use it actively to promote democratic reform.[19]

The bureaucracy remained conservative, with all ministries, in particular agriculture, controlled by traditional PNP moderate-conservatives. Political influence within parliament, the cabinet and in the party also remained by and large skewed toward the right, toward those middle-class elements which had always dominated the PNP and were most resistant to reform.

How was this reflected in the reform process? At the local level three things stood out. First, there were substantial ties and sympathy within the government for the agrarian middle bourgeoisie in the rural areas. This group encompassed not only the traditional overseers and other members of the estate staff, but also large cane farmers who felt threatened by the co-operatives. As a result, many members of the staff--discredited in the eyes of the workers--retained their positions and power within the cooperatives and managerial concerns early gained precedence over mobilization needs.

Second, there was opposition within the government to the existence of any independent political force among the workers. This intolerance extended to the mass movement, led by the left, which developed in support of the cooperatives and which was closest to the sugar workers, their needs and the needs of the cooperatives. Even though the leaders of this movement supported the democratic reforms being formulated in Jamaica, they were forced out and the sugar workers' organization was weakened.

Third, practically from the moment the cooperatives began operations they were pressed to maximize production and emphasize economic factors. While important, this not only flew in the face of certain microeconomic realities, but involved a systematic neglect of crucial political and social needs at the grass roots. As a result, neither the social relations within the cooperatives, nor the basic structures of production were altered enough to make a difference in the perceptions and attitudes of most workers.

The class contradictions embedded within the political economy of reform in Jamaica were an outgrowth of the attempt by a middle-class dominated party of reform to implement structural changes beneficial to rural workers, in a Third World context of economic scarcity and external dependence. The dynamics of the Jamaican case followed from these contradictions between the political base and orientations of the reformers and the nature of the grass-roots reforms. These contradictions by no means determined any result, but they provided the parameters within which an unfavorable outcome was likely. This study attempts to trace this interaction of choice and constraint, as it operated between the macrolevel and the grass roots, in an effort to explore and analyze the disarray which developed quickly within the reform process.

There is no attempt here to make empirical generalizations that cannot be justified on the basis of only a single case. Still, the democratic reform model is broadly applicable to a class of cases, of which the Jamaican experience between 1972 and 1980 is one. The process and responses described and analyzed in this case are, thus, suggestive of those that might be expected in other instances of democratic reform.

A JAMAICAN CASE STUDY: METHODOLOGY

The data for this study were collected in a variety of ways, First, conventional historical and contemporary materials dealing with Jamaican political economy, especially those relating to the 1972-1980 period, were consulted. These proved inadequate as a means for understanding the process of reform. They provided precious little empirical detail about sociopolitical relations and about what was actually happening at the grass roots in the course of the reform process. These data were thus supplemented by three other sources of research. The primary field research method was participant-observation. In addition, a number of unstructured interviews were conducted at both the local and national levels with individuals involved in the cooperativization process. Finally, the production and other records of the cooperatives were consulted in order to gather economic data.

Historical and Written Material

During my five-year residence in Jamaica, I collected extensive materials on the reform process as it unfolded. These were collected on a daily basis: reading newspapers, talking to people, observing what was happening, and collecting statistical and other data as they were reported in official reports and documents.
In addition, the following periodicals were systematically reviewed: Cane Farmers Association Annual Reports, Daily Gleaner, Daily News, Economic Report - Jamaica, Land Room, Socialism!, Sugar Industry Authority Annual Reports, Sugar Industry Research Institute Annual Reports, SWCC News, WISCo News, Workers Time, West Indies Sugar Company Annual Reports.
The social science and agricultural collections of the following institutions were also consulted: Institute of Jamaica, Institute for Social and Economic Research, Ministry of Agriculture, Sugar Industry Authority, Sugar Industry Research Institute, University of the West Indies (Mona). Finally, the extensive materials held by the Social Action Centre, which assisted in organizing the cooperatives, were consulted.

Participant-Observation

During 1978-1979 I lived in Lionel Town in the Vere region of the Parish of Clarendon. Lionel Town is the hub of Monymusk Estate. This sugar estate had earlier been transformed into eight cooperative cane farms and one estate-level secondary cooperative. The factory producing sugar from the cooperatives' cane had been

purchased by the government, but was not transformed into a cooperative.

My field research concentrated on two of the farm-
level cooperatives, Morelands and Springfield, and on
the estate cooperative. The period in the field encompassed a full crop cycle, from planting the cane to
reaping it. In the fall and early winter the field work
was concentrated on Morelands Cooperative, which borders
Lionel Town. This was the pilot cooperative and thus had
been operational for one year longer than the other cooperatives at Monymusk. In the late winter and early
spring, I transferred the main portion of my field research to Springfield Cooperative, about ten miles west
of Lionel Town (roughly one hour by bicycle). Field work
was also conducted at the estate cooperative which had
its office in Lionel Town.

At both cooperative farms my procedure was the
same. After receiving formal permission from the managing committee and the general membership, I became a
daily (and at times, nightly) visitor to the farm. Tra-
versing the fields and the compound by foot and by bicycle, I observed activities; talked to workers and
staff, using an informal and unstructured procedure;
attended all committee meetings and general membership
meetings; attended education sessions; worked with the
cane cutters on occasion.

I became a regular fixture at the farm, in most
cases meeting the workers and staff in the fields, at
the farm office, at their homes or at the local rum bar.
I kept a daily journal to record conversations, observations, events and thoughts.

A similar though less intensive procedure was
adopted with respect to the estate cooperative. This was
facilitated by the fact that there were fewer participants at this level, mainly the eleven members of the
Board of Management and the estate staff. I attended the
biweekly board meetings, attended the irregular general
meetings, interviewed (using both formal and informal
methods) board members and members of the staff, and
generally "hung out."

Finally, my residence in Lionel Town for nine
months, and in Jamaica for five years, provided additional opportunities to attempt to learn about the cooperatives and Jamaican politics. Numerous acquaintances
became, in effect, "informants."

Interviews

In addition to the interviews mentioned above, unstructured formal interviews were held at the local
level with politicians, sugar industry officials, staff
members of the cooperatives, union officials, cane farmers, and local cooperative leaders. At the national

level, formal interviews were held with officials from
the government, the sugar industry, the Cane Farmers
Association, the United Sugar Workers Cooperative Council, the Sugar Manufacturers Corporation, the Ministry
of Agriculture, the Department of Cooperatives, the
Frome Monymusk Land Company and the Social Action
Centre.

Farm Records

To the extent possible I used the economic and
historical record available at the cooperative farms
and the estate. Extensive cultivation records for the
entire estate and for individual farms were available
at the estate cultivation office. Where there were gaps,
the data files held at the Sugar Industry Research Institute were also consulted. Other farm records such as
daily cutting totals, use of outside labor and work
schedules were obtained at the farm level. Income data
for individual cooperative members were collected from
the estate National Insurance files. Financial information was gathered at the estate cooperative as well.
This included comprehensive month-by-month and annual
data for all agricultural categories, as well as financial reports for each cooperative farm and for the estate as a whole. Some income and production data were
also gathered at a large private cane farm in the area,
for comparative purposes. Finally, the minutes of all
committees and general meetings at Morelands, Springfield and the Monymusk estate cooperatives were reviewed.

OUTLINE OF PRESENTATION

Following this introduction, Chapter 2 provides
background on the sugar industry in Jamaica. In particular, it details the social, political and economic
difficulties which precipitated the industry's decline
after 1960 and which structured the reformist initiatives of the Manley government. Chapters 3 and 4 begin
the narrative on the sugar worker cooperatives, describ-
ing the government's early plans and the conflicts
these engendered with the sugar workers. One of the main
themes of these two chapters is the mobilization of the
workers which led to the rapid establishment of the cooperatives. Chapter 5 outlines the organization and
operations of the new cooperatives. In Chapters 6 and
7, I describe the sociopolitical dynamics of the cooperatives at the grass roots as these unfolded during
the first three years of operations. Particular attention is paid to the attempts to depoliticize and de-
mobilize the workers and how this impeded the coopera-

tives' functioning. Intracooperative social conflicts
are also described.. The following two chapters analyze
economic outcomes--how both the workers and the farm
enterprises fared. Considerable attention is paid to
putting these economic results into perspective, utiliz-
ing comparative and historical data. Finally, in Chapter 10, the evidence from this case study is summarized
and interpreted, and my conclusions are presented.

NOTES

    1. Jamaica, Department of Statistics, Labour Force (Kingston:
Government Printer, 1973).
    2. E. Ahiram, "Income Distribution in Jamaica, 1958," Social
and Economic Studies 13(September 1964), p. 337. The share accruing
to the upper income households was probably underestimated since it
did not incorporate the distribution of income in kind--perqui-
sites, undistributed corporate profits, receipts from capital
transactions--which disproportionately went to these households,
and outweighed subsistence food production of farmers which also
was not included.
    3. Jamaica, Department of Statistics, Agricultural Census Unit,
Census of Agriculture, 1968-69 (Kingston, various years). Also see
David T. Edwards, An Economic Study of Small Farming in Jamaica
(Kingston: Institute of Social and Economic Research, 1961), for a
socioeconomic description of small farming in Jamaica.
    4. Owen Jefferson, The Post-War Economic Development of
Jamaica (Kingston: Institute of Social and Economic Research,
1972), p. 45; Jamaica, Department of Statistics, National Income
and Production 1974 (Kingston: Government Printer, 1975).
    5. Jefferson, p. 281. Average labor productivity in agricul-
ture was only one-fifth what it was in the rest of the economy.
    6. Jefferson, p. 30.
    7. See Chapter 2.
    8. Jefferson, p. 178.
    9. Stanley Reid, "An Introductory Approach to the Concentra-
tion of Power in the Jamaican Corporate Economy and Notes on Its
Origin," in Essays on Power and Change in Jamaica, eds. Carl Stone
and Aggrey Brown (Kingston: Jamaica Publishing House, 1977), p. 28.
    10. Reid, p. 28. "Jamaica white" refers to Jamaicans of Euro-
pean ancestry, but occasionally with some admixture of African
heritage.
    11. Ibid.
    12. Jamaica, National Planning Agency, Economic and Social
Survey 1973 (Kingston, 1974), p. 190.
    13. Labour Force, p. 26.
    14, Economic and Social Survey 1973, p. 190.
    15. Rodney was a West Indian intellectual and political acti-
vist who taught in Jamaica in the 1960s.
    16. Michael Manley, speech to sugar cooperatives, Bernard
Lodge Estate, December 16, 1975, mimeo.
    17. Norman Girvan, Richard Bernal and Wesley Hughes, "The IMF

12

and the Third World: The Case of Jamaica, 1974-80," Development Dialogue (1980).

18. The Guatemalan coup in 1954 is one example; the Chilean coup another.

19. A useful model for dealing with concepts such as political resources, political will and political capacity is described in Warren Ilchman and Norman T. Uphoff, The Political Economy of Change (Berkeley: University of California Press, 1971).

2
The Sweet and the Sour: Sugar and Jamaica in the Twentieth Century

> "Who planted the cane?" said a slave to me
> one day, when I checked him for [stealing]
> a lump of sugar. "Who nourished its growth?
> Was it not the poor Negro? Negro man work
> all day in the hot sun; he toil through mud
> and rain. He have hunger and wet all day,
> cold all night, yet he plant the cane, he
> watch over him, he cut him down, carry him
> to the mill, he make sugar. Shall Buckra
> man, who do nothing, eat all, and poor
> Negro man, who do all dem tings, starve?"[1]

The cultivation of cane and its processing into
sugar was introduced in Jamaica around the beginning of
the eighteenth century. This agro-industry originated
in the ill-fated marriage of African labor, British
capital and European markets. Though destined to deteriorate, the marriage was quite prosperous for one hundred years; Jamaica became England's most prized possession during the eighteenth century. It was a "prosperity," however, which did not filter down to the
enslaved working class.

In the nineteenth century, the industry's fortunes
turned sour. Production declined steadily as the plantations were unable to cope with the complex of problems which confronted them. These ranged from colonialism to neo-feudal production relations.

Sugar received a new lease on life during the
first half of the twentieth century when the reorganization, modernization and growth of the sugar industry
dominated the landscape of Jamaica. The most significant aspect of this transformation was the rise of
foreign capital to a position of prominence within the
industry and society. The foreign multinational corporations could not, however, completely supplant either
the Jamaican plantocracy, which still retained political and social power into and through the twentieth

13

century, or the semicapitalist system of social relations which they inherited. But, to be sure, they did
sharply increase the level of foreign exploitation.

Hence, although production increased between 1930
and the 1960s, it engendered only a superficial prosperity. In fact, it camouflaged a number of fundamental
contradictions which were undercutting the profitability and social value of the industry. These contradictions were of three sorts: internal contradictions,
relating to the accumulation of technological deficien-
cies and microeconomic problems; social contradictions,
relating to the class antagonism and conflict between
the workers and the owners of capital; and national
contradictions, relating to the conflict between foreign capital and the national interest.

These contradictions were central to the problems
the industry experienced starting in the 1960s, when it
again began to stagnate and decline. They were in fact
exacerbated by this decline, and became open wounds in
Jamaican society. As a result, political and social in-
stability increased. One of the central political
issues of the late 1960s and early 1970s was how to
heal these wounds. Another issue was how to fashion a
viable future, if any, for the sugar industry, the
island's largest employer and second leading foreign
exchange earner. These issues were still unresolved
when Michael Manley was elected prime minister in 1972,
and provided the essential background for the reformist
policy initiatives of his government in this area.

ESTABLISHING THE FRAMEWORK FOR GROWTH

As mentioned above, the main factor contributing
to the revival and transformation of the sugar industry
in the twentieth century was the reorganization and
strengthening of the capitalist element within the industry. This involved two factors: the increasing pre-
dominance of foreign capital, and an immense movement
toward concentration of ownership and centralization of
activity.

During the first quarter of the century, the modernization of the industry was carried forward primarily on the basis of local capital, privately held.
Out of thirty-nine existing estates in 1930, only three
were foreign-owned, and only six were corporate-owned.[2]
Seven years later, however, British multinational Tate
and Lyle purchased twenty-five farms in Jamaica.[3] It
also built Frome sugar factory, the largest on the
island, in 1938. As a result, by the 1940s, Tate and
Lyle had clearly established itself as the dominant
force in the Jamaican sugar industry.

Foreign capital moved further to restructure the
industry and solidify its control through the amalgama-

tion and centralization of factory operations (Table
2.1) and the establishment of immense estates or factory-farms (Table 2.2). Between 1930 and 1943-1944,
average factory output quadrupled and the average size
of a sugar estate rose to over eight thousand acres.

In addition, the planting of new cane varieties,
increased usage of chemical fertilization, the introduction of the internal combustion engine, and the increased use of modern factory equipment transformed
operations within the industry.[4] This transformation
helped increase cane yields from 18 tons of cane per
acre on the large estates in 1927 to over 27 tons per
acre in the 1939-1943 period.[5]

GROWTH PHASE

By the end of World War II, the political, organizational, infrastructural and technological foundation
for growth had thus been laid. The foreign capitalists
and their local allies were not to be disappointed. Between the early 1940s and the early 1960s, production
and exports increased at an average annual rate of
around 10 percent. Revenues from sugar sales increased
at the phenomenal rate of nearly 50 percent per year
(Table 2.3).

The rapid growth of cane and sugar production was
manifest as well at the grass roots. The economic geography of large regions was substantially transformed.
Nowhere was this more true than in the Vere area of the
Parish of Clarendon during the post-war period. A traditional cane area, the Vere region had been largely
replanted with banana trees prior to Tate and Lyle's
involvement. Subsequently it became the most concentrated area of cane production islandwide, going from
13,000 acres planted in cane in 1941 to 37,000 acres
just twenty years later. Roughly half of all this land,
and almost 40 percent of all the land in Vere, was
owned by Tate and Lyle. It also controlled the major
sugar factory complex, Monymusk, built in 1949, and the
shipping facilities.[6]

This dynamic growth temporarily reversed traditional migration patterns in which Jamaicans characteristically _fled_ the lowland sugar areas, either to become small farmers in the mountainous interior, or for
a better life abroad or in Kingston. Starting in the
1930s, the expansion and rationalization of sugar production began to draw poor peasants and landless workers back to the cane fields. As a result, the population of Vere more than doubled during this period,
while that of the rest of the whole Parish increased by
only ten percent. The rate of growth experienced by
Vere during this period was even greater than that of
the Kingston metropolitan area.[7]

TABLE 2.1
Sugar Factories and Output, 1889 to 1944

Year	Number of Factories	Average Output (tons)[a]
1890	162	149
1900	111	187
1910	74	288
1920	66	561
1930	39	1,572
1944	26	5,842

Source: Eisner, p. 302; Jamaica, Sugar Industry Commission, Robert B. Barker, Chairman, Report of the Sugar Industry Commission, 1944-45 (Kingston, 1945), pp. 14-15 (subsequently to be referred to as Barker Report); George Cumper, "Labour Demand and Supply in the Jamaican Sugar Industry, 1830-1950," Social and Economic Studies 2(1954), p. 74.

[a]Except for 1944, the figures represent three-year averages.

TABLE 2.2
Sugar Estates in Jamaica, 1930-1943[a]

Year	Number of Estates	Total Acreage	Average Size (acres)
1930	39	25,779	661
1943	27	225,942	8,368

Source: Eisner, p. 203; Barker Report, p. 23.

[a]Estate is the traditional term in Jamaica for the factory-farm complex which both grows and processes cane.

TABLE 2.3
Basic Statistics on the Jamaican Sugar Industry,
1939-1943 and 1959-1963

	1939-1943 Annual Average	1959-1963 Annual Average
Sugar production (tons)	138,929	429,108
Sugar exports (tons)	121,310	363,368
Gross revenue from sugar sales	£1,880,557	£18,420,576
Acreage reaped – estates	33,003	70,147
Number of cane farmers	9,000	22,394
Industry employment	45,254[a]	57,750[b]

Source: Jamaica, Department of Statistics, Census Report, 1943 (Kingston: Government Printer, 1945); Jamaica, Department of Statistics, Census Report, 1960 (Kingston: Government Printer, 1960); Barker Report; Jamaica, Sugar Industry Enquiry Commission, Report of the Sugar Industry Enquiry Commission, John Mordecai, Chairman (Kingston: Government Printer, 1967), subsequently referred to as Mordecai Report.

[a]This is the average weekly employment in-crop. Out-of-crop employment dropped by about 40 percent.

[b]This is based on census figures for estate employment, plus an estimate of the number of workers on cane farms.

While Vere was perhaps the main center of growth, there was a substantial diversion of land and labor to the sugar industry throughout the island. As a result, by the 1960s about 160,000 acres were being devoted to cane annually. This represented almost one-third of the entire cultivated area in Jamaica. It included a much higher percentage of the best arable land.[8]

CONTRADICTIONS WITHIN THE INDUSTRY:
TECHNOLOGICAL AND MICROECONOMIC PROBLEMS

The substantial post-war growth of the Jamaican sugar industry camouflaged a number of serious contradictions or problems. Despite the manifest growth, the industry was actually seriously diseased. In particular, the efficiency of the industry, on many indices, had lagged far behind production.

Productivity did not increase significantly after 1940. Cane yields, the amount of cane reaped per acre, increased only 14 percent over a twenty-year period. Sugar recovery, the amount of cane needed to produce each ton of sugar, showed no improvement in this period.[9]

Costs also showed an alarming trend. Starting in the 1950s, the cost of producing cane on the estates escalated rapidly. Between 1954 and 1965 the total costs of production increased 68 percent, while cane output rose only 10 percent; costs were increasing at seven times the rate of production. By 1965, a ton of cane could be purchased from independent cane farmers at five-sixths its cost of production on the estates.[10] In other words, production costs on the cane farms, especially the larger ones, must have been considerably lower than those on the estates, a sharp reversal of the historic pattern. The latter were losing money, if field operations were taken separately. As a result, Jamaica became the highest cost cane producer in the Commonwealth, and possibly the world. In contrast, thirty years earlier only Hawaii, the Philippines and Guyana could boast lower field costs.[11]

By the early 1960s, sugar factories in Jamaica were technologically backward, by international standards. They were too small, highly labor-intensive and increasingly inefficient. Too much time was lost because of machinery failures and the amount of time needed to process all the cane reaped was considerably in excess of what experts considered acceptable.[12] Not surprisingly, the physical and technical inefficiencies were also reflected in the cost picture. Between 1954 and 1965, processing costs increased by over 5 percent annually. [13]

Adding cane production and manufacturing costs together, almost half of the factory-farms were producing

sugar at a cost above $90 per ton by the mid-1960s.
This was at least 20 percent above the realized price in
1965.[14]

It is clear that between the 1940s and 1960s, despite the great growth and profits, the Jamaican sugar
industry deteriorated significantly in terms of productivity, technology and efficiency. The factory-farms,
or estates, were mainly to blame. But why did the big
producers allow this situation to develop? What accounts
for their failure to invest, innovate and operate efficiently? Two key factors will be mentioned here. First,
commonwealth sugar arrangements protected the producers
from competitive pressure and bred inefficiency. Second,
since profits resulted mainly from processing, shipping
and refining, the larger factory-farms focused on maximizing the quantity of cane produced, and had less need
for maximizing efficiency in their field operations.
Other aspects of the situation will be discussed below:
their inability to solve the "labor question" and their
metropolitan orientation.

CONTRADICTIONS WITHIN THE INDUSTRY:
CLASS CONFLICT

For the most part, until the mid-1960s, the deteriorating technical and financial foundations of the industry were not generally acknowledged or manifest. Much
less hidden were its class contradictions. For one
thing, there were the low wages and unbearable living
conditions to which the workers, especially field workers, were subject. This was in marked contrast to the
opulence of the sugar elites. Second, the authoritarian,
hierarchical and oppressive work relationships were a
painful and anachronistic throwback to slavery. Third,
racial stratification, even more pronounced in the sugar
belt than elsewhere in the society, reinforced and over-
lay class inequality, increasing the tenseness and viru-
lence of the situation. [15]

Despite the industry's growth in the post-war
period, sugar workers were still suffering unbearable
living conditions in the early 1960s. For example,
Lionel Town, the chief town in Vere, was "one big rural
slum" in which three-quarters of the dwellings were
rented; two-thirds were tenements; 80 percent of all
households with five persons or more were crowded into
such tenements, having only one or two rooms; half of
such households were living in just one room; 95 percent
of the households were without piped water inside the
premises; one-third of the dwellings were still made of
either wattle or thatch. [16]

In addition, educational and cultural levels were
very low, as facilities and incentives were lacking.
Conditions in Lionel Town became especially serious

after 1959 when massive layoffs of field workers began
at Monymusk. Other estates followed suit in the next
decade, as field operations for loading the cut cane
were mechanized.

This material and cultural depression was in sharp
contrast to the luxury in which high-level factory and
farm staff dwelled, within sight of the Lionel Town
slums. The "compound," housing 200 upper and upper-
middle class families in quite commodious quarters,
each with one or two racially differentiated "helpers,"
was also serviced with 220 acres of recreation land, including a golf course. Yet, the 3,000 inhabitants of
Lionel Town proper were forced to make do with 20 acres
of ill-kept fields. [17] Indeed, this sort of duality,
with prosperity existing side by side with poverty, was
characteristic of practically all the estates.

Between 1963 and 1972, real incomes of Monymusk
field workers, and by extension all Jamaican sugar workers, declined by almost 40 percent (Table 2.4); they
were averaging less than $20 per week on an annual
basis. The low level of wages during this period was
also reflected, especially in the minds of the workers
themselves, by the discrepancies between earnings in
Jamaica and those available abroad. In 1971, cane cutters averaged $2.26 a day in Jamaica, compared to the
$11.58 average daily earnings of West Indian cane cut-
ters on one Florida plantation (due to both higher
rates and greater productivity). [18]

Not surprisingly, the main part of Lionel Town was
still a slum area in 1972, while sugar workers residing
on the farms themselves faced deplorable, nineteenth-
century conditions. A survey carried out in 1974 confirmed and amplified this disturbing picture. Three-
quarters of the population fourteen years and over were
either not working (and not going to school) or working
but earning less than $10 a week. Formal unemployment
stood at 22 percent, an underestimate since many of
those not in the labor force were youths who were also
not in school. But even those employed were not fully
so, averaging only slightly more than six months work
per year. [19]

Over one-third of the households were single-
parent; two-thirds were without electricity; and 90 percent still without piped water (to the house). Educationally, almost three-quarters of the population had
gotten no further than sixth grade. Certainly most of
these were functionally illiterate. By 1970, 51 percent
of the Vere population was under 15 or over 65, almost
ten percentage points more than just ten years earlier. [20]

From the 1950s, with owners of capital intent on
work force reductions, the position of the sugar workers
became quite insecure. This added to the perennial problem of only irregular employment. The one comprehensive
survey ever done found that only 21 percent of the

TABLE 2.4
Field Worker Incomes, Monymusk Estate,
1944-1972

Year	Average Gross Annual Income, Monymusk Field Workers	Price Index[a]
1944	$ 96.00[b]	n.a.
1963	656.90[c]	90.5
1972	776.71[d]	142.7

Sources:
    a. Price index (consumer prices) taken from John
Davison Shillingford, "Financial Potential and Welfare
Implications of Sugarcane Harvest Mechanization on
Jamaican Plantations," with the 1972 index extrapolated
from his 1971 figure, using the level of price inflation
for 1971-1972. (Ph.D. dissertation, Cornell University,
1974, p. 7).
    b. Jamaica, Labour Department, Report on an Econo-
mic Survey among Field Workers in the Sugar Industry,
November 1944 (Kingston, 1946).*
    c. Farm records, Springfield Farm, Monymusk
Estate.**
    d. NIS records (National Insurance Scheme), Spring-
field Farm, Monymusk (n=152, about 3/4 of all registered
and regular workers).

*
Based on a survey of 513 Monymusk field workers,
including some only irregularly employed. Average incomes at Monymusk were higher than at any other estate,
almost doubling those at Frome. One partial explanation
for this is that a much greater percentage of Monymusk
workers were classified as skilled and semiskilled, and
most were continuously employed, again in contrast to
other estates. Also more than the others, Monymusk workers tended to be male heads of households. Finally,
because most Monymusk workers did not have small plots
to fall back on it was less possible for their employers
to remunerate them below their cost of reproduction.

**
All were field workers at Farm #1, Monymusk Estate. The sample totaled 108, probably two-thirds of
all those regularly employed at that farm. Most of these
workers were working over 40 weeks. Average incomes reported were likely as much as 50 percent higher than
the average earned by workers at other estates or private cane farms.
    Data collected by author.

field workers were in fact regularly or reasonably
fully employed (working at least five days per week for
at least 75 percent of the work period, defined as a
48-week work year). The bulk of the work force was
either seasonal--working only during crop--or part-
time.[21] This is inherent in a system of work distribution in which over four-fifths of the field workers are
task workers. Most assignments were (and still are)
distributed when available, to whom overseers chose.

Racism has always reinforced the inherent contradictions between the sugar oligarchy and the working
class. Nowhere was the class-color stratification system more permanent and debilitating than in the sugar
belt.[22] This was reflected in the racial antagonisms
which still existed there into the 1970s. Estate management and ownership were almost totally white and frequently foreign. In 1943, for example, 82 percent of
all large farm operators (farms of one hundred acres
and over) were white. Only 5 percent were colored, and
less than 1 percent black.[23] Their lives were sharply
differentiated from the black workers in every way.
Traditionally, at Monymusk, for example, the only workers allowed on the compound were the maids, gardeners
and guards, almost all black (except for a few of East
Indian origin). Any other black worker found on the compound would be accosted and thrown off.

CONTRADICTIONS WITHIN THE INDUSTRY:
FOREIGN CAPITAL

Until the exploitation of Jamaica's bauxite reserves began in the 1950s, no other productive sector
was more dominated by foreign capital than sugar. In
1971, two-thirds of manufacturing capacity and roughly
half of all the cane grown was substantially controlled
by foreign interests (Table 2.5). It is this factor more
than anything else that accounted for the pattern of
"growth without development" characterizing the sugar
industry in the twentieth century.

There were a number of irrationalities--from both
a national and social standpoint--associated with this
pattern of foreign domination of the sugar industry in
Jamaica. First, the foreign capitalists tended to emphasize overseas rather than domestic linkages. Most
purchases of materials took place in the metropole. As
an example, Bookers, which controlled two Jamaican
sugar estates, imported all goods and services from the
Bookers Group of Companies, even where this source was
less efficient, more costly or had a longer delivery
time than other suppliers.[24] Forward linkages--secon-
dary processing, marketing, transportation, and secondary demand--were also heavily skewed toward the metropole.

TABLE 2.5
Estate Ownership and Sugar
Production, 1971

Estate Ownership	Percent of Total Capacity	Percent of Total Sugar Production
Foreign	54	58
Joint	12	9
Local	34	33

Source: Shillingford, p. 49.

Second, the overseas repatriation of locally generated surpluses during the 1950s and 1960s substantially reduced domestic investment levels. Few Jamaican
sugar manufacturers took any steps to modernize during
this period. During the early 1960s, especially, despite
the massive surpluses being generated, the industry was
in fact being decapitalized as two-thirds of the
estates were investing less on capital improvements than
they recorded for depreciation. This underinvestment,
more than anything else, accounted for Jamaica's competitive disadvantage.[25]

Third, a European and racially-exclusive oligarchy,
oriented toward the metropole, controlled top managerial
and decision-making positions within the industry. As
late as the 1960s, for example, the Sugar Manufacturers
Association was still dominated by whites and foreigners,
while the board of directors overseeing Tate and Lyle's
local operations was based in London until 1966.[26] This
severely restricted local opportunities for Jamaicans,
who hence tended to migrate overseas, or into other industries. This drain on middle management and skilled
workers began to affect the industry severely in the
1960s.

Finally, the agricultural economy was seriously
affected by its dependence on one crop, sugar. Multinational corporate objectives dictated that profit maximization on the entire vertically integrated sugar operations was primary. This had two major consequences.
First, it oriented Jamaican production more and more into a monocultural mode. For example, prior to its takeover by Bookers, Innswood Estate produced citrus, supported over 1,000 head of cattle and bred mules and race
horses commercially. But this did not fit in with the
sugar strategy dictated by the needs of Bookers' international operations. Hence, soon after taking over, it
sold off the cattle and horses and allowed the orchards

to deteriorate. [27]

The second consequence was perhaps even more serious. Since domestic value added came predominantly from the factory operations, cane production was extended onto economically marginal lands to ensure factory throughput. It was not important, on the whole, if these cane farming operations lost money. Cane production was maximized as long as overseas revenue exceeded the total costs of <u>sugar</u> production, and not those of cane alone. But what was profitable from the point of view of the multinational sugar producers was not socially or economically advantageous to Jamaica.

By encroaching on the best land and competing with other agricultural enterprises and the peasantry for scarce inputs, the estates restricted peasant opportunity as well as the growth of food production, including livestock and dairy. This not only led to increasing levels of food imports, but resulted in the foregoing of potential forward and backward linkages, employment and income gains. It also led to a pattern of inefficient land use for Jamaica as a whole.

STAGNATION AND DECLINE AFTER 1964

Such fundamental contradictions as we have described above--involving the stringent competitive requirements set by a world market, class relations within the agricultural economy, and the need for national versus metropolitan development--could not long remain camouflaged. By the late 1950s and early 1960s the tremors were beginning to be noticed. Then after 1964, when the Jamaican sugar industry began a period of secular stagnation and decline (Table 2.6), they became more manifest. Within a few years these were part of what became officially recognized as a crisis within the industry. By the late 1960s and early 1970s, they had become a more generalized crisis affecting the Jamaican state.

The industry's decline during the 1960s is partially recorded in Table 2.6. By 1969-1973, sugar production was down 15 percent compared to the period ten years earlier. From contributing almost one-third of total exports in 1959-1963, the sugar industry was down to contributing just over 10 percent. Starting in 1965, the estates recorded deficits each year, with the net loss in 1970 reaching over $19 million. [28] The West Indies Sugar Company (WISCo), the Tate and Lyle subsidiary operating Monymusk Estate, did not escape this trend. Between 1967 and 1970 it lost over $4 million on the cane farming operation at Monymusk. [29] These losses resulted from declining production levels, stagnation in export receipts and inefficiency.

The late 1960s and early 1970s were also marked by an acceleration of the trend toward technological

TABLE 2.6
Industry Data, 1959-1973

Year	Tons Cane Milled '000	Acreage Reaped '000	Sugar Production - tons	Export Revenue: Sugar, Rum, Molasses $ million	% of Total Exports
1959-1963 average	4,219	152.3[a]	429.1	33.8	28.7
1969-1973 average	3,984	149.2	366.6	35.4	12.3

Source: Jamaica, National Planning Agency, Economic and Social Survey (Kingston: Government Printer, various years).

[a]This is the acreage reaped in 1964; cane farmers' acreage figures prior to 1964 are not available.

deterioration. Yields and cane quality indices fell alarmingly, factory nonperformance reached crisis proportions, and average crop length increased to over 200 days, with a consequent deterioration in plant utilization. In addition, poor cultivation practices were permeating the cane fields.[30]

In 1970, reflecting the crisis in the cane fields, Tate and Lyle announced its intention to give up cane farming operations in Jamaica. The following year, the government purchased Frome and Monymusk properties (60,000 acres) for $8.4 million, though it immediately leased the cane lands back to WISCo for management purposes. Bernard Lodge Estate was taken over under similar circumstances from United Fruit Company in 1971, but without such a leasing arrangement.

By 1972 then, when the national political leadership changed hands, the structure of the industry had already begun to change. For one thing, only fifteen factories were operating, three less than in 1968. More significantly, the state owned the three largest cane farming operations, comprising about one-quarter of all the land planted in cane and as much as 30 percent of total production. In addition, the state had a 25 percent interest in Innswood Estate, part interest in

Bernard Lodge factory, and was shortly to take over Holland Estate. Finally, the Sugar Industry Authority had been reorganized and had begun to adopt an activist role.

But in other important respects things remained the same. The industry leader was still Tate and Lyle, through WISCo. It owned the two largest factories producing about one-third of all the raw sugar and 100 percent of the refined sugar; farmed and essentially still controlled the two largest cane farms; controlled the major shipping port; was overseas broker for all export sales; via Tate and Lyle was a major purchaser of the raw sugar; and continued as a dominant force in the Sugar Manufacturers Association (SMA), whose English chairperson had originally worked for Tate and Lyle. Furthermore, the plantation system was still intact, the workers continued to toil and live under miserable conditions, and production was continuing to decline.

The contradictions and conflicts permeating the sugar sector reflected those affecting the society as a whole. Sugar was a microcosm of a neo-colonial Jamaica. Poverty coexisted with prosperity, if only with difficulty, in the cane areas as throughout Jamaica. Foreign penetration and control were a national dilemma. Economic growth, even when it occurred, as in sugar before 1965 and throughout Jamaica between 1950 and 1971, was divorced from development. Only a few benefited; unemployment increased, small-scale production remained backward, and foreign indebtedness and dependence worsened.

It is in this sense that we must begin to understand the decade of the 1970s and the regime of Michael Manley. His problem was how could Jamaica transcend the economic and social contradictions which permeated the sugar industry and the society at large. In this chapter I have tried to describe the historical dialectic which defined this problem for the sugar industry. It should be clear that, to a degree, it also constrained and shaped the possible solutions.

NOTES

1. Charles Campbell, quoted in Edward Brathwaite, The Development of Creole Society in Jamaica 1770-1820 (Oxford: Cambridge University Press, 1971), pp. 207-208.

2. Gisela Eisner, Jamaica 1830-1930: A Study in Economic Growth (Manchester: Manchester University Press, 1961), p. 209.

3. James J. Phillips, "Fe Wi Land A Come: Choice and Change on a Jamaican Sugar Plantation" (Ph.D. thesis, Brown University, 1976), p. 228.

4. George Cumper, "Labour Demand and Supply in the Jamaican Sugar Industry, 1830-1950," Social and Economic Studies 2(1954),

pp. 71-74.

5. Cumper, p. 82; Jamaica, Sugar Industry Commission, Robert B. Barker, Chairman, Report of the Sugar Industry Commission, 1944-45 (Kingston, 1945), p. 32.

6. Alan Eyre, "Land and Population in the Sugar Belt of Jamaica" (Kingston: University of the West Indies, Department of Geography, n.d.), pp. 4-6.

7. The figures are for Lionel Town, the major town in Vere (Eyre, p. 6).

8. Cane acreage included about 75,000 to 80,000 acres in cane farms (not part of any factory-farm complex), 75,000 acres in estates, plus maybe 10,000 acres lying fallow. According to the 1961 Agricultural Census, cultivated area in Jamaica totaled 545,000 acres (Jamaica, Department of Statistics, Agricultural Census 1961/62 [Kingston: Government Printer, n.d.]). In 1942, only 96,000 acres were in cane, about one-quarter the total cultivated area in Jamaica.

9. Barker Report, Sections V and VI; Jamaica, Sugar Manufacturer's Association, Sugar Research Department, Annual Report (Mandeville, Jamaica, 1948 and 1964).

10. Jamaica, The Commission of Enquiry on the Sugar Industry of Jamaica, 1959-1960, H. Carl Goldenberg, Chair, Report of the Commission of Enquiry on the Sugar Industry of Jamaica (Kingston: Government Printer, 1960), subsequently referred to as Goldenberg Report; Mordecai Report; All-Island Jamaica Cane Farmers Association.

11. Barker Report, p. 7.

12. Mordecai Report, pp. 112 and 146-148; Sanderson and Porter, Inc., Jamaica Sugar, prepared for the United Nations Industrial Development Organization (New York, 1971), p. 15.

13. Goldenberg Report; Mordecai Report.

14. Mordecai Report, p. 85D.

15. Even the conservative Mordecai Commission was forced to note "the slow pace at which improvement of social conditions, particularly in relation to cane cutters and loaders, had advanced," as late as the 1960s (p. 288).

16. Eyre, pp. 11-13.

17. Ibid., p. 10.

18. John Davison Shillingford, "Financial Potential and Welfare Implications of Sugar Cane Harvest Mechanization on Jamaican Plantations" (Ph.D. dissertation, Cornell University, 1974), p. 69.

19. Joe Owens, "Report on Housing and Employment Survey of the Monymusk Estate Area" (Kingston: Social Action Center, 1974, mimeo).

20. Derek Gordon, "Housing and Population in South Clarendon," Sugar Industry Housing Ltd., Technical Report #1 (Kingston, n.d., but c. 1975), p. 3.

21. Jamaica, Labour Department, Report on an Economic Survey.

22. Fernando Henriques, Family and Colour in Jamaica (London: MacGibbon and Kee, 1968).

23. Leonard Broom, "The Social Differentiation of Jamaica," American Sociological Review 19(April 1954), p. 120.

24. George L. Beckford, Persistent Poverty (New York: Oxford University Press, 1972), p. 260.

25. Havelock Brewster, "Jamaica's Life or Death--The Sugar Industry," New World Pamphlet #4 (Kingston, 1967); Mordecai Report, pp. 102-103 and 153.

26. Richard Fletcher, Chair, Sugar Industry Authority, interview, August 27, 1977; Jamaica Daily Gleaner, May 11, 1966, p. 1.

27. Beckford, p. 266.

28. Shillingford, p. 2.

29. Carl Stone, "An Appraisal of the Co-operative Process in the Jamaican Sugar Industry," Social and Economic Studies 27 (March 1978), p. 3.

30. Jamaica, Sugar Industry Authority, The Sugar Industry Rehabilitation Programme (Draft, July 1976), pp. 53-54, 64-66.

3
Policy and Procrastination, 1972–1973

> We no not believe that the [sugar] industry
> can survive the decade of the 1970's unless
> we can transform it into a system based on
> some sort of economic democracy.[1]

> Eventually a worker-based organization must
> come forth, spanning all three Parishes if
> possible, and it must go to Government, to
> the Frome Monymusk Land Company, and to any-
> one else necessary, and it must demand what
> belongs to workers in justice on terms that
> are well within the workers' reach. Certainly
> the workers' downpayment in generations of
> blood, sweat and tears has already soaked
> deeply into the soil and cannot be ques-
> tioned. . . . If the land is ever going to be
> controlled by the people, massive educa-
> tional and motivational efforts will have to
> be made by the people themselves. In the end,
> the choice is theirs: do they want to take
> responsibility for this prime land, or do
> they want to leave the responsibility (and
> opportunity) with the busha-man?[2]

ORIGINS AND FOUNDATION OF THE PNP'S POLICY
TOWARD THE STATE-OWNED CANE LANDS

When the PNP entered office in 1972 the three largest cane farming properties in Jamaica, totaling about
48,000 acres in cane (Table 3.1), had already reverted
to state ownership. Frome Estate, established by Tate
and Lyle in the late 1930s, was situated in a high rainfall area in the western part of the island. Monymusk,
which had also been a Tate and Lyle property, was in the
centrally located Vere Plains and was dependent on irrigation. This was also true of Bernard Lodge Estate,
lying about fourteen miles west of Kingston, and

29

TABLE 3.1
Government Acquired Cane Properties,
Land Use, 1971

	Frome	Monymusk	Bernard Lodge	TOTAL
Total Acreage	23,221	37,442	13,016	73,679
Acreage in Cane	16,656	20,921	10,383	47,960
Pasture	2,418	500	–	2,918
Tenants and Squatters	842	343	30	1,215
Nonagricultural Use: Swamp, Forest, Ruinate, etc.	3,305	15,678	2,603	21,586

Source: Jamaica, Ministry of Agriculture, "Development of Frome/Monymusk/Bernard Lodge Lands" (Kingston, 1972).

previously owned by the United Fruit Company (United Brands). Following their purchase in 1971, the Frome and Monymusk properties were leased back to WISCo, the local Tate and Lyle subsidiary, to maintain continuity in the interim period while the Jamaica Labour Party government was developing its plans for the distribution and utilization of the cane lands. No lease-back arrangement was concluded with United Fruit; in 1972, the Bernard Lodge lands came under direct state administration. The three sugar factories on these estates remained in foreign hands.

The sale of these properties by their foreign owners served both political and economic ends. Politically, the multinationals were seeking to protect themselves against the rising tide of nationalism in Jamaica, as elsewhere among the underdeveloped countries. Foreign land ownership has always been a primary focus for expropriation and attack by nationalist forces. By divesting itself of the land, Tate and Lyle was protecting its more profitable milling, refining and shipping interests. Economically, the sale served to transfer the burden of decreasing agricultural productivity, an economically inefficient production process, and an organized and militant labor force onto other parties.[3] Reference has already been made (page 24) to the losses suffered by WISCo. Average yields between 1967 and 1971 were similarly unsatisfactory and much lower than in previous years (Table 3.2).

During 1972 the new PNP government deliberated on its approach to the utilization of the Frome, Monymusk

TABLE 3.2
Average Yields, 1947-1971: Frome, Monymusk, Bernard Lodge

Estate	Tons Cane/Acre			Tons Sugar/Acre		
	1947-1951 average	1957-1961 average	1967-1971 average	1947-1951 average	1957-1961 average	1967-1971 average
Frome	34.41	34.76	31.48	4.05	3.84	2.50
Monymusk	36.25	35.32	30.48	3.91	3.65	2.70
Bernard Lodge	34.81	31.36	27.68	3.80	3.71	2.48

Source: Jamaica, SMA, Annual Report, 1952 and 1961;
Sugar Industry Authority, 1976.

and Bernard Lodge lands. From its inception, the
People's National Party had supported the establishment
of rural cooperatives. In 1940, shortly after its founding, the PNP committed itself to the struggle to transform the agricultural sector into one made up of multipurpose cooperatives of small holders and agricultural
collectives. This was linked to its general objective
of establishing democratic control of all the means of
production and of eliminating capitalist exploitation.[4]
Though the party's socialist outlook and agrarian reform plans were muted beginning in the mid-1940s, in
the 1949 elections the PNP still called for the establishment of model collective farms in each parish (calling them "cooperatives") with elected worker management
committees.[5] Then again, in 1964, as the party officially rededicated itself to democratic socialism, it
reaffirmed its commitment to the establishment of multipurpose and producer cooperatives, the breaking up of
the large sugar estates, and the compulsory acquisition
of all idle land over one hundred acres.[6]

In keeping with this tradition it is not surprising that the post-1972 PNP government decided that the
fundamental principle guiding its policy toward the distribution of the newly acquired cane lands was that
they should be developed, where feasible, as cooperatives, with workers and small farmers as the beneficiaries. This approach was not only consistent with
PNP traditions and aspirations in the area of agrarian
reform and rural development, but was also very much a
reflection of Michael Manley's own ideas about rural
change and worker participation. Manley had had a long
and intimate association, as a trade unionist, with the
struggles of the sugar workers.[7] It was also a politically astute attempt to break the cane field workers'
traditional ties to the Jamaica Labour Party. Finally,
the cooperativization of the cane lands was also one of
the recommendations of the World Bank team which completed a review of the agricultural sector in 1973.[8] It
fit in well with the government's evolving commitment
to equity and social justice.

Hence, in 1972 the government initiated the planning and establishment of:

> pilot projects for the development on a coopera-
> tive basis of three blocks of cane land, one on
> each of the three Estates with provision for
> future expansion of cooperative ventures based on
> the pilot projects, if these prove successful.[9]

A second policy principle guiding the government's
approach to the distribution of the Frome, Monymusk and
Bernard Lodge lands, as well as its entire agrarian reform program, was that potential beneficiaries be given
access to land via leasehold, and not freehold, tenures.

This fit in with the Manley government's evolving ideology and tendency to emphasize the social function of
agricultural land. In this view the state must play a
leading role, and thus must have the means to influence
or control planning, intensity of land use, cropping
patterns, etc. In addition, leasehood facilitated the
use of a beneficiary's scarce capital for development
purposes, rather than as a large payment for the land.
This helped prevent both land fragmentation and land
concentration.

With these two principles, the Manley government
clearly broke from the previous Labour Party regime's
assumptions or plans for the land. The JLP planned
to sell the land in 100-500 acre parcels to local farmers or others with the capital wherewithal. In fact, its
original purchase agreement with WISCo actually contained a clause committing the government not to break
up the land into parcels of less than 100 acres.

For its part, in a plan submitted in 1972, WISCo
also suggested the gradual distribution of the land in
large parcels, but to its estate staff. It was prepared to provide training during a short interim
period, mainly by decentralizing operations and giving
greater managerial autonomy to field staff, the future
operators.[10] This plan, like the government's, proposed
leasehold tenure. The plans advanced by both WISCo and
the JLP had a clearly different class perspective than
that advanced by the PNP government during the early
1970s.

A third principle accepted by the government in
1972 was that, regardless of any plans for land reform,
cane production on the three properties had to be at
least maintained, if not expanded.[11] This fit in well
with Tate and Lyle's own plans for the expansion of cane
throughput to its two factories. In Clarendon Parish,
for example, where its Monymusk sugar factory and re-
finery were located, Tate and Lyle was calling for an
increase in the amount of land in cane, an accelerated
program of replanting, land forming and reblocking, and
the elimination of one of the two other sugar factories
in the parish.[12] The government, too, had its own plans
for a nationwide expansion of sugar production to the
450,000 tons range, up from an average of around
374,000 tons between 1969 and 1972.[13] This entailed the
necessity to maximize cane production.

The commitment to maximize cane throughput, imbedded into the policy from the beginning, had significant
implications. It meant, for example, that the considerable acreages of marginal cane land then in production,
particularly at Monymusk, would have to remain in cane
under the reform plan. This put a very heavy burden on
the future cooperatives, as it would have on any operator of the cane lands. They were not in a position,
like the vertically integrated factory-farms, to absorb

marginal losses on cane production, to be made up by
sugar processing. The added cane throughput, even if not
profitable to grow, expanded processing, shipping and
overseas operations, which contributed the bulk of their
value added and profit. In effect, for a company like
Tate and Lyle, the maximization of overall profit depen-
ded on increased supplies of cane regardless of the
losses incurred in cane production operations, taken
separately. Cane farming subsidized the other operations. However, once factory and farm operations were
separated, this economic manipulation was no longer
feasible, and the farms were saddled with the burden of
producing cane, at least in the short run, under nonviable conditions. [14]

While planners did recognize this, in part, they
were depending on rapid productivity increases on some
of the better lands to compensate for the poorer acreages. If this strategy was eventually successful, the
marginal lands could be taken out of cane without loss
in production. But there were a number of constraints
to this strategy which the planners did not sufficiently
consider. The major one, at Monymusk, was the poor
availability and quality of water. Salinity of the water
supply was a longstanding problem at Monymusk, severely
constraining any long-run plan to increase yields in the
face of unstable weather conditions. Any drought period
could critically lower the water table level, thus increasing the salinity content of the irrigation water,
and the cost of pumping it, to the detriment of most of
the Monymusk lands. When this did occur, there were significant consequences for the implementation of the cooperatives project. [15]

It was significant, too, that there was no inclina-
tion by the government either to maintain the factory-
farm complexes as integrated units--whether under cooperative or state control--or to seek state involvement
in the Frome, Monymusk and Bernard Lodge factories. It
was not until after 1976, when the cooperatives were
already established, that the government gained control
of these factories, as part of its plan for a state
sugar industry. Even then the cooperatives remained as
separate and independent entities.

Another decision taken by the government in 1972,
while not directly related to the establishment of the
sugar worker cooperatives, was to have important consequences for the cooperativization process. It decided
that the Frome and Monymusk lands, at that time leased
to Tate and Lyle, would be placed under direct state
management after the 1974 crop. This was to have a significant effect on subsequent decision-making and implementation for two reasons. First, for many in the
ruling party and sugar industry, a state farm operation
was a viable alternative to worker-controlled cooperatives, while a long-term Tate and Lyle leasehold was

not. Hence, at a later date, as this alternative gained favor it increased the level of conflict at the grass roots with workers committed to cooperatives. Second, with the government takeover, management of these vast cane acreages became the major reponsibility of the Frome Monymusk Land Company (FMLCo), the state-owned corporation set up to implement the government's policy in this area. This restricted the resources, emphasis and attention that FMLCo could devote to cooperativization, for which it was also responsible.

Finally, in addition to the various principles and decisions adopted by the government, there were two very important, but implicit, assumptions which were accepted uncritically by planners and government officials during this early period. First, an underlying assumption was that any land reform attempted, in sugar as elsewhere, would be gradual, blending pragmatism and technocratic considerations with political and social needs. According to this perspective, conflict with the local and foreign landowners was to be minimized, with amicable arrangements arrived at on the basis of negotiation and compromise, according to established bureaucratic procedures. The plan to establish the co-ops only as a pilot project in the first instance, with no explicit commitment to further co-ops, as well as the general outline of the proposed co-op structure and operations (see below), also reflected this general technocratic and moderate approach. This perspective, of course, was very much in keeping with the general tone of the regime's first two years.

Second, at no time during this early period was any consideration given to eliciting grass-roots participation in the planning process or stimulating grassroots mobilization as an integral part of co-op development and reform in the sugar belt. Attention to these aspects of the development process became salient later, but only after the workers themselves demanded them.

THE PILOT PROJECT: STRUCTURE AND
OPERATIONALIZATION

Toward the end of 1972, an interministerial planning committee, drawn mainly from the Ministry of Agriculture and the National Planning Agency, was appointed to put the government's thinking and principles into an operational plan for the development of the three properties. This included an outline of a pilot project for establishing sugar worker cooperatives as a portion of each of the estates. The committee's report became the basis of the government's planning until mid-1974.[16]

In regard to the pilot cooperatives, the report suggested that the cane lands be parceled into 30-40 acre individual units, grouped in 1,000 acre blocs.

The farmers within each section (bloc) would form a co-operative, under a project manager or co-op planning officer. Certain management and planning functions, as well as marketing, input provision and tractorage were to be provided to the cooperatives by FMLCo.

The decision to opt for an individual plot size of 30-40 acres was based on an attempt simultaneously to maximize the satisfaction of two objectives: a) that each individual holding provide an economic return; and b) that as many new farmers as possible be established on the cane lands. In practice the first objective was determinative. The planners decided that $1,500 was an adequate annual return, and estimated that 31 acres at Frome and 39 at Monymusk would realize that.

There were two main criteria for tenant selection suggested. While those with the "highest qualification for cane farming" were to be given preference, it was also considered important to provide land to those with too little land or none at all. However, the point system devised to facilitate selection was clearly biased toward those already having certain resources, in practice meaning staff, headmen (foremen) and better-off workers. For example, while general experience in farming counted heavily, those whose experience was as field workers received only two-thirds as much credit as did staff, headmen and farm operators for the same number of years.[17] Potentially even more discriminatory was the wealth criterion, with each $50 in assets worth one point. Moreover, it appeared that "highly qualified" tenants might be allowed to lease more than one holding, and that, in any case, the point system was not fully determinative. Final decisions would be made by the FMLCo board or a tenant selection committee.[18]

The still fairly vague components of the project were elaborated in mid-1973 by FMLCo.[19] In particular, the role of FMLCo and its interaction with the new tenants organized into cooperatives were more clearly developed. The thirty or so tenants comprising each 1,000 acre cooperative would form a council of tenants and elect five of their number to form the executive committee of the council. The project manager, appointed by FMLCo, was expected to be the chairperson of the committee. According to this proposal, the executive committee was to be mainly an advisory and implementing body. Major production and financial decisions were to remain the responsibility of FMLCo and the manager. The former would "direct and control the entire agricultural production." The latter was to be the local supervisory authority, controlling production operations, transportation, marketing and keeping accounts. The tenants would have to implement decisions made by FMLCo and the manager, and utilize all services provided by FMLCo, as well as pay the charges for those services and a management fee.

The principle guiding this view of the structure
was elaborated in the report as follows:

> The responsibility lies heavily upon the FMLCo to
> see that the assets invested by Government in the
> scheme remain productive and unimpaired. For this
> reason the Company should not be bound to obtain
> agreements with tenants before taking any action,
> in the management of the scheme, neither should
> the Company divest itself of full responsibility by
> submitting to arbitration any matters other than
> those governed by law.[20]

At this time the idea was clearly to establish a type of
state farm operation, letting individuals tenant the
land, but producing what FMLCo wanted in a manner that
it determined.

Thus, one major thrust of the project in this
period was toward state control of the cooperatives. A
second was toward the creation of a group of middle-
class farmers on the cane lands. One of the members of
the original planning team, who later moved over to
FLMCo as co-op officer (ultimately becoming chief executive of the sugar cooperatives) was quite explicit about
this.[21]

THE FROME MONYMUSK LAND COMPANY

The Frome Monymusk Land Company was thus given a
central role in the administration and implementation of
the government's land reform proposals for these cane
lands. Established in 1971 as a wholly government-owned
land-holding corporation, it was charged with adminis-
tering the Frome, Monymusk and Bernard Lodge lands for
the government, and with developing plans for their development or disposal. Established and staffed during
the JLP regime, FMLCo reflected the general conservative
orientation of that party.

FMLCo's original board of directors was composed
mainly of high-level, middle- and upper-middle-class
civil servants, most coming from the traditionalist
Ministry of Agriculture, particularly its Lands Department. The chairperson was the Governor of the Bank of
Jamaica. In addition, at least two of the seven board
members had close ties with the rural bourgeoisie. One,
the managing director, was also Commissioner of Lands
and himself a former United Fruit Company employee. He
was linked to WISCo via his brother, who was general
manager of Monymusk, and was married to the daughter of
a large landowner. Another board member was former general manager of Tate and Lyle's Jamaica operation. Both
were unsympathetic to sugar worker cooperatives. The
latter spoke out publicly in opposition to the PNP

government's plans as early as 1972. In general, there was little commitment or experience with either land reform or co-ops among the FMLCo staff and board members. They were much more comfortable with the JLP's plan to sell off the lands in relatively large parcels to established farmers or others with the necessary capital.

Financially, too, the Land Company was not set up to implement any sort of cooperative or leasehold system. It was heavily loaded with debt, and had no other capitalization. Its financial structure was oriented to land sales. Yet, despite these limitations, FMLCo maintained its authority, personnel and structure under the new Manley regime. Its central position was in fact confirmed and reinforced by the 1972 planning committee report.

MOBILIZATION AT THE GRASS ROOTS, 1973-1974

For a year and a half following the submission of the planning committee's report, there was very little action toward its realization by the government. There were some attempts to elaborate and refine the original proposals, but beyond this no visible activity. While the government was moving slowly, the workers were not. During 1973 and the early part of 1974, practically all the initiatives and preparations for cooperativization occurred at the grass roots. These included; a) organization of the workers and area small farmers around the need to maximize their participation in any government plans for the cane lands; b) mobilization of worker support and participation; c) education and training of workers; d) planning of worker cooperatives to operate the properties; and e) pressure activities to prod the bureaucracy out of its inertia.

The Monymusk Housing Committee, formed in late 1972, signaled a new orientation toward worker mobilization in the Vere plains. The situation on the nine major farm compounds at Monymusk Estate, housing 250 workers and their families under the most dilapidated, overcrowded and ghetto-like conditions, was one of the more obvious manifestations of the serious socioeconomic situation in Vere.[22] It was also one of a number of disturbing reminders of the semislave conditions under which sugar workers still lived and worked. The Monymusk Housing Committee was formed by the workers, with the assistance of an American Jesuit priest, to deal with their complaints in that area.[23] They demanded security of tenure and an end to all evictions by WISCo.

Early in 1973, study-action groups began appearing in the Monymusk area. These evolved partly out of the housing issue, but also in response to concern over the disposition of the Monymusk cane lands. Centering around Lionel Town, but extending throughout Vere, twenty such

groups were in existence by April. In May they amalgam-
ated together to form the Monymusk Workers Cooperative
Cane Farming Association (MWCCFA), with over 650 members, including both sugar workers and small farmers.[24]

The study-action groups began meeting twice a month
to promote the grass-roots educational, mobilizing and
representational effort to ensure participation by sugar
workers and small farmers in the distribution of Monymusk cane and noncane lands. In addition, by the fall,
roughly one hundred workers and farmers were attending
the monthly general meetings. In November, 450 paid the
50¢ dues, no small accomplishment for a young organization of poor people, some already paying union dues, and
in the out-of-crop period.

The fall of 1973 was indeed a period of intense organizing activity; nothing like it had ever before been
seen in Vere. Besides the regular meetings, there was a
petition drive with around one thousand persons signing
petitions on the land and housing issues. In October, a
delegation of workers journeyed to Kingston for a two-
hour meeting with the minister of agriculture and Frome
Monymusk Land Company officials, and also to deposit the
petitions at the prime minister's office. Even more significant, over ninety MWCCFA partisans journeyed across
the island to Westmoreland for the historic founding of
the Sugar Workers Coordinating Council (SWCC), linking
workers at Frome and Monymusk in a common struggle for
worker cooperatives.

During this same period a storefront office,
staffed by worker-volunteers and Social Action Centre
organizers, was opened in Lionel Town; three workers became SWCC organizers, paid through SAC; and the first
weekend leadership training course was held for SWCC
workers at SAC's training center in Kingston. Meanwhile
the workers were also publishing a regular fortnightly
bulletin, Land for the People.

Most significant in gauging the level of political
mobilization and activity, and its class perspective,
was the fact that beginning in October, between ten and
twenty Vere workers regularly journeyed to Bernard
Lodge in St. Catherine Parish (roughly one and a half
hours ride) to spearhead the early organizing work among
workers at that estate.

The intensity of the organizing activity during
1973 is striking. It was partly stimulated by the expectation that the pilot cooperatives would begin in 1974.
The idea at that time was still to subdivide the land
into individual leaseholds of 30-40 acres each, and workers undoubtedly had strong material incentives for
linking with SWCC. Obviously only a minority would get
access, and involvement in SWCC was a likely way of en-
hancing one's position vis-a-vis the selection process,
both as a way of showing one's interest and of providing input into the selection mechanism itself. At the

same time, this mobilization filled a longstanding political vacuum at the local level. Finally, the drive and initiative of the SAC organizers, and the support from SAC itself, were also key factors.

SWCC's aim was to ensure maximum participation by sugar workers and small farmers in the distribution of the cane lands, and from the beginning it demanded rapid establishment of worker-controlled cooperatives. Its early interaction with the government on this matter was encouraging, and raised expectations concerning the impending implementation of the pilot cooperatives. In June 1973, the cooperative officer attached to FMLCo told sugar workers and farmers gathered at Monymusk that selection of tenants would begin in August with the pilot commencing operations for the 1974 crop.[25] In July, the minister of agriculture confirmed that the design for the pilots was ready for implementation.[26] But no concrete moves followed.

In an October meeting with SWCC, the minister was still extremely supportive and suggested that SWCC's thirteen propositions submitted to him adequately summarized the government's own position. Among the most important of these propositions were calls for cooperatives of workers and "small people" on the government cane lands, with worker control and worker participation in planning being essential. Another proposition stated the need for changes of the FMLCo board with worker representatives added. However, the minister also stated that the pilots could not start until after the beginning of the 1974 crop, and that any further cooperativization would be gradual, depending on the experience of the pilots.[27]

While the workers generally accepted the government's proposals regarding the structure of the co-ops, they were still critical of other aspects. Points of disagreement included: a) the criteria or point system for tenant selection; b) the number of workers who could be accommodated; c) the degree of worker control in the new enterprises, and the future role of SWCC; and d) the retention of existing estate field staff.

Workers opposed the weighting of the point system toward the more privileged strata. Following representations by SWCC and discussions with the parliamentary secretary in the Ministry of Agriculture, the two most objectionable features of the point system—the allocation of points for every $50 in assets and the discrimination against field workers in allocating points for agricultural experience—were dropped. It was also agreed that the point system itself would serve only as a guideline, and not be interpreted strictly.[28] SWCC also demanded its inclusion in any selection committee.

Although SWCC accepted the basic form of tenure being advanced by the government, there was some disagreement on the actual numbers. In a paper written

in the fall of 1973, the SAC Monymusk organizer accepted the principle of 1,000-acre subdivisions but argued
that 20-acre allotments, providing for fifty settlers,
would be sufficient to satisfy individual minimum income requirements. This reasoning was based partly on
the assumption, not shared by the government, that any
land not yielding 35 tons of cane per acre, with a 5-6
year replanting cycle, should not be in cane. [29]

SWCC argued, more significantly, that the co-ops
should be run by seven-member boards, composed solely
of workers and answerable to the general membership.
These boards would meet regularly and take major decisions, with the manager hired by and directly responsible to them. As in the government's original 1972
planning document, it was envisioned that secondary-
level service cooperatives run by the workers would be
established, with FMLCo gradually phasing out. [30] These
proposals reflected SWCC's commitment to full worker
control of the cooperatives, a commitment definitely
not shared by the government bureaucrats.

Not only was there some disagreement on the role
of the overseers and project managers, but many of the
workers argued strongly against even the retention of
existing estate field staff. They had long been op-
pressed by many of these persons and it was uncertain
how such persons could find any place in the new worker-oriented, democratically-run, cooperatives. The
government, on the other hand, not as fully committed
to a class perspective as the workers, tried to dis-
count these sentiments, arguing that the staff's skills
were needed and they would be more sympathetic to the
workers once organized in cooperatives.

SWCC's general acceptance of the government's plan
for 30-40 acre individual leaseholds within a cooperative framework was not self-evident. Though a mass-
based group, it went along despite the obvious implication that only a minority of the workers would actually
gain access to the land. Perhaps this was because it
was considered likely that this minority would be drawn
predominantly from among SWCC's leadership since they
were in the forefront of the struggle and tended to be
headmen, small farmers and others with somewhat more
resources, experience and drive for land ownership than
the other workers. This would surely have destroyed
SWCC's viability as a mass worker organization, however.

SWCC no doubt was being influenced at this time by
the small farmers and headmen, rather than workers.
Their leadership role, especially at Frome, reflected:
a) the much greater importance they accorded to questions of access to the land and own-account farming; b)
the small farmers' relative freedom from retaliatory
actions by the sugar companies, a significant factor in
the early stages; and c) the general backwardness--
illiteracy, lack of exposure to democratic experience--

of the mass of sugar workers.

Then, too, the Social Action Centre itself reflected generally a petty bourgeois perspective, with a tendency to idealize the small farmer. There remained a significant minority of SWCC members who argued that the individual leasehold system would exclude too many workers and therefore supported a type of communal cooperative.[31]

Generally speaking, from the time of its inception as the MWCCFA, SWCC actively represented, defended and mobilized the interests of sugar workers and small farmers.[32] SWCC did not restrict its activity to the cooperative issue. It fought to get the government land-lease program to come into the Vere area, to benefit small cattle farmers, land-poor farmers and sugar workers looking for small tenancies. It demanded that the compound housing be forthwith handed over to the workers. It strove to emphasize worker unity, grass-roots power and democratic values. It initiated a cooperative education program and a political education series which was at the same time a well-developed literacy training program. Eventually, SWCC came to interpret sugar worker interests as being served best by thoroughgoing land reform and the building of a socialist society (see Chapter 4).

By the beginning of 1973, less than a year after the PNP's election victory, both the basic outline of a pilot project for sugar worker cooperatives and the administrative infrastructure thought necessary to implement it had been established. For the next year and a half, however, there was little concrete action either to elaborate or implement the proposals. This long period of procrastination had two major consequences for the subsequent development of the policy.

It helped create a crisis of confidence between workers and the government. Having sensed and welcomed the government's broad intentions, sugar workers at Monymusk, Frome and Bernard Lodge were mobilizing to maximize their participation in the process and in the expected benefits. But increasingly, as 1973 turned into 1974, they began to feel frustrated and betrayed. They felt that other groups, with goals antagonistic to theirs, were influencing the government, and that the PNP's stated social ideals and commitment to cooperativization were unreal. In the process a very important resource, the confidence of a clientele in the sincerity of their government, backed by a willingness to work alongside it, was eroded.

A second consequence was that the workers took the initiative away from the government. From late 1973 to 1976, the workers' own agenda and action dominated the cooperativization process. This mobilization, represented by the organizing and education efforts of SWCC, was at first accepted by the government which tried to establish channels of communication.[33] However, this was

not so much a sign of political support as a realistic
assessment of the resources available from SWCC, relative to the government's own financial and administrative weakness. But as time went on, and particularly
after mid-1974, there was increasing conflict. In the
end, like many other governments caught in the contradictions of underdevelopment, the Manley regime proved
unwilling and unable "to cope with the political consequences of mobilized mass constituencies."[34] For a time,
however, during 1974 and 1975 the strength of the mobilized workers, led by SWCC, carried the day.

NOTES

1. Michael Manley, in a speech to the Annual Conference of
the Jamaica Association of Sugar Technologists, Jamaica Daily News,
November 9, 1973, p. 1.
2. Joseph Owens, "Who Should Control the Government-Owned
Sugar Estates?" (mimeo, n.d., but circa 1972-1973). "Busha" is a
Jamaican term for farm overseer.
3. This is a common tactic adopted by multinationals that
control vertically integrated agricultural operations. The United
Fruit Company, for example, had earlier adopted it in relation to
its Central American banana operations (Winson, p. 34).
4. People's National Party, "PNP, a Plan for Today - 1940"
(People's National Party, n.d.).
5. People's National Party, "A Plan for Progress, 1948-49"
(People's National Party, n.d.); People's National Party, "PNP
Election Leaflet Number 1" (People's National Party, 1949).
6. "PNP Programme, 1964," reprinted in the Jamaica Daily
Gleaner, November 7 and November 9, 1964. In contrast to its verbal
support of agrarian reform favorable to the rural working class and
small farmers, it is also true that the PNP was traditionally the
strongest supporter of labor-displacing agricultural mechanization.
The party supported, for example, the mechanization of loading at
Monymusk, starting in 1961, which eventually threw thousands of
workers out of work.
7. See Michael Manley, The Politics of Change (London: André
Deutsch Ltd., 1974) and Michael Manley, A Voice at the Workplace
(London: André Deutsch Ltd., 1975).
8. Jamaica, Ministry of Agriculture, Agriculture Sector Survey, Sugar Industry Review (Kingston, 1974), p. 3. This recommendation was consistent with the Bank's support for distributional
reforms.
9. Jamaica, Ministry of Agriculture, "Development of Frome/
Monymusk/Bernard Lodge Lands" (Kingston, 1972), p. 1.
10. West Indies Sugar Company Ltd., Plan for Future Success,
(WISCo, 1972), Appendix.
11. Ministry of Agriculture, "Development of Frome/Monymusk/
Bernard Lodge Lands," pp. 1 and 6; "Sale Agreement between WISCo,
FMLCo [Frome Monymusk Land Company, see below, this Chapter] and
the Government of Jamaica," 21 May 1972; the farm lease agreement

between FMLCo and Morelands Cooperative, 1974.

12. West Indies Sugar Co., Ltd., Plan for Future Success.

13. See, for example, David Coore, Minister of Finance, "Budget Speech," Hansard I (1972-73), p. 86.

14. In other words, the private factory-farms were primarily influenced by cost considerations for the factories; hence, they emphasized reducing unit costs in factories and not on farm operations. As a group of foreign consultants concluded in 1971, "This viewpoint perhaps more than any other is responsible for the crippling estate losses of the past five years" (Harbridge House, Inc., Blueprint for the Future: A Long-Range Plan for the Jamaican Sugar Industry, prepared for the SMA [of Jamaica] Ltd. [Boston: Harbridge House, 1971], p. 12).

15. See below, Chapter 9.

16. Ministry of Agriculture, "Development of Frome/Monymusk/Bernard Lodge Lands." It is surprising that the 1972 Report really became such a fundamental document for the cooperatives project, because the planners had terms of reference much larger than just the co-ops, had only a relatively short period to prepare the report, and spent most of the report proposing a restructuring of FMLCo.

17. The latter received three points for each three years of experience; the workers were awarded only two points for each three years of their field experience. Workers over 50 were excluded.

18. SWCC (Sugar Workers Coordinating Council), "Summary of Meeting with Mr. Winston Higgins, Cooperative Officer of the Frome Monymusk Land Company" (mimeo, June 3, 1973).

19. Winston Higgins, "Frome/Monymusk/Bernard Lodge Development Project" (mimeo, August 20, 1973).

20. Ibid.

21. SWCC, "Summary of Meeting with Mr. Winston Higgins...."

22. Monymusk Estate was divided into ten farms, or administrative units, each with its own overseer, assistant overseers, headmen and workers. Some of the workers on each of these farms lived rent-free on the compounds.

23. The priest was attached to the Kingston-based Social Action Centre (SAC), a church-affiliated agency which had been active since the 1940s establishing credit and housing cooperatives.

24. The information in this and following sections is based on a study of documents relating to the development of the sugar workers movement, including newsletters, organizing materials, letters and other materials.

25. SWCC, "Summary of Meeting with Mr. Winston Higgins...." In a private meeting with SWCC leaders afterwards, however, he suggested that high FMLCo officials were conspiring to thwart cooperativization (ibid.).

26. Hansard I (1973-1974), p. 374.

27. SWCC, "Minutes of the October 25th Meeting with the Minister of Agriculture" (mimeo, n.d.).

28. Frome SWCC, Landroom (January 1974).

29. Joseph Owens, "Suggestions towards a Plan for Subdivision of Monymusk Estate into Cooperative Farms" (mimeo, September 1973).

30. Ibid.

31. SWCC, "Summary of Meeting with Mr. Winston Higgins....";

MWCCFA, "Minutes," General Meeting, May 20, 1973.

32. To be sure, it did interpret those interests from a predominantly male perspective. Though some women, mainly small farmers, were active at the grass roots, particularly during 1973-1974, the local Monymusk leadership never included any women. While the interests of the women workers were in the main fully consistent with those of the men, their exploitation was particularly acute. After 1974, when the point system was dropped and the organizational features of the cooperatives changed (see next chapter), small farmers dropped away from SWCC.

33. Horace Levy, "Report on the Social Action Centre Project among Sugar Workers in Westmoreland, Clarendon and St. Catherine" (SAC, mimeo, June 1974).

34. Milton J. Esman, "Development Administration and Constituency Organization," Public Administration Review 38(March/April 1978), p. 167.

4
Conflict and Cooperatives, 1974–1975

> Men who had for many years worked as field
> laborers, cane cutters, employees of the
> Estate who were often afraid even to complain
> about certain obvious and injurious conditions
> in their work or living situation; men who
> often tended to disparage themselves and
> others like them and who clearly behaved as
> inferiors before others; such men began to
> question, to criticize, to offer ideas, to
> develop trust for other fellow workers (or at
> least an understanding of others).[1]

RESTRUCTURING THE SUGAR WORKER COOPERATIVES PROJECT

Early in 1974, the government replaced the Frome
Monymusk Land Company's board of directors. The new
board was more sympathetic to the government's evolving
reformist perspective and more attuned to the workers'
interests. The expanded nine-member board included the
SWCC chairperson, from Monymusk, as well as two other,
non-SWCC workers, union delegates from the two other
estates. Also added were the chairperson of the Sugar
Industry Authority (SIA), who had been an early propo-
nent of the idea of sugar worker cooperatives, a university intellectual and supporter of worker participation,
and a PNP politician. The sugar manufacturers had two
representatives. The conservative managing director, the
only holdover from the old board, remained. He was replaced, however, within a few months.

The nomination of a new FMLCo board--with worker
representatives, though only one was from SWCC--was the
first indication that the government recognized the constraints to its cooperativization program. It was also
the first, minimal, manifestation of a commitment to
grass-roots participation. Unquestionably, the workers'
mobilization, and the pressure they were exerting, pro-

vided the major impetus. By 1974, the sugar worker cooperative movement had spread to all three estates under the leadership of SWCC. Whether the government
liked it or not, the workers were now a force. Neither
the workers nor their demands could be ignored, especially by a government increasingly emphasizing worker
participation, cooperatives, rural transformation and
socialism. [2]

In May, in response to SWCC's urging, and again
reflecting the government's new recognition of the
worth of grass-roots participation, several of the new
FMLCo directors attended mass meetings at the three
sites of the proposed pilot cooperatives. At Morelands
farm, Monymusk, under worker pressure, they recommitted
themselves to getting the pilot projects off the ground
before the beginning of the next crop. They also agreed
to another worker demand, that the pilot encompass
2,000 acres, rather than the original 1,000. This demand was stimulated, in part, by the Morelands workers'
recognition that the original acreage allotted to the
pilot represented the inferior section of their farm.
Even more significant, for the first time SWCC was
asked to submit plans for the pilot's structure, which
it did by the end of June.

At this time too, under mass worker pressure and
on the urging of two of the board members, [3] a major
change was made in the government's plans for the pilot
cooperatives. The original idea to provide 30-40 acre
individual leaseholds within a cooperative framework
could only have provided for a maximum of about sixty
workers on each of the twenty or so farms comprising
the three estates; this would have included about one-
third of the 200 registered workers on each farm. [4]
While it was expected that some of the excess labor
force would still be able to find irregular task work
with the co-ops, many would have been made redundant.
In an effort to avoid this social dislocation, with its
obvious political ramifications, the pilot cooperatives
were reorganized along collectivist lines, as producer
cooperatives. That is, the idea of individual leaseholds was largely dropped, the existing farm units remained whole, and all registered workers on these farms
became eligible to join the pilot cooperatives. [5]

There were other problems with the original project plan which were eliminated by the new proposal.
The varying agronomic conditions within the estates,
and even within the proposed 1,000-acre cooperatives,
implied that some of the leasehold units would have
been much better situated than others, with some units
even proving uneconomical. Keeping the farms as single
properties avoided this problem and the possible friction that would have ensued. However, at the same time,
there was still no mechanism for intercooperative, or
interstate financial adjustments.

Finally, the new approach was also more consistent with tradition and work patterns in the sugar belt. The workers on each farm, in most cases, had worked together for many years, with a well-established division of labor. Why, it was now reasoned, break this pattern up?

The decision to adopt a collective farm-type structure, however, carried with it other important implications that were not fully considered at the time, nor adequately provided for later.

First, the adoption of the new model compounded the problem, great in any case, of eliciting new behavioral and attitudinal patterns from the workers. The clients of the cooperatives project were proletarians or semiproletarians living close to the bottom of the society. Especially at Monymusk and Bernard Lodge, most had little or no land and never developed petty-bourgeois orientations. Moreover, the trade union tradition in the sugar belt was very strong, going back thirty years, and this increased the workers' proletarian orientations. They were also subject to low wages, demeaning living and working conditions, and generally menial jobs. They were individuals with limited time frames, no entrepreneurial experience, little or no literacy skills and poor self-concepts. All this of course was the reverse of the ideal petty bourgeois orientation which was needed or expected to develop: a readiness to work long hours in a self-disciplined manner, to undertake themselves whatever cultivation or harvesting tasks were necessary, and possibly to forgo immediate wage or other material rewards in exchange for long-term viability and returns.

Incorporating all existing workers in the new collectives thus greatly increased the difficulties facing SWCC and project officers. Rather than a maximum of about sixty preselected tenant farmers for each 2,000-acre farm, each co-op farm now would have a mass of roughly 200 worker-farmers all needing significant educational and social inputs. Moreover, among the 200 workers were those without any experience in private farming and those without any interest in a cooperative endeavor.

The fact that the proposed land tenure scheme would reinforce traditional work patterns was also not fully considered. Under the earlier plan, those sugar workers granted individual plots would have experienced a definite objective change in their relation to the means of production, facilitating some behavioral and attitudinal changes. This was not the case for the collectivist cooperative members. Under the new scheme the basic structure of plantation operations was little changed; hence the day-to-day experience of most workers was not drastically altered. They remained unionized wage workers, allotted the same work tasks according to the same

procedure as previously, in most cases assigned by the
same hated overseers (the "bushas").

A third implication of the adoption of the new collective farm model was that it increased the problems of
viability or profitability for the new farm units. Allowing all registered workers to join merely reproduced
within the new collectivist enterprises the labor surplus problems which existed under the old structure. It
also precluded the possibility of any substantial increase in per capita income in the short run. With an
estimated 50 percent of the workers being over 50 years
old, planners expected that this surplus could be reduced over ten years or so. Financial problems, however,
developed right at the beginning. Also, the problems
associated with retaining marginal lands in cane were
camouflaged as they could not have been had the farms
been divided up as originally planned. This contributed
significantly to the problems the co-ops faced in their
first years of existence. Finally, keeping the 2,000-
acre units intact disregarded mounting evidence of the
diseconomies of scale in cane farming on units of 1,000
acres or more.[6]

A fourth implication of the adoption of a collective farm model was that it necessitated a substantial
commitment of financial, educational, administrative and
organizational resources by the government. These needs
were substantially magnified in 1975 when practically
all the remaining farms on the three estates received
the go-ahead to become self-managed cooperatives.

The final implication of the new strategy had more
positive connotations for the workers and grass-roots
reform. This was that it allowed SWCC greater access to
the mass of sugar workers than otherwise would have been
the case. Under the original proposal, less than one-
third of the sugar workers would have actually become
involved in the cooperatives. Presumably the remainder
would have been unavailable to the SWCC organization as
it was constituted. But with the collective model all
the workers were potential beneficiaries, and SWCC members. This then increased SWCC's potential as a political force, a potential that indeed was realized during
1974 and 1975, but thwarted thereafter.

THE NEW STRATEGY AND THE FROME MONYMUSK
LAND COMPANY

From the government side, these heavy, new demands
fell primarily on the shoulders of FMLCo. Its position
with respect to grass-roots reform, however, despite the
new board, was still ambiguous. In the first place, it
continued to manifest only lukewarm commitment to a
group farming arrangement. Some within the organization
continued to support an individual leasehold scheme.

This was reflected in FMLCo's project draft, subsequent to the political decision to establish a collective-type cooperative. This new draft proposal incorporated a provision for subdividing up to half of each farm into 25-acre individual parcels for co-op members, who would still remain part of the central cooperative farm unit.[7] Others were not comfortable with a cooperativization policy at all, not to mention SWCC's notions of worker control. For example, the manufacturers' representatives on the board as well as certain advisers to the government, favored a structure more along the lines of a state farm with workers purchasing shares and with the present management remaining. They argued that this would be less experimental, hence less likely to affect production levels and thus the sugar manufacturers' interests. [8]

Second, FMLCo's unsound financial position imposed a continuing burden and constraint on the cooperativization process. Its original debt for the 1971 land purchase was increased by $8.9 million by the direct takeover of the Frome and Monymusk lands in July 1974. It estimated the cost of severance payments, working capital and equipment for 1974-1975 at $8.1 million. Therefore, FMLCo called for a $15 million government equity contribution, but received instead only a $5 million Bank of Jamaica loan repayable over four years.[9] While insisting that a substantial equity contribution by the government was unavoidable, FMLCo predicted that:

> if provided piecemeal by an irregular injection of funds to make up losses and to make severance and other payments then the entire fabric of sugarcane production will be demoralized and a golden opportunity to revitalize its structure would have been lost.[10]

It is noteworthy that the approach which FMLCo predicted would lead to chaos and ultimate failure was just that followed by the government.

Furthermore, FMLCo had other responsibilities in addition to establishing the cooperatives. On July 31, 1974, the Tate and Lyle leasehold over the Frome and Monymusk properties was terminated. These lands reverted to the direct management of the state, represented by FMLCo. FMLCo thus became the largest cane farmer in Jamaica. The significance of this was that it began to direct its attention primarily to its farming activities, and secondarily to the development of employment-generating production projects on its noncane and marginal lands. As the Land Company itself stated, its objectives were:

A. To grow sugarcane profitably.
B. To use the resources of the Estates,

particularly the noncane lands, to provide
maximum employment opportunities for redundant
workers on the Estates and for those in the
vicinity of the Estates who are at present unemployed.[11]

Conspicuous for its absence was any mention of cooperativization, which indeed was only a small part of
FMLCo's responsibilities.

A glance at its organization chart at this time re-
inforces the point (Figure 4.1). The task of transform-
ing the estate cane lands to cooperatives occupied only
a small place in FMLCo's organization and in its agenda
for action.

Fourth, while it was attempting to carry forward
the implementation of the pilot cooperative project,
FMLCo also was developing a possible institutional alternative to the co-ops, in its management and structuring of all the remaining estate cane lands under its
portfolio. Toward this end, in its state farming operation FMLCo moved to: a) decentralize decision making to
the overseer level; b) initiate a profit-sharing scheme,
to be activated when productivity exceeded "standard
yield expectations"; and c) establish worker committees
on each farm to participate in management. As it argued
at the time, these "modernized" state farm arrangements:

> will provide an alternative to the Cooperative or-
> ganization. Profit sharing and the involvement of
> workers in management provide the advantages of a
> Cooperative and yet is a more flexible arrangement.
> Therefore, in the future--particularly if the Co-
> operatives become burdened with unmanageable prob-
> lems--the workers may well opt for the looser ar-
> rangement of sharing both profits and management
> decisions. [12]

To be sure, state farms could also smooth the transition to co-ops, as the Land Company did point out.
But for SWCC, it was this sort of serious ambiguity,
when joined with the concrete anti-SWCC and anti-worker
activities that FMLCo engaged in (see below), which
raised numerous questions of trust and confidence.

By December 1974, a cabinet decision had clarified
matters, and the formal policy position was clearly toward cooperativization. The transformation would be
gradual, and the final form which the co-ops would take
was still an open question.[13] Yet there was still no
concrete plan for future cooperativization, again raising questions in the minds of the workers, as well as
one Cooperative Department advisor.[14] FMLCo was also not
preparing a pool of farm managers well versed in cooperative principles and operations, was not aiding in the
implementation of a worker training program and had no

FIGURE 4.1
Frome Monymusk Land Company, Ltd.--Organization Structure

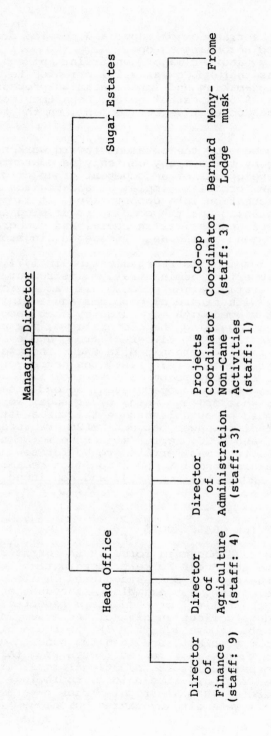

Source: Adapted from Harvard Business School, "The Frome Monymusk Land
          Company Ltd. - A Case Study" (mimeo, 1975).

plans for the transfer of input and service provision
functions to secondary co-ops.[15]

Finally, another major constraint and source of
conflict was that FMLCo was still oriented to a top-
down decision-making and implementation process. For
example, in 1975 it established a Department of Social
Planning and Cooperative Development, on the following
assumptions:

> The success of the movement toward worker partici-
> pation by the company can only be guaranteed by
> the development of a competent group of officials
> to plan, organize, implement and monitor the
> transformation into cooperatives. It is therefore
> the intention of the company to develop a small
> group of specialists in social and cooperative
> development at the Head Office in Kingston.[16]

Thus, despite its reorganization in 1974, FMLCo remained an imperfect administrative instrument in regard
to the cooperativization process. It was a growing
bureaucracy with financial problems and administrative
concerns it viewed with more urgency than cooperativization. Even regarding the cooperatives, its perspective was substantially different from, and even opposed
to, the workers' as organized in SWCC. The two main
areas of difference were: first, the degree of worker
control and autonomy to be allowed the pilot cooperatives and any future cooperatives; second, the whole
question of whether, and when, other sugar worker cooperatives would be established on the three estates. The
significant differences between FMLCo, representing the
government, and SWCC, representing the workers, on these
and other matters was fertile ground for sowing the
seeds of future conflict. Such conflict became manifest
during the second half of 1974, and continued throughout 1975.

CONFLICT AT THE GRASS ROOTS

During 1974 the main force at the grass roots continued to be the Sugar Workers Coordinating Council.
This was true despite some stagnation in its organizational development. For example, although the number of
members on the rolls increased, to a reported 1,200 in
mid-1974, dues collection did not increase. The November
figure reported above (Chapter 3) was the zenith. There
were probably somewhat more than two hundred dues payers, though there was a fall-off even from this in the
out-of-crop period. It is traditional in Jamaica for
worker organizations, like unions, to include as members
far more persons than are regular dues payers, and
sugar workers were already paying union dues (via check-

off).

For a short while, the local councils set up by SWCC were meeting only monthly, and the SWCC bulletin, now called <u>SWCC News</u>, became a monthly in 1974. There were reports of too many members only on paper, and of the need for cutting down the rolls, to be based on the more reliable workers. Organizing activity also seemed to be stagnant, and tended toward more bureaucratic modes--press releases, reliance on the work of the SWCC nominee on the FMLCo board, meetings without concrete action or results, and training in co-op principles and managerial practices for potential management committee members. No doubt a major factor here was the procrastination and bureaucratic maneuvers by the government, which helped trim the sails of the workers after the April-to-November mobilization and buildup of expectations.

Nonetheless, once the government finally decided that the pilot cooperatives would start in 1975, it was SWCC which played the major role at the grass roots in mobilizing and preparing the workers for the changeover. During the summer and fall, SWCC organizers actively assisted the various farm steering committees in their preparations. Indeed, the concentration of SWCC's resources on the pilots at this time constrained its activity on the other farms.

However, by the fall, with worker steering committees formed for the pilots and operating well, SWCC's full attention returned to the other workers on the three estates. SWCC after all had been formed by sugar workers to ensure their participation in the distribution of the government cane lands. To this end, local worker councils had been formed at many of the farms on the estates. At this time, SWCC took this one step further, setting up Workers' Management Committees (WMCs) at each of the farms and the tractor and transport department. These committees were meant to facilitate, and exemplify, the government's stated commitment to worker participation. But more important, according to SWCC, the WMCs were necessary in order to train and prepare the workers for their forthcoming managerial responsibilities as cooperators. The WMCs would give the workers access to information, experience in decision making and provide a morale booster for them while they awaited cooperativization, by showing them that progress was being made.[17] They operated parallel to the existing farm management structure.

Membership in the WMCs was drawn from the existing SWCC local councils. At Monymusk it was expected that these fifteen or twenty of "the most competent and interested members" would be the vanguard, the basis of a successful transition to cooperatives. The local councils continued to operate, though meeting only half as frequently as before, or once each month. By the begin-

ning of October, WMCs were in place and functioning,
with monthly meetings, on all the farms at Monymusk.

In order to function properly, the WMCs needed to
be recognized formally by the Land Company, which was,
after all, in charge of the estates and the cooperativization process. SWCC called on FMLCo to "instruct
present farm management to enter into collaboration
with them (the WMCs) in all matters pertaining to the
operation of the farms." SWCC insisted that the WMCs be
given real authority, that they not be limited to "a
merely advisory capacity, so that management could disregard their wishes."[18]

While FMLCo reportedly praised and gave its
tacit approval to SWCC's plan, in fact it had other intentions.[19] With the active support of local-level
field staff and the two major trade unions, FMLCo began
to organize its own worker committees, in opposition to
SWCC's WMCs (Table 4.1). SWCC was too independent and
too committed to worker mobilization for FMLCo, too
committed to worker control for the staff, and too much
an organizational competitor for the unions. FMLCo in-
tended to isolate and, if possible, destroy SWCC, and
co-opt the workers movement at the local level.

In addition to being an anti-SWCC local-level power
base, the FMLCo worker committees were vehicles of that
agency's notion of worker participation. In FMLCo's
case they were not seen as a preparation or training
ground for cooperativization. While giving workers some
management experience in case further cooperatives were
started in the future, these committees, it was hoped,
would also add to the efficiency of the existing state
farming enterprises. And for many in the government and
sugar industry, as we have said, a state farm was the
preferred long-term operating structure for these cane
lands. And, for many, this was the appropriate model of
worker participation.

The Land Company withheld all assistance and support to SWCC's organizing efforts. That organization
was denied even lists of the names of all registered
workers on the farms. But in the main, FMLCo relied on
its local-level field and administrative staff and the
unions to carry forward its anti-SWCC grass-roots campaign.

The unions, both the PNP-affiliated National Workers Union (NWU) and the JLP-affiliated Bustamante Industrial Trade Union (BITU), opposed SWCC for four
reasons. First, SWCC was viewed as an alternative and
competing workers organization. This view was reinforced by the fact that it was often critical of the
unions, more democratic in its operations, and much more
vocal and active in defense of workers' interests.
Second, the cooperativization reform posed a potential
further threat to the labor unions, that of eliminating
their working-class base, by turning the workers into

TABLE 4.1
FMLCo and SWCC Worker Committees, 1974-1975

FMLCo	SWCC
General Orientation	
"The Committee is an Advisory Consultative Body and it may not by resolution or otherwise reverse or amend any instructions given by management," nor intervene in disciplinary matters or any union function, such as salaries. The Land Company's idea was to get some worker input, improve communication and "to encourage the feeling that management and workers must work together cooperatively to achieve common goals."	The WMC was meant to "represent and implement the will of the workers at the workplace." Ultimately the WMC was to be the main authority on the farm, with staff answerable to it. The WMCs were also meant to represent the workers in relation to the unions and other bodies, and to educate, motivate and mobilize the workers to transform the farms to co-ops.
Membership	
The FMLCo Committee was to have no more than 11 members, with the overseer, or Head of Department, as the chairperson. The estate manager was an ex-officio member of each committee, and up to two other staff members were eligible to be members as well. Staff members of the Committee were selected, not elected. The secretary was an elective position.	The WMCs did not include staff, but they were expected to work alongside staff. They were to be independent, with their own officers and answerable only to the workers as a whole. The WMC should be large enough to "resist intimidation and victimization from the management," with 11 members considered a good number.
Elections	
Workers were to be elected by occupational groups, with at least one from each separate work category, but no more than 8 altogether. The Ministry of Labour would supervise elections. Workers would be elected to two-year staggered terms, with reelection disallowed.	Worker elections were to be on an at-large basis, held annually. Reelection was allowable. The Department of Cooperatives was the valid supervisory body. The first WMCs were not elected, but nominated or co-opted.

(Continued)

Table 4.1 (Cont.)

FMLCo	SWCC
Meetings	
The Committee was to meet at set times, but not less than once per month during crop, and once every two months out-of-crop. The chairperson could request a special committee meeting anytime, as could any three members.	The WMC should meet with management at the start of every week to review operations, and at least once per month by itself.
Relation to General Membership or Work Force	
There were no provisions for meetings of the general work force.	All workers were invited to the monthly WMC meetings, and the WMCs were to report regularly to the workers.
Participation in the Planning of the Committees	
The Committees were basically set up by FMLCo and local staff, without worker inputs at either the planning or implementation stage.	The WMCs were formed from within SWCC, hence, with worker participation. Traditional cooperative principles generally prevailed.

Source: Frome Monymusk Land Company, "Constitution and Rules of Procedure of the Committee," n.d., in Minutes of the Board of Directors, FMLCo, January 28, 1975 (in FMLCo files); SWCC, "The Role and Function of the Workers' Committees of Management" (mimeo, October 1974); SWCC, "Rules and Functions for Workers' Committees of Management" (mimeo, October 1974); SWCC, "Propositions concerning Workers' Committees" (mimeo, December 1974).

small farmers. The local-level leadership of the BITU and supporters of the JLP had other fears—that cooperitivization was aimed at weakening their influence among the workers. The fact that many of SWCC's early leaders had ties either to the PNP or to the NWU reinforced this perspective and provoked partisan opposition.[20] Finally, the generally conservative local and national trade union leaders were quite threatened and alarmed by SWCC's leftist orientations and ties [21] and were influenced by their generally close relationships with management in the industry.

Estate field and administrative staff had long-standing strained relations with the workers, in a pattern dating back to the days of slavery. At Monymusk,

when the pilot cooperative was established on Morelands
farm, the worker steering committee demanded the ouster
of the existing farm overseer. He was well known for his
authoritarian manner and disrespect for the workers, and
was widely disliked by them. Their eventual success in
firing this overseer caused other field staff to sit up
and take notice. [22] Shortly after this event they formed
a staff association at Monymusk, with others following
at the two other estates. The staff associations, particularly the one at Monymusk, strongly opposed SWCC. They
were particularly in conflict with its notions of worker
control, its success at worker mobilization and its
radical perspective. In addition to agitating actively
against SWCC at the local level, as in the conflict over
the WMCs, they also played a leading role at the national level in opposing both the workers' demands for
full cooperativization and SWCC's leadership.

SWCC called the FMLCo committees "company committees" or "busha committees," and launched a strong coun-
terattack. [23] Its position was that:

> No committee set up by management will be given any
> real authority or power. Such a committee will only
> be for show, to give the workers the _feeling_ (but
> not the _reality_) of power. [24]

Early in 1975, two thousand sugar workers signed SWCC
support petitions, destroying the basis of FMLCo's key
argument--that since SWCC was not "truly representative"
of the majority of workers there was no justification
for recognizing them. The Land Company's own counter-
mobilization effort faded after this.

The pilot cooperatives represented another locus of
conflict between SWCC and the Land Company. FMLCo carefully cultivated the allegiance of the pilots as a
source of local power that could be used against SWCC
and in support of its own interests in the cooperativization process. This was relatively easy because once
the pilots began operations their main interaction was
with FMLCo, which provided them with all services, including management. Meanwhile, all of SWCC's resources
became occupied with the struggle to convert the other
farms into cooperatives. Most of the members of the
pilots quickly lost interest in this continued struggle
once they were established as cooperators. FMLCo and
the Co-op Department reinforced this split. The sugar
workers' business was now cane farming and not "agitation," they told the pilot cooperators.

In 1975, FMLCo attempted to take its advantage a
step further by forming an association of cooperatives,
comprising in the first instance the three pilots. This
was another obvious attempt to compete with SWCC. Although meetings were held, the association never got off
the ground. [25] Nevertheless, FMLCo, through its co-op

director and education officers, continued to cultivate
ties with the pilots, while attempting to split them
from the wider sugar worker movement. For example, during 1975, SWCC's first chairperson, who had also become
chairperson of Morelands Co-op, gradually split with
the larger movement. His co-op did not join the other
farms at the Estate Cooperative level until much later
(1978). Neither Barham Pilot Co-op (Frome) nor Salt
Pond (Bernard Lodge) ever affiliated, and they continued to be centers of resistance to SWCC. The splitting off of the pilots during 1975 "had a profoundly
debilitating effect on the whole cooperative movement,"
according to one organizer.[26]

This was particularly frustrating to SWCC because
it considered worker unity to be an essential prerequi-
site of any sort of progress for sugar workers; this
and worker control were its two cardinal principles.
Hence, SWCC always resisted any tactic that would divide
workers or set them against each other in the kind of
destructive intraclass conflict so common in modern
Jamaican history. FMLCo's tactics, in their eyes, were
leading to the destruction or weakening of the workers'
movement. That was, they felt, its major goal.

During 1975, there was also increasing opposition
to SWCC from within the PNP. By 1976, high-level party
opposition was being translated into concrete support
for strategies aimed at wresting control of the co-op
movement from SWCC. SWCC was seen as a political liability, for a number of reasons: a) it was an independent
political force competing with the PNP for sugar worker
allegiance; b) it was "two-faced" in its relation to
the PNP, sometimes adopting "underhand anti-PNP tactics"; c) its strong socialist orientation and anti-
union postures made it susceptible to political attacks
by JLP political and trade union leaders; and d) the
hostility of some of the workers toward SWCC could be
projected onto the PNP.[27]

The increasing level of conflict and opposition to
SWCC during 1974-1975 was directly related to the workers' own political mobilization. As SWCC came out of
its brief period of dormancy in the latter part of 1974,
it became more active and more of a threat to certain
political, administrative and economic interests. As
these interests mobilized against SWCC, it intensified
its rhetoric and militance, rather than retreat. For
example, the traditional class antagonism between workers and overseers was not used or emphasized by SWCC
during its early organizing.[28] Organizers in fact tended to play down the very significant worker hostility
to the "busha." The conflict over the worker committees,
however, with the field staff playing a leading role in
opposition to SWCC, led to an intensification of the
manifest levels of hostility between workers and staff,
and to more self-consciousness and rhetoric among SWCC

members about the need for <u>class</u> struggle.[29]

Then, too, in keeping with national trends, it was around this time that socialist and left-wing orientations became more of a focal aspect of the sugar worker movement. For example, in December, at SWCC's invitation, Guyanese communist Cheddi Jagan presented a public talk to workers in Lionel Town. In February, also in Lionel Town, left-wing student groups organized a rally and talk in support of human rights in Dominica, particularly those of lumpen youth called "dreads."[30]

In April 1975, SWCC's Second Congress adopted a much more militant line than previously. The assembled WMC chairpersons and other worker delegates demanded that all the farms and departments on the estates ready to become cooperatives must be allowed to do so immediately after the harvest season. Just a few months earlier, SWCC had called for only four to five new co-ops on each estate. Also at this congress, SWCC for the first time openly called for complete worker control of the entire sugar industry, with SAC expanding its program of worker education and cooperative development as a first step. Significantly, SWCC also extended internationalist support to striking oil-field and sugar workers in Trinidad: "We urge you all to maintain the utmost pressure on the oppressors of the working class."[31]

SWCC was also strengthened by heightened levels of worker support during the latter part of 1974 and into 1975. One manifestation of this was the two thousand signatures on the SWCC petitions in 1975. At this time, too, over 650 sugar workers were regular monthly dues payers, and the newsletter returned to a fortnightly basis.

In addition to supporting SWCC's commitment to worker control and the establishment of cooperatives, and its grass-roots organizational approach, many workers were also drawn to SWCC after the pilots began operations and the sugar worker-cooperators on those farms received severance payments. At that point the demand for cooperatives became entangled with the expectation of windfall severance payments. The payment of severance to all workers, as their farms became cooperatives, was based on previously negotiated union agreements, originating with an agreement between the unions and the previous government. When the land was originally purchased in 1971, it was expected that it would be parceled out in large blocs to cane farmers, with many workers losing their jobs. To protect the workers at least partially, it was agreed that any future transfer of the lands out of government hands would justify workers' severance claims. The payment of severance to all workers was justified further by the recognition that if severance were paid only to those workers opting not to join the cooperatives, and hence losing their cane

jobs, then this would have pulled many workers away
from the co-ops. Finally, the Manley government was
buoyed by its revenue windfall in 1974-1975 from sugar
sales and the new bauxite tax; it appeared to have the
financial resources.

The expectation of these severance payments, following the example of the pilot cooperatives, was an important carrot drawing workers into active support for
the cooperativization movement, and in effect for SWCC.
While the quality of this expanded base of support for
SWCC was questionable, the increased level of SWCC political capacity that resulted was not.[32]

FURTHER COOPERATIVIZATION

All this--the successful struggle with FMLCo over
the worker committees, the increasing worker support,
its political momentum, and left-wing trends nationally
--strengthened SWCC's position in 1975 despite opposition from administrative and other forces. The level of
worker mobilization during 1975 was indeed impressive.
This immensely strengthened the workers' position at the
same time that it alarmed the local and national bourgeoisie, sugar industry leaders, and many PNP and government officials. This even as the latter were express-
ing pro-socialist sentiments. From this position of
strength, the workers' movement on the three estates
undertook to resolve the key question facing them and
the government in 1975--how many new cooperatives would
be formed?

The government's position was that financial and
managerial constraints restricted the pace of cooperative development, and that the possibilities and consequences of failure, in terms of cane production and for
the future development of cooperatives in Jamaica, suggested a cautious approach. Thus, only three more cooperatives were planned for the 1976 crop.[33] Because of
SWCC's opposition to this, however, the prime minister
convened a special committee in 1975, including all the
major interests, to deal with the issue of the pace and
extent of co-op development on the three sugar estates.

At their meetings (four sessions were held before
the major report was submitted), despite intense opposition coming mainly from staff association representatives, SWCC's preparation, diligence, commitment and
political support were decisive. Manley's apparent sympathy for SWCC's position was also an important factor.
The planning committee concluded that "the highest
priority should be given to initiating as many new Cooperatives this year as are possible," with pre-cooper-
atives being formed where lack of finance, management
and training personnel, and low levels of readiness of
the workers constrained the formation of full coopera-

tives.34 Those farms that were ready, according to a set of criteria developed by the Cooperative Department, could begin farming operations as co-ops beginning in 1976.

There was also agreement on the importance of establishing secondary and tertiary cooperatives, responsible to the primary cooperatives, and providing the technical and support services then being provided by FMLCo. Toward this end, the major parties agreed immediately to set up a transitional service body. There was no agreement on membership of this transitional body. SWCC felt only it and FMLCo were critically involved, but others argued for additional membership for the Sugar Industry Authority, the Cooperative Department and the trade unions.

Third, the committee stated that all workers, as well as staff, should be eligible for membership in the cooperatives, and that members of staff would continue in employment with the new co-ops. Finally, on the issue of jurisdiction, SWCC was given responsibility for grass-roots organizational and mobilizing work, with some participation in training and education. This latter was the major preserve of the Cooperative Department. FMLCo would retain training responsibilities for managerial staff, and continue to advise on technical and financial matters.

This decision, to move forward rapidly if the workers proved their readiness, was favorable to SWCC, and could not have been approved without Manley's support. He was obviously impressed by the workers' determination and organization, and was influenced by the government's revenue windfall as well. In addition, the impending elections in 1976 could not have been very far from his mind. The agreement, however, was also a compromise with staff, the unions, FMLCo and the Cooperative Department in a number of ways. SWCC did not get the whole cake. Hence, the basic conflicts between SWCC and the others remained.

To reinforce its advantage and to ensure the workers' readiness, SWCC launched a massive, grass-roots education campaign. Due mainly to this campaign, practically all the remaining farms on the three estates were able to satisfy the criteria established for determining which farms were ready to be transformed into cooperatives.

SWCC had always been aware of the debilitating legacy of illiteracy, self-doubt, worker disunity and attitudes of dependency on those of higher class status among sugar workers. It was also mindful of the importance of worker education and consciousness in its efforts to mobilize the sugar workers. Indeed, from the outset, SWCC organizers set as their goals:
  a. the promotion of social-psychological change among workers, emphasizing worker unity, worker

capacity and self-reliance, and, in particular,
the development of a "democratic" consciousness;
b. educational advancement--the promotion of literacy, political education, cultural education,
education in co-op principles and cane farm
finances;
c. the promotion of a more realistic perspective on
the mechanism of social change, as requiring
struggle along with one's co-workers and others
in a similar position against capitalist and
reactionary forces. [35]

At Monymusk, not only were certain activities
geared to these ends, but the actual practice of the
movement sought to embody them. From the beginning sugar
workers took effective leadership roles within SWCC. The
main SAC organizer never accepted a formal position,
though still providing considerable initiative, energy
and leadership. This was part of the commitment to worker control, both in the farm enterprises and in the
political organization. The rhetoric of the movement emphasized, possibly more than anything, the need for worker unity as the key to progress and that workers alone
could do whatever they set themselves.

Nonformal educational experiences had high priority. Through mid-1975, almost 400 workers from all three
estates had attended at least one of the eighteen SAC-
run residential courses, each running up to five days. [36]
These courses emphasized leadership training. Beginning
in 1974, Monymusk workers were periodically also attending Cooperative Department residential courses on co-op
management. The Cooperative Department also conducted
courses locally. For example, early in 1974, two twelve-
week programs were run concurrently in Vere.

The most significant education effort, however,
most significant because of its depth, intensity,
method, and emphasis on the mass of workers and not just
the leadership, was launched by SWCC in mid-1975, with
the assistance of SAC. This campaign incorporated three
aspects:
a. literacy training--it was hoped that three weeks
of intensive training would have everybody reading and writing at least at a third-grade level;
b. political and cultural education--"workers must
learn the history of poor man's struggle, the
tactics of the oppressors, the strategy which
workers must follow to gain back control over
their lives, their lands, and their labor"; [37]
c. cooperative education--imparting knowledge of
the basic organizational, operational and financial principles and practices of cooperatives,
and trying to instill a new co-op consciousness
and new work habits.

Readers were written and published for use in this
educational campaign. There were five readers incorpo-

rating 23 lessons. Each used visual as well as written material, with the latter constructed and presented so as to provide literacy training as well as information and consciousness-raising. The readers also used Jamaican patois, the "people's language," and teachers were encouraged to use this language in their classes, in direct contravention of traditional practice in Jamaican schools.

The intensive education program, like the whole movement of which it was a part, was designed to exemplify and reinforce the principle of worker control. It was education by and for workers. Though it was never fully implemented, the campaign was based on teams of worker-educators at each farm: twenty of the more politically conscious and literate workers, at least one from each work gang, and with no more than half being members of the worker management committees. They were to receive three weeks of on-the-farm training from the fourteen SWCC/SAC teachers and five resource persons.

The education program never fully got off the ground, especially at Monymusk. There it did not start until September, and the worker-educators were never a significant feature, as SWCC teachers carried the load. Sessions were only infrequently held in the fields, tended to be haphazard and never utilized all readers.[38] Still quite a number of workers were reached, an average of almost one hundred for each farm.[39]

The grass-roots education and mobilization drive resulted in seventeen more farms—seven at Monymusk, six at Frome and four at Bernard Lodge—being approved to become cooperatives beginning in 1976. The cooperatives averaged 1,867 acres in cane at Monymusk, 1,366 at Frome, and 1,861 at Bernard Lodge. It was also agreed to establish three estate-level or secondary, cooperatives, one at each of the estates, and one national, or tertiary, sugar worker cooperative body.

While the pilot cooperatives had received individual leases of forty-nine years, SWCC argued that the remaining lands should be leased en block to the estate cooperatives. An estatewide lease with subleases to each farm would, it was felt, ensure that the individual farm cooperatives remained linked together, would increase the possibility of intra-estate economic transfers between farms, and would strengthen the degree of worker solidarity and worker control. It was also felt that a lease to the estate cooperative would, by strengthening and legalizing the workers' control at that level, provide a bulwark against expected attempts by FMLCo to reassert its authority via an attempt to influence decisions at the estate level.

This issue became the basis of the most serious local-level campaign against SWCC up to that time. A number of workers did indeed favor individual farm leases, because of their concern that any other arrange-

66

ment would wrest direct control from them. FMLCo and
members of staff built on this legitimate fear, using
and stimulating the issue and the recrimination, conflict and hostility surrounding it to divide and weaken
the workers' movement. This served two purposes: to
break SWCC's hold and to establish an estatewide governing system that could more easily be controlled by managerial staff and be answerable to FMLCo.[40]

A major campaign of propaganda, agitation and even
violence at the local level ensued. Land Company officials, staff, local political leaders (both PNP and JLP)
and a few ex-SWCC supporters were all active participants and leaders of the anti-SWCC, anti-estate lease,
anti-SAC campaign. It continued even after the government formally approved an estate lease around the end
of November.

The hostility generated had a lasting influence. At
Monymusk, for example, three of the farms and the tractor and transport department continued to oppose SWCC
into 1976. The general recrimination and conflict which
surrounded the establishment of the co-ops created a
most inhospitable and difficult atmosphere in which to
implement this major agrarian reform and experiment in
social transformation. Nonetheless, starting January
1976, twenty self-managed farm cooperatives, three
estate-level cooperatives, and one tertiary-level cooperative were in operation. The "workers' time" had
come, but it was a tense beginning.

NOTES

1. Phillips, p. 523.
2. In September 1974, the PNP officially declared itself a
democratic socialist party.
3. Richard Fletcher, SIA Chairperson and Dr. Carl Stone, Lec-
turer in Government at the University of the West Indies. Their
leading role was described in a personal communication by Stone.
4. The farms averaged about two thousand acres. Actually, the
average number of workers placed on the farms would have been less
than sixty since significant portions of the land on many of the
farms, especially at Monymusk, were completely inappropriate for
cane cultivation.
5. The original 1972 planning document had rejected producer
cooperatives because of the assumed association with low work productivity due to the lack of sufficient individual incentives. It
is interesting, and important, to note that FMLCo's two major cooperative planning and implementation officers between 1973 and 1975
were included in the 1972 interministerial planning committee, were
in fact its "co-op experts." Hence, it is not unreasonable to con-
clude that they concurred with the conclusions of the 1972 report.
Yet, after 1974, they were deeply involved in implementing collectivist cane farms.

6. The diseconomies tended to be due to higher overhead costs and management problems on the larger units. One study estimated that cane holdings of less than 1,000 acres were 10 percent more cost-efficient than larger ones (Harbridge House). Also see Ministry of Agriculture, Agriculture Sector Survey, p. 3 and E. A. Sims, "Sugarcane Production Cost in Jamaica" (Mandeville, Jamaica: Sugar Industry Research Institute, 1977).

7. Winston Higgins, "Bernard Lodge, Frome and Monymusk Pilot Project Design and Operations" (mimeo, n.d.). Higgins was one of the two co-op officers identified above in fn. 5.

8. At that time, almost all of the manufacturing capacity was still in private, mostly foreign, hands. Stone has denied that there was any significant political opposition on the board (personal communication). But SWCC documents, based on reports from its chairman, who was also a member of the board, suggest otherwise.

9. The Frome Monymusk Land Company Ltd., "Operational Plans," Draft (mimeo, August 1974), pp. 9-17.

10. Ibid., p. 1.

11. Ibid., p. 3.

12. Ibid., p. 5. This lack of commitment to cooperativization was reflected in statements by other government officials as well, in which they referred to cooperative farming as just one possible development model among many.

13. N. A. Lyon, "Managing Director's Report on the Frome Monymusk Land Co. Ltd., August 1974 - December 1974" (mimeo, December 1974).

14. E. Parnell, "Sugar Cane Cooperatives Operating on Lands Leased from the Frome Monymusk Land Co. Ltd." (mimeo, February 1975).

15. Ibid.

16. Jamaica, Ministry of Agriculture, "Annual Report, 1974-1975" (Kingston, n.d.).

17. SWCC, "Organization of Workers' Management Committees at Frome, Monymusk and Bernard Lodge" (mimeo, June 1974).

18. Ibid.

19. SWCC News, July 1974.

20. Interview with Joe Owens, SAC organizer, June 5, 1978.

21. Interview with Holroyd Thompson, President, National Workers Union, June 12, 1978.

22. Interview with W. Madden, President, FMLCo Staff Association, April 16, 1978.

23. "Busha" was the traditional worker term for the overseer.

24. SWCC, "The Role . . . ."

25. Personal communication, Horace Levy, SAC organizer.

26. Personal communication, Joe Owens.

27. These charges were contained in a private document presented to a meeting of the PNP executive committee in early spring, 1976.

28. This was less true at Frome than at Monymusk.

29. See various organizing materials put out during the conflict with FMLCo over the WMCs, as well as the various SWCC newsletters, especially Landroom, put out by SWCC Frome.

30. In 1974, Dominica passed the "Prohibited and Unlawful Societies and Associations Act," aimed particularly at the dreads,

but also considered to be a tool against the left. The dreads were
similar in appearance to the Jamaican Rastafarians, and the negative
middle-class reaction to them was also similar.

31. SWCC, Chairman's Congress, April 4-5, 1975, "Resolutions
Passed" (mimeo, n.d.).

32. Severance was paid on the following basis: for each year
of employment up to and including the tenth year the worker received three weeks pay for each year; from the eleventh year of employment on, the worker received four weeks pay for each year. At
the end of 1975, staff members also demanded and received such payments (for them, like the workers, regardless of whether they were
still working). In their case, there was no previous commitment to
pay them such severance in the circumstances. They staged a strike
and other actions to enforce, and ultimately secure, their demands.
The severance payments ended up being a significant financial drain
on the government and were considerably higher than anyone expected
in 1971 when the agreement was made. This was due to the rapid escalation of wage rates, especially in 1975, and the industrywide
increase in severance protection for workers. Severance payments
totaled over $11 million. In 1976, when the government took over
the Frome and Monymusk factories, workers there also demanded severance though none were made redundant. The government refused and
this became a continuing source of industrial unrest among factory
workers. As late as October 1979, Monymusk factory workers struck
over the same issue.

33. Michael Manley, speech at the lease signing for Salt Pond
Workers Cooperative Society, Jamaica Daily Gleaner, April 10, 1975.
Also see the opening remarks by FMLCo Board Chairman and Ministry
of Agriculture Parliamentary Secretary, Desmond Leaky, at the first
meeting of the Prime Minister's Committee on Co-operative Development, in the minutes.

34. Prime Minister's Committee on Co-operative Development of
the Frome, Monymusk and Bernard Lodge Estates, "Report" (mimeo,
May 21, 1975).

35. Horace Levy, "Report on the Social Action Centre Programme
among Sugar Workers in Westmoreland, Clarendon and St. Catherine
(SAC mimeo, June 1974).

36. SAC, radio broadcast, "Education for the Sugar Worker Co-
ops," Spring 1978 (SAC, typescript).

37. SWCC, "SWCC News and Study Sheet #11" (mimeo, June 1975).

38. Among the problems impeding progress with the education
program at Monymusk were the following: opposition from management
at both the estate and farm levels, manifest in the refusal to allow workers any time off to attend education sessions in the field
during the work day; a lack of adequate meeting places in the
fields; a less developed system of work gangs than at other estates
such as Frome.

39. Jim Schecher, "Report on Co-op Member Education Programme
Carried Out by Social Action Centre in Conjunction with USWCC Member Services Department" (Kingston: SAC, 1976).

40. Carl Stone, "Statement to Workers" (mimeo, November 28,
1975).

5
Structure and Organization
of the Cooperatives

Between June 1974 and December 1975, the three largest sugar estates in Jamaica were almost wholly transformed into twenty sugar worker cooperatives. The first stage involved the establishment of three pilot cooperatives in 1974, with the worker-cooperators on each of these approximately 2,000-acre farms granted collective 49-year leases. Beginning with the 1976 crop, seventeen additional cooperative farms were carved out of the three estates. At the same time, secondary-level cooperatives, made up of the farm-level cooperatives at each estate, took over the functions and responsibilities of the Frome Monymusk Land Company at that level. The usurpation of FMLCo, and with it the elimination of direct state authority over the cooperatives, was completed with the additional formation of a central sugar worker cooperative body, operationally and physically supplanting FMLCo at the national level. In effect, by 1976, the Frome Monymusk Land Company, a state farming entity, was completely replaced with a cooperative structure (Figure 5.1). Meanwhile, a state-owned National Sugar Company was formed, and it began to buy out Tate and Lyle, the owner of Frome and Monymusk sugar factories, and the local syndicate that controlled Bernard Lodge factory.

The multitiered structure, with functionally and politically oriented secondary and tertiary levels, was directed to serving the needs of the primary level cooperative farms and the worker-cooperators who composed them. They were functionally oriented in the sense of providing necessary services, like finance, planning, central purchasing, etc. At the same time, they were politically oriented in that they cemented the unity of the sugar worker cooperative movement within each estate and between estates. The United Sugar Workers Cooperative Council (USWCC), based in Kingston, also provided the cooperatives with a national political presence.

In the post-1976 period, however, neither the

70

FIGURE 5.1
Sugar Workers Cooperative Structure

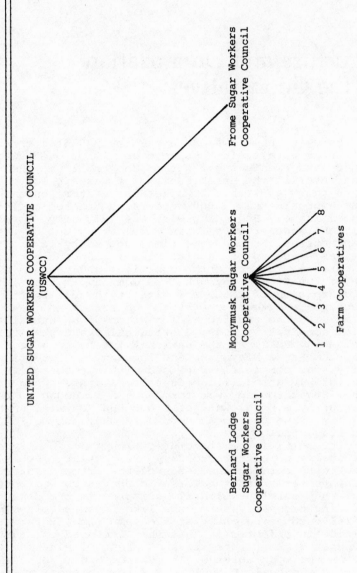

UNITED SUGAR WORKERS COOPERATIVE COUNCIL
(USWCC)

Bernard Lodge
Sugar Workers
Cooperative Council

Monymusk Sugar Workers
Cooperative Council

Frome Sugar Workers
Cooperative Council

1 2 3 4 5 6 7 8

Farm Cooperatives

<u>Source</u>: Adapted from <u>Workers Time 1</u> (March 1976).

Workers' unity nor their organization were ever as
strong as they had been between 1973 and 1975. Thus,
for example, there was never any question of intercooperative redistributive mechanisms--whether intra-
estate or between estates--and this was not solely at-
tributable to the absence of anything to redistribute.
Nor, in the post-1976 period, was the sugar workers'
movement as self-consciously a movement with a political
content and a bias toward worker mobilization as it had
been previously. In part this was an expected consequence of the cooperatives' new business-oriented
roles, but it also was a reflection of wider political
realities (Chapter 6). This topic will be taken up more
fully in the following chapter. Before doing that, this
chapter will detail the structure and organization of
the cooperatives which were established.

THE FARM-LEVEL COOPERATIVES

Nature and Membership

The sugar worker cooperatives were collective farms
established and organized according to traditional cooperative principles. According to Galeski, collective
farms are:

Farms operated by groups of producers who are not
members of the same family and not workers hired
by a manager, but who are members of a group organized on the principle of sharing among themselves
property, work and the results of work.[1]

The cooperatives were collective farms because all the
land, machinery and buildings were owned by the collective membership organized as a cooperative society, and
legally registered as such under Jamaican law. Even the
members' houses were owned by the cooperative. While
there were also generally accepted usufruct rights to
house plots, these plots were usually quite small. In
addition, some members also kept cattle on or cultivated "outskirt" lands. Though they had no formal right
to do so--as in the past it was still often considered
"capture land"--their tenure went generally undisturbed.
The membership of each of the cooperatives was made
up of all workers previously registered by the Frome
Monymusk Land Company to work on the particular farm.
As an additional condition of membership, each worker
had to agree to deposit 50 percent of his or her severance payment in the cooperative as an interest-bearing
loan deposit callable in two years and yielding 8 percent, or 1 percent above the normal rate for savings.[2]
If the need arose, additional members could subsequently

be admitted by decision of the committee of management. Members were also required to purchase twenty shares at $1 each (payable over an extended period), and pay a 10¢ entrance fee.

Most sugar workers registered with FMLCo did avail themselves of the opportunity to join the cooperatives. As a result, Morelands began operations with 182 members in 1975, and Springfield with 181 in 1976. There was significant variation among the cooperatives in this regard. Another cooperative farm at Monymusk, for example, had 250 members.

In general, the worker-members tended to be older, male and illiterate (Table 5.1). Estimates of illiteracy ranged between 50 and 80 percent. Only a small minority of the cooperators at Monymusk had any significant small farming experience. The same was true at Bernard Lodge, but not Frome, where peasant traditions were strong.

TABLE 5.1
Membership Data: Springfield Cooperative

	Average Age	% Males	Years Working with the Estate
Springfield Workers	47	89	22

Source: Farm records, Springfield.

According to the rules and regulations, members of each cooperative agreed to subject themselves to the authority and instructions of general membership meetings, and secondarily, the committee of management, or its duly authorized representatives. They also agreed to give the cooperative first claim on their labor power: they were obligated to work on the cooperative's property, as long as work was available, and at rates determined by the committee of management.[3] Nonworkers could not be members. Special permission was required from the committee of management for any members to absent themselves from the farm for a period of time as, for example, when workers went overseas to do farm work. It was further expected that the workers would take an active interest in the running of the farm, including seeking ways of controlling expenditures, working extra hours or days without pay, and taking more care and interest in the planting, cultivating and reaping of the crop.

Management System

The system of cooperative management (Figure 5.2)

reflected the interplay of three main groups: the general membership, the committee of management, and the hired managerial and administrative staff. From the beginning the cooperatives were plagued by the difficulties encountered in efficiently combining or meshing these elements.

The members of the cooperative societies meeting in duly constituted general meetings represented the supreme authority within the cooperatives, making the most important decisions and electing or removing members of the management committee. According to the rules, at least one such meeting, the annual general

FIGURE 5.2
Cooperative Authority Structure

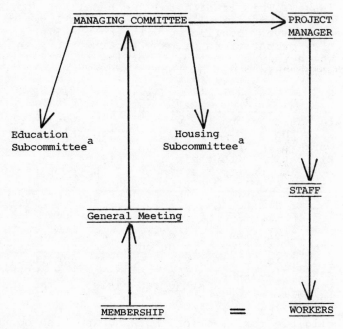

(Arrows signify
flow of authority)

[a]Functioning education and housing subcommittees
were rare.

meeting, had to occur each year. This took place following receipt of the financial audit for the previous year. At this meeting members were to: a) receive and discuss the committee of management's annual report together with the financial statement of the previous year's business and accounts, and any other reports; b) decide on the appropriation and distribution of profits, if any; c) make any other policy decisions that arose; d) elect members of the committee of management, and one floor member as a delegate to the estate cooperative; and e) amend the rules of the cooperative, if necessary. Voting at all general meetings was according to the "one person, one vote" principle, regardless of shareholdings, and with proxies disallowed.

The cooperatives were not obligated to hold any other general meetings during the year. "Special" general meetings, however, could be called, either by the committee of management, or by the members themselves, via a petition from twenty-five members or 15 percent of the membership, whichever was less. According to the rules, such meetings were held only to discuss specific issues. This traditional "Rochedalian" approach, which evolved historically with regard to large consumer cooperatives, conflicted with the populist and participatory orientations of many sugar workers and the movement which they supported. According to this view, general membership meetings should be held regularly, perhaps monthly. Certainly the need for more regular meetings was consistent with the collectivist and participatory nature of the cane farm enterprises, and the close interaction among the workers. It was also consistent with the need to promote attitudinal changes among the workers and to stimulate a high degree of worker identification with their cooperatives.

In practice, a number of the cooperatives, including Morelands, did try to adhere to a pattern of monthly meetings. Others, like Springfield, made no effort along these lines. A closer analysis of these variants is taken up in Chapter 7.

Operational and decision-making authority within the cooperatives was delegated by the general membership to an elected eleven-member committee of management. Elections to the two-year terms on the committee took place, on a staggered basis, at the annual general meeting. Those from a list of at-large nominees who received the most votes were elected. Only members were eligible for election, but any who also occupied staff positions requiring that they report directly to the committee were ineligible for election. According to the rules, committee members were eligible for reelection, but were also recallable by a majority resolution of any general meeting. They received no remuneration, nor were they entitled to any special benefits as a result of their positions.

Meeting at least monthly, the committee of management functioned as the executive arm of the cooperative with delegated authority over all business matters and other affairs--within the guidelines set by the annual general meeting or other general meeting. It directed and oversaw the activities of the farm manager and, through him, the entire staff. In addition to its responsibility for the economic functioning of the enterprise, the committee of management was also responsible for organizing the institutional affairs of the cooperative, including the provision of member education, the registration of new members, and discipline. Subcommittees or special farm committees were sometimes established. Such subcommittees were rarely very active or successful.

The chairperson of the committee of management played the key individual role within the cooperative. Like other officers of the committee, the vice-chairperson and secretary, he/she was elected from within the committee and not by the general membership. The rules stipulated that these elective positions were voluntary--no additional payments were made to cooperative officers except that they could be reimbursed for time spent off the farm on cooperative business. This rule was widely breached (Chapter 7).

A farm manager (also called project manager), two or three assistants, and an accounting clerk were the usual staff complement of a farm-level cooperative (Figure 5.3). Under the coordination and direction of the farm manager, the staff were responsible for day-to-day managerial and administrative functions. According to the cooperative rules, the farm manager and the entire staff were directly responsible to and employed by the committee of management, and ultimately of course to the entire membership. However, there was ambiguity and conflict here. For one thing, until January 1978, they were actually employed by FMLCo, with their employment in fact guaranteed (between 1976 and 1978) by that body. After that date, according to the staff contract negotiated by the staff association and USWCC, a contract which merely reproduced longstanding estate practices in this regard, the farm manager took direction not from the committee of management or general membership, but from the chief executive of the estate cooperative. The chief executive was responsible to the estate cooperative board of management.[4]

Organization of Work, Principles of Distribution
and Structure of Incentives

With the cooperativization of the estates, the formal socioeconomic status of the sugar workers changed from being "workers hired by a manager" to

76

FIGURE 5.3
Management Chart -- Springfield Cooperative

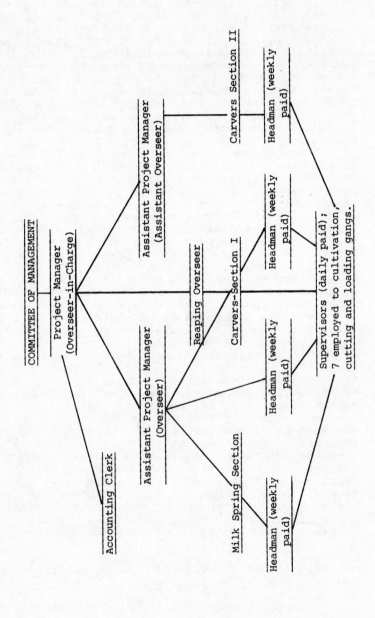

"groups of producers." They were "groups of producers," however, who continued to work for wages much as they always had. In other words, other than the potential for after-crop bonuses or dividends based on surplus genera- tion, distribution within the cooperative, in prin- ciple, remained identical to the precooperative situa- tion. Members worked as before and were paid as before. This had the following implications. First, the repug- nant task rate system remained intact, carrying with it incentives for corruption and the legacy of the semislave system. Second, pre-existing inequalities, il- legitimate in the eyes of the workers, were reproduced within the cooperatives. For example, the superior eco- nomic position of the headmen continued, and in fact was intensified. Third, there was little possibility, especially given the poor economic position of the farms, of increasing incomes for the mass of cooperators in the short run.

The major tasks performed on the cane cooperatives, as on all cane farms, included planting, weeding, irri- gation, drainage, harvesting, fertilizing. Each task had its own rate, and sometimes there was a series of rates, as many as sixteen for the same basic task. Such tasks were graded according to the difficulty of the opera- tion, as determined by the headman, and the appropriate rate assigned. The eleven rates for weeding out main canals, for example, ranged from 29¢ to $1.72 per chain, usually depending on how much weeding was neces- sary. Some jobs were daily paid, and sometimes task work was given out on a day work basis. Only certain headmen were weekly paid; all other workers were paid by the day or task.

Both before and after the establishment of the co- operatives, the determination, allocation and pricing of the work done was carried out by the overseers, headmen and supervisors. Work was allocated either on each Mon- day for the week, or on a daily basis. Work was not always on an individual basis; groups or "gangs" often worked together (a gang was composed of from two to up- wards of fifty persons, the latter comprising the reap- ing gang). In general, both the allocation and pricing of work was a very arbitrary process. Often workers would not know what their pay was for the work done un- til the end of the week, when the headmen came around and "priced" their work, or worse, even later when they got their paycheck. This arbitrariness also led to many disputes between the overseers or headmen and the wor- kers, with the latter often objecting to the price given a particular task.

Thus, as in the past, it continued to be true under the cooperative system that overseers and headmen had enormous power. And this power was often used in an ar- bitrary or even cruel manner, with certain workers vic- timized and others favored. It also led to a great deal of corruption.

To be sure, under the cooperative system there was some modification of this pattern. Managing committees and/or chairpersons occasionally did make suggestions about the work to be done, and would arbitrate disputes over pricing and the distribution of work.[5] In this regard, however, the possibilities inherent in the new system of worker control were not fully realized. This was due to a number of factors: a) most staff were retained from the precooperative period, and they preferred doing things the old way; b) many chairpersons were themselves headmen; and c) the old work structures and patterns, as discussed above, were retained.

Degree of Socialization of Work

The degree to which members of the cooperatives were actually involved in the work of their enterprises is another important aspect to consider. This breaks down into two issues: first, the percentage of the work potential of the members that was used in the cooperative endeavor. Soviet kolkhoz members, for example, are required to work at least 200 days for the collectivity if they are to retain their membership rights. At the other extreme, on many single-purpose cooperatives very little, if any, work is done by the membership.

The second consideration is what percentage of the work done was done by members and what by hired labor or outside voluntary labor. In the example of many single-purpose cooperatives, almost all is done by hired labor. At the other extreme, the traditional Israeli kibbutzim were strongly resistant to any outside wage labor. Almost always, though, at least some tasks are and often must be performed by outsiders.[6]

Given the high degree to which capital was socialized within the sugar worker cooperatives, it is not surprising that labor was too. The rules bound each member to work the land personally, while restricting the employment of nonmembers.[7] Nonmembers could not be employed to undertake work which a member could do while members themselves were not fully employed. If a nonmember was employed full-time for three months continuously, he/she could apply for full membership.

Despite this, the hiring of outside wage labor (often called contractors) was not minimized. This was a surprise to policy elites and organizers who expected that: a) the traditional specialization of work would be reduced, with members willing to take on more varied tasks than previously; b) the intensity of work would increase with the new "owners" having greater incentives than when they were mere "workers"; c) as owners the workers would have a greater commitment to cutting costs, such as, for example, were incurred by hiring

outside labor to do work that members could take on
themselves as part of their contribution to the collectivity. On all counts their expectations were not realized.

A number of other factors further contributed to
the use of nonmember wage labor. First, some members,
usually the older ones, left the cooperatives and received their severance deposits back, but then kept
working more or less as before, though as nonmembers.
Second, the workers' commitment to their less fortunate
brothers and sisters militated against the effort to
restrict work to members, as did the ethic of spreading
available work in a labor-surplus situation (a paternalistic and politically astute tradition of the plantation system). Third, cooperativization apparently
increased the members' reserve price for certain types
of labor, like manual weeding, for which only low levels of pay prevailed. This necessitated the hiring of
outside workers for these tasks.[8] This phenomenon was
widely remarked on and criticized by many opponents or
critics of the cooperatives. Finally, the cooperatives
were often able to pay outside wage labor less than members. For example, government taxes were often not deducted from contractors' wages.

So, though the members still devoted most of their
labor time to the cooperatives, they did not account for
as high a percentage of the total labor effort as had
been expected.

Capital Structure and Financial Operations

The financial base of the sugar worker cooperatives
was very weak at the outset. The capital structure was
composed of three components: a) share capital, which
amounted to less than $4,000 for each cooperative; b)
severance loan deposits by workers, which averaged between $200,000 and $300,000 per farm, but were callable
after two years; and c) SIA and crop lien loans.[9]

Initial capital was almost wholly in the form of
interest-bearing loans. There was no equity finance to
speak of. This only exacerbated the poor operating positions of the estates at the outset, especially Monymusk.
WISCo had been suffering deficits on its cane farming
operations for some years, and the situation at Monymusk was particularly acute. Moreover, a drought in 1976
and skyrocketing irrigation costs made matters much
worse; 1977, in particular, was a catastrophic year.

The peculiar financing arrangement for the large-
scale cultivation and reaping of cane was also significant. In cane farming significant operating costs are
incurred twelve to twenty-four months before payment for
the crop occurs; hence, the need for significant levels

of crop financing.

Writing in 1976 and using a five-year financial projection as his base, USWCC's financial controller identified this as a major problem. But the substantial inflow of interest-free or low-interest, long-term capital which he called for, as FMLCo had before him, never materialized.

Financial problems were exacerbated because the cooperatives were totally dependent on the revenue generated by cane sales. While diversification was given lip service, only a few of the co-ops made any real efforts in this direction.[10] This was an unhealthy situation, especially in a period of low world sugar prices.

Financial operations of the cooperatives were also affected, or potentially affected, by the Cooperative Societies Law. Among its key provisions were: a) 20 percent of all profits had to be transferred to a reserve fund; b) not more than 10 percent of the balance could be used for educational or charitable purposes; c) dividends were not to exceed 6 percent; d) cooperatives were not liable for income tax or stamp duty; and e) annual independent audits were mandatory.

THE ESTATE-LEVEL COOPERATIVES

The three estate, or secondary-level, cooperatives were composed of the farm and branch (service departments) cooperatives at each estate. However, when the estate cooperatives were first constituted, in December 1975, none of the pilot co-ops opted to join. As late as 1978 only Morelands had joined its estate co-op, though the other pilots were regularly attending estate cooperative meetings. A few other independent-minded farm cooperatives, those opting for individual leases, also did not join at first, but then linked up with the other farms in the estate cooperatives shortly after. The estate cooperative was actually the lessee of the lands from the government, providing in turn subleases to the farms (except in the case of the pilots and those farm co-ops opting for individual leases). Members of the estate cooperatives were obligated to market their cane through it and obtain all services from it, at rates set by the estate board of management.

Supreme authority in the estate cooperative was vested in the general meeting of delegates, composed of the chairperson from each primary cooperative, plus one additional delegate for each fifty members, to a maximum of six from each cooperative. Ongoing authority was delegated to the board of management composed of each chairperson plus three at-large worker delegates (elected at the annual general meeting of delegates). At Monymusk there was also an executive committee, composed of board members, which met weekly, with the full board meeting biweekly. Day to day management was in the hands of the chief executive and his staff (Figure 5.4).

The estate cooperative's responsibilities included: a) accounting and internal auditing services; b) agricultural planning, research, monitoring and coordinating agricultural operations, and advice to the farms; c) irrigation services; d) tractor and transport services; e) member education and other member services; and f) central purchasing of all supplies and their distribution to the farms.

The Member Services Department was unique and possibly the most significant operation of the estate cooperative, especially in terms of its potential for reaching the mass membership. Each estate had a member services coordinator plus two or three assistants or education officers. In addition, at Monymusk there were three "organizers" or worker-educators. Most of the Member Services Department workers were former organizers for SWCC, paid and assisted by SAC.

The general aim of the Member Services Department was to ensure that members got the services and benefits they needed or were eligible for. It focused on three main activities: a) cooperative development—assisting the estate board and farm-level committees of management, and in general seeking to ensure the smooth and efficient functioning of the cooperatives; b) cooperative administration—ensuring that programs or services aimed at members, such as pension, medical, credit, housing and insurance, did actually reach the grass-roots members; and c) cooperative education—promoting cooperative principles and practices, business methods and cultural consciousness through a regular on-farm education program supplemented by residential (off-farm) training.

THE UNITED SUGAR WORKERS COOPERATIVE COUNCIL

The United Sugar Workers Cooperative Council (USWCC), or central cooperative body, was actually a federation of the three estate cooperatives financed by an annual charge on their cane production. When it was first established in December 1975, USWCC took over the central operations of FMLCo, even moving into its office in Kingston. In its first year of operation, to reduce administrative costs and promote greater efficiency, USWCC hived off certain of its functions to the estate cooperatives, and just eliminated others. Among the activities no longer performed were: personnel administration, agricultural planning, central purchasing, certain accounting services. It retained the following functions: a) financial planning, including arranging finance, establishing and overseeing standardized accounting procedures, and effecting overall cash

FIGURE 5.4
Monymusk Sugar Workers Cooperative Council - Administrative Structure

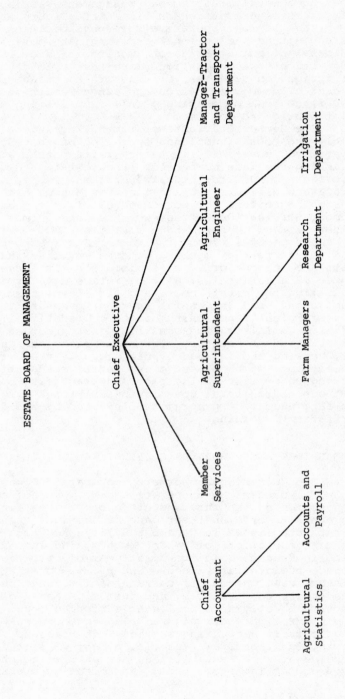

control, in association with the Sugar Industry Authority; b) interestate communication, public relations and
education; c) contract negotiations; and d) central
policy making. Figure 5.5 provides an overview of the
administrative structure of USWCC.

In other respects, USWCC was an organization very
different from its predecessor. Supreme authority was
vested in the general meeting of delegates, with each
estate cooperative appointing two delegates, plus one
additional delegate for each 25,000 tons of cane it produced.   An eleven-member board of management was
elected for two-year terms, with no estate cooperative
allowed more than four representatives. In addition, up
to five nonvoting advisors were appointed by USWCC to
sit with the board. The general secretary was the key
official. Following a short interim period when a local
management consulting firm supplied this service, the
former assistant director of cooperatives for FMLCo was
named to this post. Upon his retirement in 1978, the
chief executive of Frome SWCC moved into this position.

GOVERNMENT AGENCIES INVOLVED WITH THE
COOPERATIVES

The political and administrative environment in
which the cooperatives operated included a number of
important entities. Despite the importance of the sugar
cooperatives to the Jamaican political economy, however,
no single government agency was given the resources and
responsibility to oversee and guide the development of
the cooperatives. Prior to 1976, this was not the case,
with FMLCo clearly the responsible body. After 1976,
a multiplicity of government bodies "colonized" various
aspects of the cooperatives' operations and the government's interaction with them.

The Frome Monymusk Land Company

FMLCo was the government's primary agent involved
in the cooperative process prior to 1976. It provided a
centralized locus of policy formulation and implementation, with direct links to the political directorate
and the sugar technocracy.[11] But with the establishment
of the cooperatives, FMLCo was left without a substantive portfolio, staff or office. During 1976 it existed
mainly to negotiate the lease and, formally, to oversee
operations of the three precooperatives at Frome and
the staff contract. The USWCC took over most of its
head office staff, its facilities and many of its functions.

84

FIGURE 5.5
USWCC--Administrative Structure

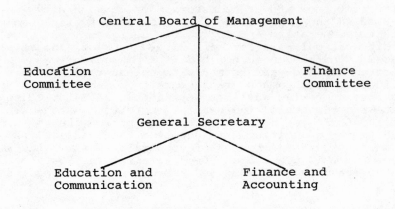

The Sugar Industry Authority (SIA)

Following its reorganization in 1971, SIA spearheaded a more vigorous involvement of the government in
the sugar industry. Following Manley's election, this
role became even more pronounced. During this period,
the state, acting through SIA: a) took over responsibility for the research arm of the industry, previously
part of the Sugar Manufacturers Association (SMA); b)
began to handle the international marketing of Jamaica's sugar, while continuing to utilize the domestic
marketing system of the SMA; c) initiated the reorganization of the SMA into a joint public-private sector
body, the Sugar Manufacturing Corporation of Jamaica,
with a mandate to revitalize and rationalize the industry; d) established a state sugar company to provide
overall planning, management and finance for the rapidly
expanding state sugar sector, totaling almost two-
thirds of processing capacity by 1978; e) took over
direct responsibility for a number of cane farming properties; and f) established a series of loan schemes
for farmers and manufacturers.

In terms of the cane farming subsector, including
the sugar cooperatives, SIA had a number of specific
functions. First, it was a major source of crop finance
and loan capital. Here it actually played a much
greater role vis-a-vis the cooperatives than other
farms since the commercial banks refused to grant the
co-ops the needed crop lien loans without government
guarantees. This was provided through SIA, which thus

became the financial overseer of the sugar cooperatives.
Second, it ran a field extension service, with extension officers assigned to each cane growing region.
Third, in conjunction with industry interests it established a fixed price for sugar. This was set at $168/
ton in 1974, rising to $270/ton in 1975 and $300/ton in
1977. According to a longstanding formula, cane farmers
received approximately two-thirds of this fixed price
for the sugar produced from their cane. For example,
assuming an average of ten tons of cane needed for each
ton of sugar, farmers received $18/ton of cane in 1975.
Manufacturers received the remaining one-third of the
fixed price for each ton of sugar they produced. Fourth,
SIA attempted to regulate and penalize poor quality
cane delivered to the factories. Fifth, it conducted
research on many phases of cane agronomy, harvesting
and economics.

The Sugar Industry Authority became in effect the
financial overlord of the sugar cooperatives, guaranteeing their bank loans, providing separate loans of
its own, collecting cane sale revenues, and in general
attempting to oversee their financial activities and
budget preparation. In addition, SIA's first chairman
was the single most active, aggressive and influential
government official with respect to the co-ops.[12] The
director of SIA's research arm was also a very influential USWCC advisor.

Registrar and Department of Cooperatives

The twenty cooperative farms established between
1975 and 1976 were not only cane farms but also cooperatives. As such they, and the four secondary and tertiary-level cooperatives, were registered and regulated
by the Registrar and Department of Cooperatives. The
Registrar of Cooperatives had full and ultimate authority over all cooperatives in Jamaica, including the
power to annul any cooperative's registration if it was
felt that the society was no longer a bona fide cooperative, was financially insolvent or was not adhering to
regulations. The registrar had full access to cooperative records, had to approve the annual audit and could
hold a special inquiry into the affairs of any cooperative, whether on his own volition or upon application
by one-third of the general membership or by a majority
of the committee of management.

A number of field officers were assigned by the
Department of Cooperatives with responsibility for
assisting cooperatives in adhering to the regulations
of the cooperative law and the rules of each cooperative body, providing education on cooperative principles, and providing advice on business management and
accounting practices. Since the Cooperative Department

was part of the Ministry of Agriculture, such officers also assisted in carrying out government policy in the agricultural sector.

At Monymusk there was one field officer covering all the farm and service cooperatives, as well as other co-ops in the region. He had only irregular contact with the farm-level cooperatives, occasionally attending committee of management meetings and general meetings.[13] When present he did often play an active advisory role. The field officer also, more regularly, attended estate cooperative board meetings, again frequently proferring advice on a wide range of issues. He rarely provided or assisted in the provision of member education.[14] In general, the field officer was the major source of government assistance to the cooperatives at the local level. While having more contact with the workers at the grass roots than any other government official during the implementation phase, this interaction was still very limited.

Ministry of Agriculture

The Ministry of Agriculture retained overall authority over the sugar cooperatives, setting up a desk to oversee cooperative affairs. It also provided an advisor to the USWCC board. Through its parliamentary secretary, with special responsibility for cooperatives, it was a major conduit for political pressure and interaction.

The Prime Minister

Finally, the prime minister was a sort of ultimate arbiter of cooperative conflicts. He was especially effective because of his influence and prestige with the co-op leaders. In this role he often acted independently of other government agencies.

The existence of a multiplicity of administrative interests dealing with the cooperatives in the post-1976 period reflected a number of factors. First, the government was unclear that any special role was necessary for it. There was a lack of leadership and no concrete plan of assistance during this phase. Furthermore, it was assumed that an appropriate administrative structure had been set up, with most of the FMLCo staff and its headquarters transferred to USWCC. In other words, since most of FMLCo's functions had been transferred to USWCC, further government inputs could be channeled through it, just as they had previously been channeled through FMLCo.[15] But USWCC had only limited impact on the grass roots. Third, the cooperatives were established as bona fide cane producing organizations, and the pattern of government interaction with such enterprises was well established . As agricultural institutions, they related to the Ministry of Agriculture; as cane producers to SIA and SIRI (Sugar Industry Research Institute); as cooperatives to the Department of Cooperatives; as an important government program to the political directorate. So the multiplicity of administrative relations was not unusual, except on the assumption of special needs. But this was not assumed to be the case. Rather it was assumed that the major problems or areas of concern were mainly technical, and the existing channels and structures could facilitate government technical inputs. Political and social concerns were deemphasized by the government after 1976.

Fourth, the cooperatives' history of antagonism to government intervention and their commitment to worker control restricted the government's role, largely ruling out any administrative or political approach which appeared to encroach on workers' territory or reflect a paternalistic orientation to them. After 1976, however, the cooperatives repeatedly requested stronger government intervention at the grass roots. For example, as early as March 1976 the farm chairpersons and board members petitioned the prime minister to delegate a representative to sit with each estate board. Later, in 1977, the USWCC board requested more local-level assistance from the newly formed Cooperative Development Centre, despite the fact that its director had long been considered an arch-enemy of SWCC. These petitions went unheeded.

Finally, strong and active government involvement was constrained by its limited financial and administrative resources, especially at the grass roots.

Hence, though the needs of the sugar workers and the new cooperative institutions may have called for innovative political, social and economic strategies at the local level, interaction between the government and the cooperatives after 1976 was generally unorganized and mostly centered at the USWCC level or channeled through it. But communication and authority flows between the central and local levels within the cooperatives' own structure were very weak. Thus, both the primary and estate-level cooperatives had little direct or indirect interaction with government or even with Kingston-based nongovernmental sugar industry bodies, like the Cane Farmers Association.

NOTES

1. Boguslaw Galeski, The Prospects for Collective Farming (Madison, Wisconsin: Land Tenure Center #95, 1973), p. 1.

2. Morelands workers agreed to deposit 60 percent of their severance payments, with some also signing up for longer terms.

3. The regulations stipulated that the worker-cooperators should be paid on a task rate basis wherever possible. This was the traditional pattern. The cooperatives also adhered to the rates established under existing collective bargaining agreements.

4. Unlike other recent examples of a Third World government supporting the establishment of cooperatives for development and social purposes, the Jamaican government had no direct subsequent involvement in the units so formed. In Algeria, for example, the managers of each self-managed enterprise also represented the state, with the power to veto plans which did not conform to the national plan and generally to safeguard the public interest (Odida Quamina, "Autogestion: Workers' Self-Management in Algeria," Transition 2[1979], p. 54). A similar situation existed in Peru.

5. The grievance procedure of the unions was never used significantly.

6. This framework is developed by Galeski, who also suggests a correlation between the degree to which control over the means of production is socialized within the co-op and the degree members work on the cooperative activity.

> It is not only true that the socialization of the means of production implies or even requires socialization of work, but it is also true that socialization of work implies or more often requires the socialization or possession of means of agricultural production (Galeski, p. 29).

7. This was actually meant more as a protection for than as a restriction against outside labor.

8. A similar process developed among the Israeli kibbutzim. See H. Barkai, "The Kibbutz: An Experiment in Microsocialism," in Self-Management, ed. Jaroslav Vanek (Baltimore: Penguin, 1975).

9. Among the loans available to the cooperatives from the state, and which were also available to all cane farmers, were the following:

   a. replanting loans--providing $200/acre with a one-year grace, repayment in two years at 10 percent interest;
   b. field development loans--$300/acre, with two years of grace, then eight years to repay at 6 percent;
   c. equipment loans--2/3 of the cost of heavy equipment, with five years to repay at 10 percent;
   d. liquidity or crop lien loans--$2/ton, carrying no interest, but repayable annually through automatic deductions at the factory before payments were made for the farmers' cane;
   e. fertilizer advances--from the Cane Farmers Association, bearing no interest and repayable each year.

10. The lease agreements between the cooperatives and the government restricted the cooperatives to planting only cane, unless a case could be made that this was economically not feasible.

11. The chairman of FMLCo was also parliamentary secretary in the Ministry of Agriculture. The board included the chairman of SIA.

12. He left the SIA in 1977.

13. He attended about 15 percent of such meetings at Morelands and Springfield.

14. Starting in 1978, and lasting for less than a year, a newly-formed agency of the Ministry of Agriculture, the Cooperative Development Centre, tried to revitalize the education program for sugar co-op members. At that time, the field officer increased his activity in providing cooperative education.

15. This was a long-established pattern of government interaction with quasi-independent nongovernmental agriculture organizations, such as the Jamaica Agricultural Society and the Cane Farmers Association. Government influence was often dominant at the national level, with leaders closely allied to the ruling party, and with finance often supplied by the state.

6
Counter-Reform: Demobilizing the Sugar Worker Movement

We are a great country for ideas,
but we're damn short of implementation.[1]

It appears that there is a conspiracy to
deprive workers of good education--for
fear that if the workers ever <u>do</u> become
conscious and competent, they really <u>will</u>
take control.[2]

The implementation of the sugar worker cooperatives project after 1975 coincided with a marked transformation in the organization and activity of the sugar
worker movement. A change in priorities and a change in
the framework of action followed the establishment of
the cooperative farms. In particular, the political and
social basis of the movement seemed to vanish, leaving
the cane farming enterprise as the main or sole concern. Yet, important political and social tasks associated with the development of the cooperatives and
their membership remained, and this greatly affected
implementation. Between 1973 and 1975, under the banner
of the Sugar Workers Coordinating Council, such tasks
had primacy; sugar worker mobilization dominated the
scene. This mobilization emphasized social transformation, distribution issues, mass participation, and worker organization and representation. After 1976, however, with the cooperatives actually functioning and
faced with immense economic tasks, the workers' movement
began to institutionalize itself along bureaucratic,
productionist and business-oriented lines. Conspicuous
for their relative absence were many of the previous
themes, in particular the emphasis on political mobilization. While to a large extent this phase of the implementation process did primarily involve the need for the
workers to adopt certain bourgeois patterns or orientations, they were also heavily influenced in their new
direction by national trends and political pressures.

91

The importance of sugar worker organization and
mobilization in the cooperativization process through
1975 has been described in detail (Chapters 3 and 5).
SWCC's position prevailed at almost every major decision point in 1975. FMLCo was defeated in its attempt
to form and control the worker committees; the decisions of the prime minister's Committee on Cooperative
Development led to the establishment of seventeen new
co-ops in 1975, not the three originally proposed; the
estate-level cooperatives were structured as worker-
controlled bodies; and finally, the leases were given
to these estate cooperatives and not the individual
farms. Without this level of participation by SWCC in
1975, culminating a three-year process of organizational
development and activity, it is almost certain that
only a handful of farms would have been converted to
cooperatives that year, and quite possibly none thereafter.[3] The structure and operation of the co-ops, moreover, would certainly have been more paternalistic,
with less scope for worker participation and control.

The sociopolitical matrix of interests, classes
and power surrounding the cooperativization policy resulted in favorable outcomes for SWCC mainly because of
SWCC's mobilization successes at the local level and
the supportive political trends in the wider society.
At the local level, SWCC was assisted by the poor arti-
culation and relative weakness of both the PNP and the
state administrative apparatus, represented mainly by
FMLCo. This weak grass-roots political-administrative
capacity made effective opposition to the workers'
movement difficult. While the estate hierarchy, field
staff and BITU were much stronger countervailing forces
at the local level, they too could not match SWCC's organizational strength or the momentum of the workers.
In addition, because these latter forces also often represented anti-PNP and anti-progressive political tendencies, they conflicted with and were not supported by
the government during this period. The political leadership was predisposed to favor SWCC over these forces,
as more consistent with its own long-run interest,
though its position became more ambiguous and contradictory over time.[4]

In addition, SWCC contributed to, and was a beneficiary of, the national political tendency during 1974-
1976 toward democratic reforms, socialist ideology and
worker mobilization. Manley, in particular, attempted
to identify with and support these trends, which were
especially strong among youth and petty bourgeois
strata within and outside the PNP. The revenue generated by the bauxite levy and the rise in international
sugar prices also strengthened SWCC's position.

Finally, and fundamental to the success of SWCC,
it responded to the sugar workers' deep yearnings for
social transformation, provided a channel for mass par-

ticipation and tapped their volatile class consciousness.

By late 1975, however, the pendulum had begun to
swing in the other direction. On both the national and
local levels, SWCC began to experience increasing resistance and opposition. Reinforced by factors related to
the establishment of the cane farming cooperatives, and
by weaknesses internal to SWCC, these forces stimulated
a process of demobilization of the sugar worker movement. This was most manifest in the actual replacement
of SWCC by a three-tiered cooperative structure in 1976.
But demobilization had many other manifestations as
well, including: a) the reorganization of SWCC; b) the
depoliticization of the sugar worker movement; c) the
weakening of the leadership; d) the bureaucratization
of SWCC; e) the resurgence of localism; and f) the dis-
solution of the education program.

DEMOBILIZATION

Reorganization of SWCC

In 1976, SWCC, a grass-roots political organization,
was changed into a three-tiered cooperative structure.
SWCC itself had been operating, at least in a rudimentary way, on a local, estatewide and national basis.
For example, what was to become the board of management
of the estate cooperative had actually been functioning
from around September 1975, and even before that on a
more informal basis. However, the organizational transformation or restructuring which occurred in 1976 was
more than merely nominal.

The new cooperative structure was legally and otherwise set up primarily as a business organization. Its
major function was the operation of the cane farming
enterprise, the assurance of viability and the generation of surplus. To be sure, as a self-managed worker
cooperative it was different from a joint stock or private enterprise. Nonetheless, its raison d'être was
business and this was reinforced by government officials
and others. For example, from the time of the establishment of the pilot cooperative at Morelands, a con-
tinuous refrain heard from officers of the Cooperative
Department was that the co-ops' main business was now
business, and that all other activities ought to be
dropped. Furthermore, the farms were in such poor shape
it was apparent that achieving viability was not only a
primary, but an immediate problem, and one of great
proportions. This task was generally interpreted in
purely economic terms.

One striking manifestation of what was implied by
this restructuring and the new emphasis was the hiring

in late 1975 of a prestigious accounting firm as management consultants to USWCC. In January 1976, a member of
this organization became temporary chief executive of
USWCC. Other high staff officials of the workers' organization had all worked previously with FMLCo. Perhaps
predictably, the consultants advised the USWCC board
that its core function was business, and that this must
get priority. Cooperative development could proceed
separately, but only where it supported the business
aspects.[5]

Another implication was the paradoxical reduction
in the availability of funds after 1976 to carry forward organizational tasks which were not traditional
cane farming activities. Though the workers took over
multimillion dollar businesses, their new responsibilities and pressures as cane farmers and their loss of
independence actually meant that they had less access to
financial resources than previously. In other words,
faced with the pressure of money-losing businesses, and
with this pressure reinforced by advisors, government
officials, the media and others, the legitimacy of any
expenditures not directly related to cane production
and economic viability was greatly reduced. This was the
basis, for example, for the elimination of USWCC's
thrice weekly radio program, which had been aimed at
keeping cooperative members and others throughout the
society fully informed of the cooperatives' activities.
Though a low-cost operation, it was eliminated as "too
costly."[6] Of course there had been financial constraints before 1976, but these were of a very different
sort, related to the absolute availability of funds.
The new financial constraints were a source of increasing friction between newly cost-conscious cooperative
leaders and a frustrated cooperator work force.

Depoliticization of the Sugar Worker Movement

The major implication of SWCC's organizational restructuring was that it changed SWCC from primarily a
grass-roots political movement, without any economic
functions, to a cane producing, surplus generating, more
diffuse organization, with only peripheral political
functions. While trying to steer clear of party or partisan politics, SWCC's explicit political commitments--
to the sugar workers--had always been primary. Indeed,
increasingly between 1973 and 1976, SWCC had moved to
the left. It began calling openly for a greater national
commitment to a socialist orientation and a broadening
of the worker control movement to other segments of the
sugar industry and other areas, and had begun establishing closer linkages to other left-wing groups and parties. After 1976, however, though still committed to
the interests of the sugar workers on the three estates,

it began interpreting these interests almost wholly in
terms of economics, for the cane farming enterprise.
Business responsibilities began to push all other considerations to the background.

As a result, political and socialist manifestations were largely jettisoned, and the sugar worker
movement rapidly dropped its ties to and support of
other workers in the sugar and other industries, not to
mention overseas workers. The leaders began to see
themselves more as cooperative directors or business
managers than worker-leaders. Almost overnight, <u>mobili-
zation roles became managerial roles</u>, and bureaucratic
and technocratic norms became dominant. As one USWCC
board member has written:

> The establishment of co-operatives on the three
> estates meant that the time had come for a change
> in strategy from agitation to one of "healing the
> breach" and making co-operatives work. [7]

For many workers, indeed, the government's agreement in 1975 to establish most of the remaining farms
as co-ops beginning with the 1976 crop, the subsequent
registration of the estate and central cooperatives,
and the successful battle for an estate rather than individual farm lease, undoubtedly signaled that the
years of struggle were now to bear their fruits. Indeed,
the movement's immediate goals were substantially
achieved by December 1975. It was felt then that new
behavioral patterns were necessary and the movement
would have to reorient its focus from transformation to
production, from politics to business. This tendency
was further reinforced by the explicit proscriptions
against partisan political activity incorporated into
the cooperative rules and deeply imbedded in cooperative traditions in Jamaica, as elsewhere.

But the tendency toward depoliticization greatly
conflicted with the fact that significant political and
social tasks remained. These included: first, support
for the general transformation of Jamaican society without which the cooperatives could hardly succeed in the
long run; second, continued political intervention in
the national policy arena to ensure favorable outcomes
for the workers in the face of continuing opposition;
third, ensuring the transfer of management authority
from field and estate staff to worker committees, the
implementation of an appropriate staff-worker relationship on this basis, and the resocialization of staff to
their new roles; fourth, the liberation of the workers
from the culture of oppression, including apathy, self
doubt, dependence and distrust, which necessarily would
impede the proper functioning of the co-ops; fifth, the
reorientation of worker behavioral dispositions away
from a proletarian wage focus and trade union loyalties,

toward an emphasis on the cooperative movement, and the
importance of profits, accumulation and efficiency;
sixth, the diffusion of education on cooperative principles, operations and finances, as well as political
education, and the widespread dissemination of information on co-op activities and operations; seventh, the
mobilization of broad worker support for the sugar worker movement and the elected worker leadership at all
levels; and, finally, ensuring that the cooperatives
functioned in a fully democratic manner, with members'
needs serviced and channels established for worker participation and control.[8]

While there was an economic rationale for cooperativization of the sugar estates, political and social
factors had always been primary. The future viability of
the enterprises, as well as the dignity of the sugar
workers, were seen to require a significant transformation of political and social relations in the sugar
belt. Yet, at a crucial time, with the transformation
only really beginning, a political reaction set in. Political and social tasks were subordinated or repressed,
as the cooperatives were still expected to perform economically, increasing yields, labor productivity, efficiency and managerial effectiveness.

Another aspect of the movement's trend to depoliticization and demobilization was the weakening of its
class character. While prior to 1976 SWCC was decidedly
a workers' organization, the cooperatives incorporated
staff and others in key positions and even as members.
Whether as members or not, the field staff, historical
antagonists of the workers, were working within the cooperatives in what was supposed to be a common struggle
with the workers. This was politically confusing to the
sugar workers, who just the previous year were deeply
engaged in a hostile struggle with the same staff. Key
administrative positions throughout all levels of the
sugar cooperatives were held by nonworkers, including
some who had been among the most bitter opponents of
the cooperative movement between 1973 and 1976. Finally,
middle-class technocrats and politicians, as well as the
generally traditionalist Department of Cooperatives,
were involved with the workers after 1976 as advisors
and confidants in ways they could not have been before
1976.

Weakening of the Leadership

The post-1976 SWCC leadership was weakened in two
senses. First and most important, cadres from the Social
Action Centre suspended their local-level activity, for
the most part, and did not significantly participate in
USWCC affairs.[9] SAC had been active from the beginning,
providing key leadership, logistic and financial

resources. By 1975, however, it had become a target of those working to halt the sugar worker mobilization, as well as those opposing the socialist upsurge nationally. This was especially so since the increasing militance and socialist orientation of the sugar worker movement, and its commitment to spread the benefits of worker control to other parts of the sugar industry, were supported strongly by and identified with SAC.

In the last quarter of 1975, two developments added fuel to the anti-SAC campaign. One was SWCC's strong opposition to the imposition of certain education officers on them by FMLCo. These officers were seen as inadequately trained and as having different views from SWCC on cooperatives and worker control. Then too, SWCC had established its own education program, with the assistance of SAC, and wanted it carried forward.

The second was the virulent battle over the estate lease. This especially provided the occasion for a sustained campaign against SAC, particularly at Monymusk, including attacks against leading organizers there. At one and the same time, propaganda painted SAC as both communist and as being a CIA agent bent on getting an estate lease so it could control the cooperatives for the United States. [10]

Under heavy political attack, conscious that the workers had been largely victorious in the struggle over the distribution of the cane properties, and committed to a model of worker control, SAC for the most part removed its nonworker cadre from the local scene. But the workers were still not adequately prepared for the heavy demands on leadership resources which the new cooperatives placed on their shoulders. There were not enough class-conscious and capable workers to carry on without SAC's assistance. The government, for its part, did not in any way replace the local-level leadership and other organizational resources which SAC had provided.

The second factor which weakened the movement's leadership after 1976 was the divisions which developed within that leadership. For example, beginning in 1975, SWCC's first chairperson began to separate himself and his farm from the SWCC movement. A few other early leaders also split with SWCC, especially during the conflict over whether to opt for an estatewide or individual farm lease. They favored the latter and got caught up in the virulent struggle which ensued. Thus, at the beginning of 1976, three of the eight cooperative farms and the tractor and transport department at Momymusk remained outside the estate cooperative (they subsequently rejoined).

Bureaucratization

A fourth manifestation of the process of demobilization which took place after 1976 was the increasing tendency for bureaucratic modes of interaction to replace participatory modes. The old WISCo administrative structure had been marked by overcentralization. This same structure and its personnel were taken over by FMLCo, and then by the cooperatives. As a result, apart from the worker boards, much remained the same.

The secondary and tertiary-level cooperatives were very much removed from the mass membership, and there was little effort made to reduce the gap. In particular, there was a very serious communication gap between the farms within each estate, between the workers and the estate and central cooperatives, and between estates. At Monymusk, after 1976, there was no newsletter or organizational bulletin. For a time, USWCC did publish a newsletter but it was not widely circulated and little read. Only Workers Time[11] existed as a viable communication channel, but it could not adequately cover the three estates, and was not always widely circulated. As a result, many decisions taken at the estate and central levels were rarely known by the mass membership, except as rumor.

In addition, the problems and conflicts which developed after 1976, such as the prolonged conflict over the terms of lease, the problem of securing crop lien loans, the conflicts with the staff over terms of employment and emoluments, and the inadequacy of the education program and the dispute with the government over its funding, were generally dealt with along bureaucratic lines. The mass of cooperators rarely knew what was happening, and they were not asked to involve themselves or commit their resources to the struggles. Thus, basic issues affecting them were decided without their involvement, knowledge, or, in some cases, consent, tacit or otherwise.

As the gap between leaders and led grew wider the workers grew more and more wary of the estate and central boards. The potential benefits of such a multi-tiered structure were never adequately explained to them, nor made evident in practice. The higher-level cooperatives appeared as distant and alien with the workers having little or no control over their operations. They were thus seen as having too much power.[12] The worker-leaders at these levels, furthermore, were either not conscious enough of the importance of such mass participation or not experienced enough to develop mechanisms for stimulating it.

Resurgence of Localism

The cooperatives were established on a pyramidal basis, with power and authority emanating from the base, where the workers were organized into their farm-level cooperatives. While this authority structure was always characteristic of SWCC, after 1976 it became more localized and diffuse, with the workers less united at the estate and national levels.

Before 1976, the workers in the movement were clearly recognized, and recognized themselves, as members of SWCC, a national organization, with local chapters. They cemented this affiliation, subjectively and objectively, by paying dues. But with the establishment of the cooperatives, the workers' main organizational affiliation became their different cooperative farms. They were no longer formally members of SWCC, or anything like it. They were members of this or that Workers Cooperative Society, with affiliations to the estate cooperative, and, through it, to USWCC. Second, the local SWCC organizational bulletins, for example, SWCC News at Monymusk, ceased publication and nothing replaced them as a means of intra- and interstate communication, integration and mobilization. Third, there were no longer regular estatewide general meetings as occurred during the mobilization phase. Fourth, the importance of having a vibrant estatewide organization of the workers, with political, social and educational, as well as economic, goals, lost salience under the new cooperative structure. This was largely due to the factors cited above, resulting in the estate cooperative becoming primarily a bureaucratic facility serving the cane farming enterprise, at best.

Localization was reinforced by the workers' own tendencies to focus primarily on their local situations, as being more concrete and immediate. Hence, many favored individual farm leases and were unwilling at the beginning even to join the estate cooperative.

Dissolution of the Education Program

The general demobilization was also manifest in the cooperative education program run by USWCC and the estate cooperatives. For example, after 1975 no new education materials were written other than occasional (monthly for a time) centerspreads in Workers Time. While SAC was willing to supplement the existing materials which it had originally provided, USWCC resisted paying the costs. The USWCC board was being pressured both to cut expenditures and to keep SAC out of the picture.[13] Promises of government assistance, meanwhile, never materialized.

An additional factor was that the personnel available to carry out an education program were insufficient. During most of the 1976 to 1978 period, there were only two active education officers at Monymusk, covering eight cooperative farms and two service co-ops, or roughly 2,000 workers, and education formed only part of their functions. So despite their energy and commitment, during 1976 only four of the farms at Monymusk even had education programs. These did not commence until the second half of the year and reached only a small minority of the workers.[14] During 1977-1978, except for one specially arranged financial education session at each farm, education work was practically nonexistent. This situation was not materially altered in 1978 when the government took over the education program for one year.

A number of factors affected the program. On the one hand there was a scarcity of finance and other resources. This could have been alleviated by the Inter-American Foundation of the United States, which approved an education grant to USWCC of US$200,000 in 1976. High Ministry of Agriculture officials, however, blocked it mainly because SAC was slated by the IAF and USWCC to provide the bulk of the services for the project. Still, the government could provide no alternative source of finance.[15]

At the local level, the farm and estate committees of management provided little leadership for the education program. None of the co-ops at Monymusk had active education committees. There was no substantive support for the plan to organize a corps of worker-educators at each farm, nor was there any willingness to alter work schedules to provide time during the day for education.

Also at the local level a host of problems and the persistence of unresolved conflicts after 1976 created an agitated atmosphere in which little serious education work could go on. For example, throughout 1976 the inability to finalize an acceptable lease document, joined with the still simmering fallout from the previous fall's disputes, created a good deal of tension. Then in 1977 there was a delay in providing the previous year's audited accounts.[16] This was followed by the intense loan deposit dispute (see below). At times of such uncertainty, doubt and conflict, the workers generally were not prepared to hear about cooperative principles, rules and practices. It was the current issues, and their demands for resolution, that mattered. But the education officers were not always flexible or imaginative enough to fashion an attractive education program, and it stagnated.

HOW WAS DEMOBILIZATION POSSIBLE?

The demobilization of the sugar worker movement--

its adoption of certain tendencies, such as economism
over politics, bureaucratization over mass participation, elitism over democracy, mild reformism over thoroughgoing social transformation, class collaboration
over class consciousness and conflict--was neither spon-
taneous nor accidental. That is, it was made possible by
a number of factors. Broadly speaking, these included
external pressures and internal weaknesses.

External Pressures

The sugar workers faced opposition pretty much from
the beginning of their struggle. This opposition came
from a number of different quarters: the local estate
staff, the Frome Monymusk Land Company; both major
unions; and, in a looser fashion, by landowners and
other of the more reactionary elements in the society.
As SWCC gained strength and moved in a left direction,
however, opposition also began increasingly to come from
within the PNP and the government.

SWCC's mobilizational strength and its moves in a
left direction have already been described. The publication of Workers Time starting in February 1976 was another step in this regard. Published by SAC in conjunction with USWCC, Workers Time was primarily addressed to
the cooperative sugar workers on the three estates, but
looked also to the entire working class and peasantry.
Evolving out of the cooperativization campaign, Workers
Time was a working-class newspaper, particularly covering the sugar industry. It saw cooperativization there
as "the most important step towards socialist land reform and workers' power" to have arisen in Jamaica.[17] It
dedicated itself to struggle for cooperativization and
worker control of the whole sugar industry, and indeed
throughout Jamaican society--"worker's time."

> For too long it has been Minority's Time or Capi-
> talist's Time in this country. Things will have to
> be shared differently from now on. We must move to-
> wards WORKER'S TIME.[18]

But this required continued progress and class struggle.
"Sugar Barons Next!" was the emblazoned message of the
first-page cartoon in the first issue.

> It is only if we the workers at Frome, Monymusk and
> Bernard Lodge understand the gospel of cooperatives
> that you will be able to free the Halsehall workers,
> the Yarmouth workers, the Waterwell workers, the
> Rowington workers. All of them have to come under
> worker control whether they are owned by government
> or not.[19]

By late 1975 and early 1976, increasing opposition to these tendencies was evident within the PNP and the government. The PNP had always been essentially a middle-class, if reformist, party. Many party members accepted only with reservations the rededication to democratic socialism in 1974, and the party's increasingly populist, left-oriented manifestations.[20] Their commitment was mainly to a "mouth-water socialism"-- essentially a paternalist, capitalist, welfare state.[21] Like the bourgeoisie, these elements were not comfortable with any sort of mass mobilization, unless it was strictly controlled for their own political gain. Hence they were increasingly sympathetic to the anti-SWCC arguments of the agrarian middle and upper bourgeoisie, government technocrats, and others.

The government also was generally dominated by a similar technocratic, productionist and gradualist perspective. This was reinforced after 1976 by national and international economic pressures. By 1976, the balance of payments was in a crisis and the economic situation as a whole was deteriorating. This constrained the government's receptivity to radical change in the sugar belt, or to anything that might affect production. In addition, it faced large operational deficits at Frome, Monymusk and Bernard Lodge, the debt carryover from the original land purchases and large severance payments to workers and staff. The need now, it was felt, was for the cooperatives to "repay" the government for its "generosity," and this was pressed very hard. A "no-nonsense" hard line approach was adopted, epitomized by the chairperson of the Sugar Industry Authority. As he stated, early in 1976, in reference to sugar cooperatives that lose money, and then request a subsidy:

> Tough on you. . . . If you lose money go out of business. I've told them that already. I've told them if they don't like it, sell it back to me, and I'll take it back on the same terms you have it and I'll run it and make money off of it. Because they have to learn, and there is no way they will learn if they feel they are a political movement.[22]

Behind the scenes, elements within both the PNP and the government began mobilizing to "discipline" the cooperatives. In particular, they aimed to weaken SWCC and to ensure its separation from USWCC and the cooperative movement. A high-level anti-SWCC faction within the party argued that SWCC had become a political liability for the PNP. This was mainly because it had developed into an independent political force competing with the PNP for worker allegiance, and sometimes adopting what were perceived as anti-PNP tactics. To counteract this, the following strategy was proposed.

First, the PNP should give its support to anti-SWCC workers and attempts to weaken SWCC's support among the workers. Second, it should strive to increase the linkages between PNP groups, affiliates, PNP youth and cane farmers and the co-ops. Third, technical and managerial aid should be provided to the cooperative farms, as a carrot to wean them away from SWCC. Finally, the involvement of the unions and other agencies in the education program should be expanded.[23]

High government officials, including the Minister of Agriculture and the SIA chairperson, also lobbied against SAC, blaming it for the "poor performance" of the cooperatives (after only four months in operation!). In particular they criticized SWCC for: a) its overemphasis on politics rather than farming, which led to wasteful and bitter power struggles, the dissipation of valuable energy in agitation, alienation of the trade unions, cane farmers and party organizers, and an incentive to overspend the budgets; b) its wider political objectives; c) its attempts to extend the co-op movement to other cane farms and factories; d) its "inventing an enemy" through attacks on staff, which led to poor staff-worker relations and management difficulties; e) its attempts to monopolize the education work.[24]

There was also pressure, apparently, from the World Bank. The same document just cited also stated that "any attempt to extend the co-op movement is likely to cause the World Bank to have grave doubts about the viability of our programme" for a factory rehabilitation loan.[25] A World Bank review of the sugar industry did indeed raise objections and reservations about the cooperative program.[26]

The media also contributed to the anti-SWCC, anti-cooperative atmosphere. In March 1976, two very significant interviews were published in the pro-government Daily News. Both were highly critical of the cooperatives.[27] Starting at this time too the anti-government Daily Gleaner began to publish a number of anti-cooperative articles. Since 1976 was an election year, the Gleaner seized the opportunity to certify the cooperatives a "failure" so as to weaken the PNP.

At the same time, the strengthening or resurgence of the estate staff also weakened SWCC. After strike action on all three estates in November 1975, members of staff received severance payments (in some cases over $50,000) as had the workers. They also received a 22-month guarantee of employment from FMLCo, with FLMCo formally "assigning" them to the cooperatives. At each of the estates, then, the co-ops had to retain in high administrative positions staff members who had been vocal opponents of the cooperatives. Most government officials, too, were sympathetic to the views of the staff members, especially in terms of cane farming operations and the workers' role in their management.

Finally, between 1975 and 1976 there was a campaign within Jamaica, spearheaded and supported by the reorganized JLP, against the PNP's socialist mobilization which occurred between 1974 and 1976. SWCC and the co-operativization of the three estates were part of that mobilization, and they were affected by the reaction to it which encompassed large sections of the middle class and bourgeoisie.

Internal Weaknesses

The process of demobilization was also rooted in certain contradictions or weaknesses affecting SWCC and the workers' movement between 1973 and 1975. The momentum and successes of these years served to camouflage these weaknesses.

In the first place, the mass of the workers were at very low levels of political and social consciousness and never rose much above these. This of course was a fundamental problem of the plantation economy. Among other things there were very low levels of literacy, almost complete inexperience with democratic processes, and a tradition of subservience and dependence on others. Related to this was the tendency for some of the organizers to adopt an "idealistic overestimation of workers' capabilities and levels of consciousness."[28] While there were certain significant attempts at political and social education before 1975, they hardly matched the needs. Hence, only the organizers and a few workers retained awareness of wider political realities. This more advanced political consciousness was never internalized by the mass of the workers in anything other than a rudimentary form.

In addition, the worker leadership was motivated for the most part by individualistic goals and ambitions—both material and political.[29] Indeed, these leaders tended to have better jobs, higher pay and more education than the mass of cutters and cultivation workers (see Chapter 7). It was the petty bourgeois potential of the cooperatives which they grasped, and in general their political consciousness never advanced beyond this level. Furthermore, the period of struggle and mobilization was neither long enough, nor was it intense enough, to alter this situation.

Another weakness was the failure to link the struggle in the cane fields seriously with that of the workers in the sugar factories, as well as with the working class in general. The factory workers tended to be far more advanced educationally, socially and politically than the field workers, with significantly higher income levels as well. While SAC organizers did see factory organizing to be a priority, they were hampered in their efforts to stimulate a cooperative movement there by a number of factors. These included their own lack of resources (finance, personnel, time); the more concentrated opposition there from the unions, management and government (attempts to organize factory workers occurred subsequent to the establishment of SWCC in the cane fields, and hence the forces of opposition were more sensitized to what they perceived as a threat); the greater difficulties in reaching the workers at their workplace since organizers were systematically barred from the factories; and the better conditions of the factory workers.

But in addition there was a strong tendency within SWCC, as well as within SAC, to see cooperativization as a sectional struggle of the field workers for land and justice and not as part of a wider class struggle. This attitude strengthened over time, especially after agitational efforts in the factories were set back. Also, there were never substantial links to the Workers Liberation League (Workers Party of Jamaica after 1978) and its leaders who represented the national communist movement. This was partly due to the WLL's own conflicting attitudes toward the cooperative movement as well as to anti-communist tendencies or fears of the WLL within SWCC and SAC. Hence, in general, the struggle at the three estates adopted a community rather than a class perspective, and tended to emphasize the short-term reform struggle to the detriment of larger political needs.

A fourth weakness in the movement was the concern from 1974 on for "quality rather than quantity," at least at Monymusk. This decision, to focus on the minority best able to manage cooperative farms, responded to certain immediate short-term needs, but weakened the mass movement over the long run. It also reflected the continuing contradiction between political mobilization and business management or economism. After this period there were very few new entrants from among the mass of workers into the leadership.

Fifth, a good deal of the mass support for SWCC and the co-op struggle was superficial because it was based on purely materialist and transient motives. In particular, the level of mobilization achieved in 1975 was related to the workers' recognition that large severance payments awaited them upon the transformation of their farms to cooperatives. Many, if not most, were most immediately concerned with this factor.

A final weakness of the sugar worker movement which facilitated its subsequent demobilization and reorientation was its ambiguous relationship to the PNP. While some in SWCC saw the need to remain independent of party politics, there were a disproportionate number of PNP supporters in the organization, and they retained commitments to the party. This was not surprising, given the tendency in Jamaica for interest associations to be

more closely associated with one or the other party,
often depending on which is in power. SWCC tended to
fall into this pattern. This of course weakened SWCC
when it became apparent that the PNP was one of the forces anxious to clip its wings. It was less resistant,
making it more pliant and responsive to the party's
wishes.

THE GOVERNMENT AND THE IMPLEMENTATION PROCESS
IN THE CONTEXT OF A DEMOBILIZED WORKERS' MOVEMENT

   The demobilization of SWCC and the sugar worker
movement reduced significantly the resources available
to sugar workers to carry forward the implementation of
the cooperatives project. Yet, despite its active involvement in this campaign, the PNP government did not
move to replace the lost resources or to introduce new
resources at the grass roots. This was doubly unfortu-
nate because with the demobilization of their movement,
sugar workers became increasingly dependent on government initiatives and action.
   A good example of this dynamic was the education
program, already described. Unable, for financial and
other reasons, to implement a viable education program
for the worker-cooperators, something all concerned considered crucial, the USWCC looked for outside assistance. But the Inter-American Foundation funds granted
to it were blocked by government action, and no alternative was forthcoming. Finally, in 1978, the newly formed
Cooperative Development Centre took over the cooperatives' education program, but it too proved short of
manpower and finance, as well as imagination and commitment, and its program fared poorly.
   Another example was the loan deposit issue. These
worker investments in the cooperatives, drawn from their
severance payments, became callable at the beginning of
1978. Given the tenuous financial position of the cooperatives, however, it was agreed by USWCC and the government that repaying the deposits at that time would be
inimical to the financial and social viability of the
co-ops. [30] But pressing this decision on the workers was
difficult. The local cooperative leaders argued that it
was beyond their ability, and that since it was the government that was controlling the finances, its representative must come down to the farms to present the issue
and win over the people. The government was slow moving,
administratively unprepared, and felt it was the local
co-op leaders' role to do this. As a result the situation festered, eventually erupting in strike action and
general disruption. In fact, it would not have been very
difficult to convince the majority of the cooperators of
the importance of retaining their loan deposits, only

requiring sincere, sustained and imaginative communication efforts.[31] But this was not forthcoming.

In general, between 1976 and 1978, governmental input into the implementation process was mainly focused
on the USWCC where government officials interacted
closely with board members in the determination of policy. The Ministry of Agriculture, Sugar Industry Authority and Department of Cooperatives maintained advisors
formally attached to the USWCC board. Informally there
was further interaction and consultation. Moreover, the
cooperatives' precarious financial position made them
dependent on the government, with the SIA guaranteeing
and seeking loans for them, and with finance consequently channeled through and controlled by the SIA. In
general, the workers' representatives at the central
level considered seriously, and usually heeded the arguments of their advisors.[32] The implementation of this
advice, however, and the board decisions which embodied
it were always problematic. This was because of the
chasm separating national and local levels within the
cooperative movement.

At the estate level, interaction between the government and the cooperatives was much more tenuous than
at the national level. This was mainly because of the
multiplicity of administrative interests dealing with
the co-ops and the lack of any coordination of government interaction. Further, there just was insufficient
personnel. Only the Department of Cooperatives' field
officer interacted at all with the local level, but
this was mainly with cooperative leaders and was only
of a limited nature. The estate Member Service Department provided an ideal mechanism for dealing with the
mass membership and coordinating policy and programs.
However, it was completely independent of the government, was not given appropriate leadership or authority
by the elected cooperative leadership, and in fact often
acted as an independent force under the circumstances.
At the base of the cooperative structure, then, government influence was practically negligible.[33]

As early as 1976, the government was concerned
with this situation and sought to develop strategies
for strengthening its presence and control. Yet, at the
same time, paradoxically, it ignored SWCC's pleas for
a representative of the prime minister to sit with the
estate boards.[34] Rather, its first initiative in this
direction revolved around the formation of the Cooperative Development Centre in 1977. Though the CDC could
have played a viable role at the local level in both
the education program and as an influence among the
mass membership, it was constrained by financial and
personnel problems. In addition, the director of the
Centre had previously been with FMLCo and was considered an "enemy" by many co-op leaders.[35]

Later in 1977, convinced that the existing cooper-

ative structure was unable to implement measures needed
to correct existing problems, the Minister of Agriculture appointed a committee to investigate the need for
and possibility of restructuring the cooperatives. In-
explicably, no worker was on this committee, though two
union leaders were.[36] In its report submitted in 1978 it
recommended a radical restructuring of the cooperatives,
but this was never implemented, largely because of worker opposition.[37] A variant of this restructuring plan,
however, was implemented beginning in 1979. By then, indeed, the social and political infrastructure of the cooperatives was in substantial disarray, as we see in the
next chapter.

NOTES

1. Keble Munn, in a speech to a seminar on community enterprise organizations, September 26, 1978. Munn was then Minister of
Regional and Parliamentary Affairs, and had been Minister of Agriculture between 1972 and 1976.

2. SAC radio broadcast, p. 1.

3. Using hindsight we can see that the following factors would
have constrained further cooperativization, on the assumption that
only three co-ops, the government's original proposal, had been
established in 1975:

   a) the economic difficulties the existing cooperatives would
      have faced, under any circumstances, in 1976 and 1977;
   b) the macroeconomic crisis faced by the nation;
   c) the strengthened position of anti-cooperative and right-
      wing forces;
   d) possible World Bank and IMF pressure.

All these factors would have combined to weaken the already tenuous
political-economic resolve of the government to carry forward fully
its cooperativization policy. On the other hand, 1976 was an election year and this would have created strong pressure contrary to
the above scenario.

4. In this sense, the PNP-linked NWU was a much stronger opponent of SWCC since it was more legitimate and powerful within the
PNP. It opposed SWCC at least as strongly as did the BITU and
other anti-PNP forces.

5. Peat, Marwick and Mitchell, "Progress Report" (mimeo,
February 9, 1976, in USWCC files).

6. Politics was involved, too: the radio program had been a
SAC-initiated and assisted project.

7. Matthias Brown, "The Sugar Cooperatives in Jamaica (A Cooperator's View)," presented at the First West Indies Sugar Technologists Conference, Kingston, November 1976.

8. Adapted in part from Carl Stone, "Socio-Political Aspects
of the Sugar Cooperatives" (Kingston: University of the West Indies, Department of Government, 1976), pp. 3-4 and p. 38.

9. SAC began to get more involved again at the local level
starting around 1979.

10. The leading SAC organizer there was an American, a Jesuit priest.

11. Beginning in 1976, Workers Time was published for the sugar workers by SAC. It started as a monthly, then became bi-monthly.

12. Apparently, a similar process took place in the Peruvian sugar cooperativization program, with workers there also developing a deep skepticism of the benefits from such higher-level cooperatives (Douglas Earl Horton, Haciendas and Cooperatives: A Study of Estate Organization, Land Reform and New Reform Enterprises in Peru (Ithaca, NY: Latin American Studies Program, Cornell University, 1976), pp. 296-297.

13. Personal communication from Jim Schecher, SAC.

14. Jim Schecher, "Report on Co-op Member Education Programme Carried Out by Social Action Centre in Conjunction with USWCC Member Services Department" (Kingston: SAC, 1976),

15. In 1979, the grant was revived and approved, with SAC still involved.

16. The financial year ended September 30, 1976, but audited accounts were not received by the Monymusk cooperatives until the following summer. The one exception was the pilot cooperative, Morelands, whose members recieved their financial statements much earlier.

17. Workers Time 1 (February 1976), p. 2.

18. Ibid.

19. Joe Owens, SWCC organizer, in Workers Time 1 (February 1976), p. 6. Halsehall, Yarmouth, Waterwell and Rowington were large, privately owned, cane farms in Vere.

20. The PNP was originally established, in the late 1930s, as a democratic socialist party along British Labour Party lines. This ideology lost credence in the 1950s and 1960s. In 1974, the party formally renewed its commitment to this philosophy and program.

21. PNP General Secretary Ralph Brown popularized the phrase "mouth-water socialism" contrasting it with real socialist commitment and action. No definitions were provided. The occasion was an intraparty debate, during 1978, on the meaning of Democratic Socialism.

22. Richard Fletcher, in an interview with Ric Mentus, Jamaica Daily News, March 7, 1976. Some form of subsidy was actually justified on a number of grounds: a) the government's requirement that the co-ops retain all the farmland in cane, even though some was marginal; b) the fact that some of the farms taken over were already unprofitable, and possibly could never be profitable; c) allowing all registered workers to become members filled certain important social needs, but it also meant the retention of a labor surplus on the payroll; and d) the very low level of factory efficiency, particularly at Frome and Monymusk, due to long years of neglect.

23. The charges and the strategy were contained in a private document presented to a meeting of the PNP Executive Commitee in the early spring, 1976.

24. A.U. Belinfanti, "Sugar Cane Cooperatives at Frome, Monymusk and Bernard Lodge," unpublished Cabinet Note, April 2, 1976.

·Belifanti was Minister of Agriculture. The note was actually written by Fletcher of the SIA.

25. Ibid.

26. IBRD, Staff Appraisal Report - Sugar Rehabilitation Project, Jamaica (IBRD, Report #1732a-JM, 1978). The loan agreement finally signed between the government and the World Bank for the rehabilitation of the sugar factories contained a clause committing the government not to grant any subsidies, in any form, to the cooperatives which were not also made available to all other cane farms. This was at a time that the co-ops in particular, and the sugar industry in general, were facing severe problems.

27. Ric Mentus, "Interview with Carl Stone," Jamaica Daily News, February 15, 1976, and Ric Mentus, "Interview with Richard Fletcher, Jamaica Daily News, March 7, 1976.

28. Horace Levy, "What's Wrong with the Sugar Co-ops," Part I, Public Opinion, February 24, 1978, p. 12.

29. Stone emphasizes this point (Carl Stone, "The Morelands Sugar Cooperative," Jamaica Sugar Digest 1 and 2 [1973 and 1976]).

30. Not only were these deposits "on loan" from the members significant to the cooperatives' balance sheets, they also signified an important personal commitment by the workers in their cooperatives.

31. This conclusion is based on the author's experience in the field.

32. Interview with Una Saunders, Ministry of Agriculture, sugar co-op desk officer, and advisor to the USWCC board, November 2, 1977.

33. Attempts by the state to control the cooperatives--to intervene in decisions, to generate political support, and to appoint or influence the elected leadership--was a much more salient factor in the Peruvian cooperativization experience. There the state was well represented at the estate level. See Horton, pp. 334-335.

34. USWCC, "Urgent Petition to the Prime Minister Concerning Sugar Worker Cooperatives" (mimeo, March 2, 1976).

35. For example, see Workers Time, March-April 1977, for a description of a public protest directed against this individual and against his having any responsibility for or role with the education program.

36. The only representative from the cooperatives on the eleven-member committee was the USWCC general secretary, a staff member.

37. Committee Appointed by the Minister of Agriculture, Michael Shaw, Chairman, "The Rescue and Development of the Sugar Cooperatives" (mimeo, April 1978).

7
Social Relations at the Grass Roots Among Workers, Managers, and Staff

What is the production society? The ending
of the duel between the employer and the
wage earner.[1]

The ejido as a cooperative enterprise will
generally be unable to break the framework of
individualism, corruption, private profit-
seeking, and exploitation which characterize
the wider society. The ejido cannot become a
sociological and economic "enclave" within
the framework of a society that collectively
rejects it. . . . It can only function as an
institutional alternative if it manages to
cut the umbilical cord that links it to the
society which generated it. But this is of
course impossible unless that society itself
becomes totally transformed.[2]

This is farm ten. The ten commandments mash
up here. We picking up the pieces, and the
first piece say work.[3]

The sugar worker cooperatives were a radical departure from the existing pattern of production relations
on the sugar estates, as from established practices in
Jamaica as a whole. They were democratically owned,
socialist-oriented, self-managed bodies in a political
economy heavily imbued with the importance of class,
private property and capitalist values. And they were a
major factor in an important sector of the economy.

Not surprisingly, the pattern of social relations
which developed during the first few years experience
with the new arrangements did not fully correspond with
the ideal, or with corresponding expectations. Many
problems cropped up during the implementation process,
and these frequently were not dealt with or dealt with
in a haphazard manner.

WORKER-STAFF RELATIONS

From the beginning, the sugar worker cooperatives
project was affected by the cleavages and social contradictions that existed between workers and estate staff.
Field staff in particular had resisted the workers'
movement for control of the farms. This conflict was
carried over into the new cooperatives as most of the
field staff retained their positions despite the organizational transformation. As before, they continued to
resist the implementation of a democratic and worker-
controlled management structure.

The project managers, overseers and assistant overseers who composed the field staff, together with other
technical and middle management elements among factory
and estate administrative staff, were part of a hetero-
geneous agrarian bourgeoisie. This class also included
larger farmers, contractors (for example, owners of
heavy agricultural equipment) and local merchants. The
linkages between the estate staff, who did not directly
exploit labor, and the bourgeoisie who did were based
mainly on the fact that most of the staff had worked
long years managing and controlling workers for foreign
capital, in particular Tate and Lyle (Frome and Monymusk) and the United Fruit Company (Bernard Lodge). It
was not, however, uncommon for staff members also to
have local business interests, including interests in
farms, shops and contracting operations.

The specific cleavages between the field staff and
the workers were based mainly on the staff's role within the neo-colonial, semislave system of social relations which, as late as 1972, still bore heavily on the
sugar workers. The field staff managed, enforced and
symbolized the plantation system, which was widely rejected by the workers, though they had few employment
alternatives. The frequent use of disciplinary action by
the bushas, their brutality and their corruption, only
reinforced the workers' resentment.[4]

Many examples highlighting the oppression experienced by the workers can be cited. For example, sugar
workers at Springfield cooperative recalled the work
distribution practice of one busha in the precooperative
period. He would meet the workers at the farm office
and then ride off on his horse to the field that was to
be worked on, sometimes a good distance away. Those workers who were able to keep up with the horseman, arriv-
ing at the site before the others, were given the work.

The farm managers and their headmen, as above, generally had complete discretion in the distribution of
the often scarce field work. It was characteristically
menial, paid on a task-rate basis, and only accepted out
of necessity, by a work force of self-conscious "wage
slaves."[5] To reinforce their subordination, the workers
were never allowed to approach too close to the busha's

office, except in special circumstances. This system
heightened the oppression of the workers, the power of
the bushas and senior management, and the level of corruption.

The deep cleavages apparent in the relations between the two classes also involved social and economic
factors. For one thing, the color-class stratification
system characteristic of Jamaica right up to the 1970s
was perhaps most manifest and most strongly rooted in
the sugar estates. While sugar workers were mostly
black, their bosses, from the overseers to the owners,
were predominantly white, with an admixture of some
light or brown-complexion people in a hierarchy of
color.[6] This racial stratification was reinforced by seg-
regated living arrangements. Working-class blacks were
essentially barred from the Monymusk staff compound, except for those employed as gardeners and household workers. This was enforced by fences and security guards.[7]

A huge gulf in living conditions also separated
workers and field staff. As late as 1977, the field
staff earned up to fifteen times the average worker's
earnings. Historically this inequality had been worse.
The income of staff members, moreover, was guaranteed;
they were employed on an annual basis and paid monthly,
while the workers' remuneration was on a task or daily
basis, and tended to be irregular, even during the harvesting season. The workers were very conscious of this
injustice, and it also affected their relations with
weekly-paid headmen. Income differentials were translated into disparities in living conditions. For example, wooden barracks consisting of one- or two-room
dwellings for the workers existed side by side with
commodious housing having all the amenities, including
a private golf course, set aside for members of staff.

The agrarian bourgeoisie tended to interact socially only among themselves, often living together on
the estate compound. They eschewed the public education
system for private schools which were especially provided for them.[8] There was little, if any, social interaction between the two classes.

The workers did not outwardly rebel in their inter-
personal relations with the field staff; rather, paradoxically, they adopted deferential attitudes. Moreover,
they developed a strong dependency syndrome, needing
and responding to the leadership and initiative of such
higher-class others, mainly the agrarian bourgeoisie.
The latter in turn adopted a paternalist orientation.
However:

> Dependence, while it dominates, is coupled with
> discontent, with a yearning to reverse the situa-
> tion. . . . He relies heavily on managerial staff
> and headmen, even as he abuses them. [9]

Stone makes an analogous point:

> While individual survival on the part of the worker
> often required acceptance of or accommodation to
> 'overseer paternalism' or 'role-playing' at servile
> or deferential behaviour to staff personnel, these
> outward forms of acceptance of a self-denigrating
> lower-lower class status often masked and obscured
> anger, bitterness, resentment, as well as counter-
> vailing feelings of firmly rooted self confidence
> and personal dignity. Militant trade unionism pro-
> vided one channel through which to restore the
> wounded dignity and pride of the worker through the
> catharsis of collective action and the demonstra-
> tion of collective power over the highly placed
> estate establishment.[10]

The class divisions between the two groups became
politicized during the cooperativization struggle. From
the beginning, SWCC was generally critical of the staff.
For example, as early as 1973 at a meeting with the
FMLCo cooperative officer, SWCC workers made clear their
hostility to the existing field staff.[11] In mid-1974,
SWCC recommended formally a complete overhaul of farm
management, starting with the acceptance of a policy of
changing farm overseers around at regular intervals so
as to restrict their victimization of workers.[12] Around
the same time, the Morelands workers, with the support
of SWCC, successfully resisted an attempt by FMLCo to
impose on their new cooperative their old farm manager.
Worker opposition to staff hardened during 1974-
1975 in the face of sometimes virulent opposition by
staff members to the cooperativization project and especially to SWCC. The staff associations, among other
things, agitated strongly for employment security. They
were supported in this by the government and FMLCo. In
this regard, the Prime Minister's Committee on Cooperative Development stated in its second report: "Staff
currently employed by the Frome Monymusk Land Company
are expected in almost every case to continue to provide
this service to the new Cooperatives."[13]
In November, however, with the cooperatives ready
to become operationalized, SWCC conducted an evaluation
of staff members on the three estates. They were rated
on a three-point scale: to be retained without conditions; to be retained but on a probationary basis; not
to be retained, either because they were judged unsuit-
able, for their dishonesty, incompetence or hostility
to the workers' organization, or unnecessary. At Monymusk, of thirty-six staff members associated with field
operations, ten were recommended to be displaced, and
three more were recommended for probation.[14]
The staff associations responded with demonstrations and even a staff strike. They demanded severance

pay and guaranteed employment of at least one year. In
the end, even though some were indeed fired by the cooperatives, all members of staff received a two-year
guarantee of employment by FMLCo, and all were paid
severance, whether they were actually severed or not.

While there was an obvious need for managerial and
technical expertise, the weakness of the field staff in
this regard was not widely recognized. Few, if any, of
the project managers had any experience managing auto-
nomous agricultural units, let alone any of the size of
the co-ops. Under the Tate and Lyle/WISCo system, decision-making authority in most cases resided with
higher levels, with farm overseers mainly responsible
for implementation and bookkeeping. Worse, there was a
shockingly low level of technical and educational training among the staff. Few of the project managers had any
formal agronomic experience at all. Analogous arguments
could be made concerning holdover estate-level administrative elites, who often had little formal training
or even educational qualifications. Partly for these
reasons, the farm staff were peculiarly resistant to
diversification. They were traditionalists without any
agricultural experience or confidence outside of cane
production.

The latent and manifest conflicts between staff and
workers were not significantly eased by the removal of
some of the more repugnant bushas. Nor were the conflicts overcome after the cooperatives began operations.
If anything, during the first three years they worsened. Rather than alleviating existing problems, coop-
erativation produced additional sources of conflict,
emanating from attempts to implement the new cooperative structures.

The role of a hired manager within a worker-controlled cooperative is not a clear one. Four functions
of such a managerial type can be suggested: a) entre-
preneur; b) administrator; c) technical advisor; and
d) agent of social transformation.[15] Farm management
under any circumstances certainly involves the first
three functions. However, where cooperative farm management is concerned, and where the cooperative is a
producer cooperative with implicit or explicit goals
of social transformation as well as economic viability,
the farm manager must at least also be sensitive and
sympathetic to the fourth role as well. This means,
among other things, that the hired manager must work
actively to support the development of the cooperative,
in distinction to, but also in addition to, the enterprise. In other words, while in one sense cooperatives
are business enterprises like any other, in another
sense they are not. They are working-class or small-
farmer institutions in which: a) member education and
uplift have a high priority; b) members do not merely
work together or just pool their resources, but must

also participate as fully as possible in the day-to-day
life of their cooperative, including sharing as far as
possible in the solution of problems confronting the enterprise;[16] and c) members are often linked to a wider
movement which seeks to surmount the basic contradictions of capitalism.

The manager must be sympathetic to, and attempt to
support, these goals. This includes being willing to
stimulate the development among the cooperators of certain administrative and entrepreneurial capabilities,
and being willing to share such functions with them;
being concerned with maximizing member participation in
an organized and disciplined fashion; and assisting in
member education.

In general, the farm staff of the sugar worker cooperatives hardly saw their functions this way, and
this resulted in increased conflict and hostility between workers and managers, and significantly constrained the implementation process.

From the beginning the role and authority of the
field staff was an unresolved issue. The staff members
would, for example, express uncertainty as to whom they
were actually working for, whether it was the Frome
Monymusk Land Company, by whom they were guaranteed employment for two years; the Sugar Industry Authority,
which ultimately controlled the purse strings; the central cooperative (USWCC), which negotiated their contracts and by whom they were in fact employed after
1977; the estate cooperatives, to whose chief executives
they were formally responsible; or the farm cooperatives, whose members generally assumed that the farm
staff worked for them. While there was some diffusion
of authority, the expressed uncertainty by members of
staff was mainly a mechanism for clouding reality--a
reality of worker control. In this, nonetheless, they
were supported by many others--cane farmers, government
officials, sugar industry elites--who also sought to
reinforce, wherever possible, the authority and resources of the staff.

The workers, for their part, retained their ambiguous distrust of the staff; they were convinced the
staff were not acting in the workers' interests, but
were uncertain of themselves otherwise. Hence, while
formally the cooperatives were structured as democratic,
worker-controlled institutions, informally there was an
enormous and debilitating "tug of war" reinforced by
high levels of mutual distrust, dislike and conflict.

The issue was joined early in 1976, right at the
start of the first crop under cooperative management.
Acting in response to staff refusals to recognize the
authority of the new farm and estate-level worker committees at Frome (where the harvesting of the crop was
scheduled to start first), and resisting continued attempts to force the cooperatives to accept previously

rejected members of staff, all three estate boards voted not to start the crop until the issue was satisfactorily resolved.[17] They relented only when the government symbolically confirmed their authority, with letters granting the estate cooperatives possession of the land, while the formal lease documents were being finalized.

The conflict, however, continued thereafter. In the first place, co-op members insisted that the staff should be responsive and responsible to them and to the cooperatives, but class consciousness among the staff led them to resist this strongly. The staff would not accept their subservience to "illiterate" sugar workers. In general, older members of staff especially had too much of a commitment to the plantation system to be able to accept this transformation in social relations willingly or readily. This conflict was exacerbated by certain populist excesses by the workers. For example, they sometimes demanded individual authority "at the shop floor" over management.

Another manifestation of this serious problem affecting the cooperatives' management structure was the ongoing "tug of war" between the farm-level staff and their respective management committees. Project managers did not regularly attend meetings, did not present adequate reports, nor did they provide monthly budgetary information. This served, possibly in a calculated fashion, to weaken the authority of the management committees, and to reinforce a rank and file view that their elected leadership was incapable of overseeing the overseers.

Similarly there was little or no effort to support, let alone stimulate, general member education and participation. In effect, few of the staff were able or willing to alter substantially their behavior and traditional way of doing things, under the cooperative regime. They were no more willing to listen to workers' suggestions about farm operations, and were only slightly more willing to share financial and other information about farm operations. They had, moreover, to be forced to attend general meetings. Most often they did not attend.

In terms of the organization of work, a similar pattern prevailed. While field staff formally derived their authority and power from the workers themselves, and hence were restrained from employing their traditional autocratic patterns, the basic system of work organization, with its hierarchy, its task work pattern, its irregularity and dependence on favors and good relations with overseers remained. All this contributed to the reinforcement of dependency patterns and the maintenance of existing social relations of production (despite their nominal transformation).

In addition, with the cooperators now filling the roles of owner or operator as well as worker, new

sources of conflict developed. These arose out of the
workers' critical perception of the managers' performance qua managers. At Morelands, for example, the workers felt that work was not being authorized when it
should have been. For one thing, they argued that the
fields were not being weeded enough. As workers, this
affected them in two ways. When they were called on to
weed, the work was extremely difficult because of the
"bad grass," and was not compensated enough even with
the flexibility of the rate system. Second, there was
less work to give out, with fields being weeded once
per crop rather than the more usual three times. But
this now also affected them as owners and exacerbated
the conflict, since they assumed that failure to weed
properly was affecting yields. This became a very sore
point with the cultivation workers but, significantly,
they never utilized existing organizational mechanisms
to review the matter or air their grievances. A similar
situation developed around the irrigation workers who
felt that not enough water was being applied to the
cane. In both cases, the issues were not sufficiently
aired, nor were they used as an occasion to discuss or
educate the workers about farm economics, as an essential element in management. But they contributed to what
was a general dissatisfaction with the work performance
of staff. By 1978, only about one-third of the workers
surveyed on four Monymusk farms believed the staff was
"pulling its weight," with only a similar proportion
agreeing that proper care was being taken of the cane.[18]
    Existing class patterns were therefore not altered
significantly by cooperativization. To be sure, for the
workers there was now a greater potential for mobility
into, or at least to the fringes of, the agrarian middle
class. For one thing, there were constant reminders that
they were now small property holders, members of the
petty bourgeoisie and "part owners" of properties equal
to the largest in Jamaica. Second, workers were
accorded preference for promotion into available junior
staff positions, and some workers did indeed make the
jump. But for the most part this mobility, this breaking down of class barriers, was predominantly restricted to a minority of workers who were committee members
and headmen. These select workers now had considerable
influence, with income levels approaching that of junior
staff members, and in some cases residences closely approximating those traditionally accorded only to the
overseers.
    Hence, overall the position of the agrarian bour-
geoisie, represented by the staff, remained strong and
was reinforced by the implementation process. This
strengthening was due to a number of factors: a) the
political demobilization of SWCC and the sugar worker
movement; b) the increasing national political support
for staff elements after 1976, culminating in the

restructuring exercise in 1979; c) the strong propaganda
campaign in Vere and in the press against cooperativization, in which one of the prominent themes was alleged
worker mistakes and stupidity in attacking the staff;
d) the economic and other problems encountered by the
co-ops in the early years of their existence; and e) the
staff's retention of power and privilege at the local
level, reflected in the continued payment of bonuses,
their favorable staff contract and, in general, in their
continued dominance on most farms.

So for the vast majority of sugar workers, class
remained as salient as ever.[19] The continued power of
the staff significantly affected the implementation process. As Soliman has put it:

> As long as the power tends to concentrate in the
> hands of a few, whether influential families or the
> cooperative staff, there is great risk of accentu-
> ating old structures in making, or creating new
> systems similar to the old one.[20]

The workers understood this as they saw their hired
managers use their position and power to undermine the
cooperatives. They were aware that most members of staff
had opposed the workers from the beginning of the cooperative movement, and continued frequently to hear them
point out problems and failures within the cooperatives,
blaming them on the workers. Further, the unwillingness
of the managers in general to act in a manner consistent
with worker control and democratic cooperatives fueled
the cleavages. Behind it all, many workers felt, was the
fact that the staff continued to covet the opportunity
to gain control of the cane lands for themselves.

RELATIONS BETWEEN ELECTED LEADERS AND WORKERS

There are three ways that leadership can relate to
the mass movement, according to one famous formulation:

> To march at their head and lead them?
> To trail behind them, gesticulating and
> criticizing?
> Or to stand in their way and oppose them?[21]

After 1976, local-level cooperative leaders generally
followed the middle road.

Despite their working-class origins and background,
the elected cooperative leaders at the farm, estate and
central levels tended not to be representative of the
whole membership. This was particularly true of the
chairpersons. In particular: a) they were disproportionately drawn from supervisory categories (weekly and
daily paid), mainly headmen, and to a lesser extent

irrigation workers; b) they tended to have higher socioeconomic levels than the mass of workers; and c) their
literacy and education levels were significantly higher
than the average, which was low.

Morelands, for example, was led in the early stages
by a group of supervisors, tractor and transport operators (who lived on the Morelands worker compound) and
one member of staff. As a group they were more advanced
than the other workers at Morelands in terms of having
the resources to participate, including education,
greater self-confidence, less dependency, etc. Second,
they tended to be more upwardly mobile; hence they also
had greater incentive to participate. It was this group
that moved most strongly in 1974 to replace the then
farm manager, a very strong and authoritarian figure,
possibly seeing him as a stumbling block to their own
ambitions. A similar class pattern prevailed at Springfield cooperative during 1977-1978, with seven of eleven
management committee members being supervisors. At another Monymusk farm, nine of eleven were supervisors.[22]

Educational, socioeconomic, and work role differentiation between management committee members, in particular the chairpersons and secretaries, and the mass of
cooperators was usually reinforced during their tenure
in office. For workers election to the committee offered
mobility into supervisory positions and higher income
levels. Practically all the chairpersons began to draw
weekly salaries as chairpersons, though this was formally disallowed by the cooperative rules.[23] To legiti-
mize this, they were often made into or classified as
headmen. In addition, there was a tendency for any open-
ings which developed at the supervisory level to be
filled by committee members. The Springfield secretary
became a supervisor, then a weekly-paid headman in this
manner. Its chairperson became a headman more or less in
the former manner.

Committee members had disproportionate access to
training and other learning experiences. Other benefits,
like housing and allowances, also tended to accrue disproportionately to committee members. For example, few,
if any, of the staff houses on the farm compounds which
became available to the cooperatives were distributed to
ordinary workers. Chairpersons and secretaries, or other
committee members, got first choice.

Supervisors, who were heavily represented in leadership positions, were also able to reap extraordinary
windfalls. One of the first official acts of the Monymusk estate board was the quite unusual recommendation
that the pay rates for weekly and daily paid supervisors
be increased significantly. The increase, which averaged
roughly 50 percent, was extraordinary in its magnitude,
in the fact that it went outside traditional contract
procedures, and in that it established a new parity between these categories and all other daily and task-

rated work (see Chapter 8). This act had a strong impact
on the membership, suggesting that grass-roots workers
were not in control; that others would benefit from
their struggles and the changes made in their name; that
worker demands for justice and equality would go unheeded; that the estate board and the management committees on the farms were a clique of supervisors and
others not serving the interests of the majority of worker-members.

As a result of these phenomena, one of the most
significant economic patterns related to the cooperative
implementation process was the tendency for incomes of
chairpersons and supervisory categories to rise to the
level of junior staff, moving away from general worker
levels.

This "new stratification" should not have been un-
expected. The reproduction of class and inequality within cooperatives--sometimes regardless of any formal commitment to democratic mechanisms and ideals--is a common
experience.[24] It also fulfilled certain traditional expectations of the workers concerning leadership and what
roles leaders were expected to play. In such a class-
stratified and elitist society as Jamaica, workers had
come over the years to expect that those having leadership or management responsibilities would and should be
differentiated from the mass along socioeconomic and
other dimensions. Those elected to leadership positions
with the co-ops easily fell into this pattern.

On the other hand, sugar workers traditionally were
sensitive to illegitimate attempts by other workers to
raise themselves too high above the mass. This was reinforced by the instruction they received concerning worker cooperatives, and by their experience of the mobilization process between 1973 and 1975. Hence, they re-
acted negatively to this development among their elected
leadership. As they perceived it, though this leadership
had working-class origins like their own, in their
leadership roles they quickly became "ex grass-roots."
Workers cited the following behaviors to exemplify their
contentions about the leaders. Workers elected to leadership positions managed to receive larger paychecks;
they began to avoid walking and bicycling, using cars
and jeeps instead; they tended to spend a lot of time
off the farms; they spent more time with staff members
than with the workers; they would no longer work in the
fields; and they frequently went to meetings, and just
sat around.

The workers' contentions here contained both sense
and nonsense. In part they were objecting to legitimate
functions and needs of cooperative leaders, such as to
attend meetings, interact with staff, etc. But they were
also being sensitive to a very important observation,
that the workers who became leaders often did begin to
lose or throw off their roots in the cane fields. This

was correctly seen as an anti-democratic tendency, a weakening of the cooperatives' commitment to full democratic control and participation.

Divisions between the rank and file and the leadership were also reflected in and reinforced by the actual performance of the leadership. At the root here was an unresolved contradiction between the economic needs of the cane operations, on the one hand, and the political and social needs of the cooperatives and cooperators, on the other. The leadership's main responsibility--qua committee of management--was to manage the affairs of their cooperatives, and this came to be interpreted mainly in terms of the economic needs of the enterprise. But this did not always coincide with the workers' interests, as these were interpreted by the rank and file. Hence the leadership often ended up struggling against the rank and file workers. The experience of many of the workers, then, was of an <u>adversary</u> relationship between the committee and the membership.

This sort of conflict was not unique to the Jamaican case:

> In a production cooperative, owned and controlled by members with management elected by the members, the role and position of management is ambiguous. There is a tendency for a growing-apart of management and members, with the latter coming to look upon themselves as "we the workers" and viewing management as "they the bosses." This tendency of a we-they dichotomy is characteristic of most production cooperative-collective enterprises, especially after they have been in existence for some years.[25]

This phenomenon was most marked in those cooperatives generally thought to have "stronger" or "better" management committees, such as Springfield. The "stronger" committees were those which operated most according to traditional hierarchical and business norms, with less legitimacy accorded other concerns. But it was these other concerns--the need to maximize democratic participation, initiate strong worker organizations, and devolve resources and power to the workers--to which many workers were attracted. In other words, certain of the farm-level committees which were stronger in their commitment and ability to manage the farm enterprise appeared weaker in their relationship to the cooperative as a sociopolitical institution. To be sure, the co-ops did have a far greater commitment to democratization than traditional farm enterprises, but economics and efficiency became increasingly more important over time. If the co-ops had flourished and material rewards had been provided to the rank and file, it is likely that this deficiency would have been ignored. But the economic results were very poor, and this exacerbated the conflict. In 1979, at Springield's annual general meeting, all the "strong" committee members up for reelection, including the chairperson and secretary, were soundly rejected.

Other aspects of the elected leadership's performance were also unsatisfactory. There was a general tendency among the Monymusk cooperatives for the committee of management to schedule regular biweekly meetings. This was Springfield's standard practice and committee members attended diligently. Between February and June 1978 there were fourteen regular committee meetings at Springfield, with an average attendance of nine (out of eleven members). At Morelands, however, committee members exhibited far less discipline and leadership. Biweekly meetings there regularly fell through for lack of a quorum. This, rather than the experience at Springfield, was more the norm for Monymusk as a whole. In fact, there was at least one cooperative at which the committee of management did not meet for three months.

The elected leadership abdicated or failed to fulfill its role in other ways as well. In a number of cases, the leaders failed to perform important functions adequately. Budgets were often perfunctorily reviewed, or not reviewed at all. The estate board of management, for example, did not review or discuss the 1977-1978 budget before passing it. In effect, the board members were too inexperienced and too deficient in the necessary skills either to recognize the importance of this job or to carry it out adequately. But staff members were also to blame, since they tended to be extremely reticent about budgetary matters. In addition, when they did present budgetary information to the workers they made no effort to clarify or simplify the material. This may have been calculated, since it fostered a relationship of dependence by committee members on the staff personnel. Of course it was also true that many of the farm managers themselves had only a formal understanding of the mechanics of preparing adequate budgets, or of developing cost-efficient operations. In terms of the elected worker leadership, the experience in this area only pointed up their continuing need for outside support, assistance and guidance. But this too was lacking.

Most committees, such as at Morelands, tended to shrink from their authority. They seemed afraid of it, or did not know how to use it. Another sense in which they shirked their true responsibilities was in not adequately overseeing farm-level or estate staff. Neither the Morelands nor Springfield management committees were, for example, able to ensure even the presence of their farm managers at committee or general meetings. At Morelands, in particular, the farm manager generally refused to attend general meetings, and most committee meetings. Consequently such meetings often were failures, since the manager was needed to answer

124

basic questions. Furthermore, the chairperson at Morelands was unclear that he could do anything other than
"request" the manager's presence, a ludicrous situation.
For these and other reasons such committees tended not
to fulfill their responsibility to oversee farm operations.

Other examples of the near abdication of leadership
can be cited. It was common, for example, for elected
leaders to fail to attend general meetings and special
education sessions, not to mention, as we have said,
committee meetings themselves. At Morelands, less than
half of the committee members could be expected to attend general meetings, with Springfield having only
slightly better participation. The leadership must also
share the blame with the staff for its gross malfeasance
and inaction with regard to the need to diversify operations. They lacked confidence in themselves, the membership and the staff and did not seem to know how to go
about developing a plan for diversification of production and acting on it.

In addition, there was a general failure to develop
and implement appropriate procedures and mechanisms
whereby the elected leadership could relate to and communicate with the mass worker-membership. A good example
occurred at Morelands. In response to a worker's insistence that he be paid for a weeding task which was in
fact inadequately done, the committee reaffirmed an implicit policy, that any work not done properly was not
liable to be paid. But the committee at the same time
did not develop any mechanism for implementing this decision, in particular a means of communicating it to the
workers as a whole. Hence it was never reliably done.
Informal modes of communication were generally relied
on, mainly committee members disseminating decisions
among the workers. But only a very few committee members
took this seriously. Hence, decisions were either inadequately communicated, or communicated in a distorted
manner. Sometimes the farm managers were relied on to
communicate decisions to the workers, but they were as
uncommitted to the task as the majority of committee
members. The relative lack of vertical communication
within the farm-level cooperatives was duplicated in
terms of the dissemination of information to the rank
and file concerning estate and central board delibera-
tions and decisions.

All of this weakened the legitimacy of the elected
leadership in the eyes of the workers. This reinforced
the tendency toward division between the rank and file
and the leadership. This development was manifest in a
number of other areas as well. The leaders often appeared uncomfortable or incapable of relating to the
rank and file in their new roles as cooperative officials. They tended to be extremely defensive at times,
and appeared to have little patience with the grass-

roots members. They seemed to have lost touch with the mass, talking _at_ them rather than _with_ them or _for_ them. They seemed to fear, rather than respect, the mass movement (and indeed it was volatile at times!). Thus, for example, the leadership often looked to the government to intercede for them with the workers on touchy issues. Like the staff, they often had to be forced to listen. Part of the problem was that the management committees were often dominated by headmen who had internalized inappropriate attitudes or established tense relationships with the workers through their on-the-job interactions. Local leaders appeared highly frustrated by the low levels of enthusiasm and participation of the rank and file. Yet, at the same time they seemed to fear much higher levels of participation, both in numbers and intensity. They quickly resigned themselves to the apathy, and were slow to develop viable strategies for reversing it.

There was, moreover, even a tendency to restrict rank and file participation or even attendance at meetings of the committees of management. This was partly because the facilities were inadequate for attendance by large numbers (the normal meeting room for the eleven-member committee was a small office). This was also due partly to a restrictive understanding of the democratic process. The committee was the duly elected authority and the feeling was that there was no need for member inspection and involvement. In fact, even when rank and file workers were invited to discuss a specific matter, they usually had to wait outside until they were called. There was one instance when the committee met to discuss some corruption discovered at the farm and scores of interested workers came to the meeting, all attempting to crowd into the office used for meetings. The committee did not move to change the venue, to take the meeting outside where all could be accommodated, until it was urged to do so by the head of the member services department, who was present. What was in effect a general meeting then ensued, and all were satisfied.

While this tendency to restrict worker participation was standard practice elsewhere in the economy, the workers had come to understand the cooperative enterprise differently. Moreover, being traditionally distrustful and suspicious of local leaders, the workers were prone to disapprove of closed-door meetings.

There was a similar pattern at the estate level. For example, despite an early decision that each of the members of the estate committee of management could bring one or two persons from their cooperatives to the meetings, only one of these leaders made any effort to do this. The estate board's concern was stimulated by the low visibility which it had among workers at Monymusk, a problem shared with the farm committees at their respective cooperatives. In 1975, more than two-thirds of the Morelands members could not name half of their management committee.[26] This was a reflection of the low participatory levels and also of the fact that there was extremely little interaction or communication between the committees and the members.

As the level of mutual suspicion increased, the rank and file began to lose their identification with and respect for the cooperatives. Poor work discipline and lowered levels of effective participation ensued. Particularly significant here in affecting the attitudes of the rank and file were the relatively large number of instances of corruption which were detected among elected leaders.

An early case occurred at Morelands. By 1977, both the chairperson (a headman) and secretary (an accounting clerk) had been expelled by the membership for stealing cooperative funds. The cooperative had set up a small shop on the workers' compound in 1976, but shortly afterwards funds were discovered missing, and these leaders were implicated. The chairperson of one other Monymusk cooperative also had to be expelled for corruption. Other instances of corruption were also discovered among the staff and headmen. While corruption within cooperatives and grass-roots groups has always been a problem in Jamaica, its reoccurrence reinforced worker feelings of distrust and disenchantment.

All this contributed to a decline in the credibility and legitimacy of the chairpersons and management committees. While they had started out with considerable reserves of support and legitimacy, with the staff at low levels, within a few years the situation was reversed. By 1978, less than one-quarter of the workers at four Monumusk cooperatives believed that their committees were pulling their weight. The figure, as low as 10 percent at one farm, was 16 percent at Morelands.[27] While a committee like that at Springfield was more capable of identifying and fulfilling traditional management roles, its members were less adept at fulfilling the peculiar democratic leadership tasks of a worker committee of management. Hence, it too fell into dis-, favor, as pointed out above.

In defense of the elected worker leadership, it is true that the cooperatives experienced a number of serious economic, social and political problems right at the outset, and the brunt of these fell on their shoulders. Among other things, many of the workers, especially the cane cutters, were extremely undisciplined, aggressive and disruptive. Many neither understood nor supported the cooperatives, and had no respect for the elected local leadership. Lacking political direction and adequate leadership, their activities often appeared to border on anarchy.

Not only had the leadership hardly been prepared for such a situation, but they received, after 1976,

precious little outside assistance. In view of these
circumstances and the general demobilization of the workers' movement, a different operating pattern would have
been unlikely.

In summary, the grass-roots leadership was weak,
and often acted in ways inconsistent with the democratic
principles on which the cooperatives were based, and
hence inconsistent with the expectations of the workers.
In effect there was a vacuum of politically conscious,
dynamic and worker-oriented leadership at the grass
roots. Those elected to provide leadership seemed more
concerned with management than leadership, with business
organization than political organization, with production than transformation and the needs of the workers
they represented, with institutionalization than continued class struggle.

THE WORKERS AND THE COOPERATIVIZATION PROCESS

The pattern of social relations which arose out of
the cooperativization process was also affected by the
rank and file workers themselves. The worker response to
cooperativization was complex and shaped by a number of
factors, in a dialectical way. That is, they not only
responded to and were molded by events, but themselves
helped shape those events and the cooperative institutions. The conflicts inherent in their own situations,
how these conflicts were resolved, and with what implications, were crucial determinants of the project's
outcomes.

Individualism vs. Collectivism

One such conflict was that between individualism
and collectivism. One of the fundamental impediments to
the development of the cooperatives was the pervasive
proletarian or wage consciousness of the workers. For
example, the farms at Monymusk were high cost operations. Their long-run viability clearly required increased productivity and/or cost cutting. Here, however,
long-run entrepreneurial motivations confronted the
short-run needs and incentives of the workers. Would it
have been rational for the cane cutters to give up their
weekend work days, at time and a half and double-time
rates, so that the cooperatives could save money and the
factories could run more efficiently? Would it have been
rational for the irrigation workers to pray for rain so
as to benefit the crop and save money on costly irrigation water, when this would also have temporarily put
them out of work and reduced their earnings? Was it
rational for the workers to give up their union member-
ships and the demand to be included in industrywide con-

tract agreements, now that they were in effect cane farmers, as some suggested?

More than thirty years of trade union struggles, focused almost exclusively on the wage issue, hardly prepared the workers for the collectivist, entrepreneurial outlook needed in their roles as cooperators. It was the weekly paycheck and the lack of viable employment alternatives that were their rationale for being sugar workers, as it was for nearly all unskilled farm labor in Jamaica. Most of the cooperators had never known any other incentives than these. The cooperativization process did not substantially change this pattern after 1976, mainly because the old work organization and task-rate system which conditioned and nourished the workers' individualist, survival outlook for those thirty years and more, remained. When they came to "paybill" every Thursday after 1976, it was still as proletarians. When earnings appeared low, or the system unjust, they complained just as bitterly as they always had, often in the same manner and with the same single-mindedness of purpose. They did not see, nor were they adequately supported in seeing, that with the cooperatives they had more constructive avenues to achieve justice.

This is just one example of how the incompleteness of the transformation process, the retention of plantation roles and structures of exploitation, constrained the cooperativization process by reinforcing dysfunctional incentives. It also impeded attempts to change attitudes because in the perception of many of the workers neither the social relations of production nor their material conditions had changed substantially. At the time of this study, most workers retained their orientation to individualist, material incentives. Few workers seemed prepared to contribute any work effort for the cooperatives that was not directly remunerated.

To be sure, the development of a "collectivist (cooperative) consciousness" was not completely absent. Especially at the outset--1975 for Morelands, 1976 for the others--there was some enthusiasm and commitment to the cooperatives. By 1978, however, with the changes that had occurred appearing to lose their substance and significance, and with old patterns reasserting themselves, this outlook lost strength. While it still retained its salience for at least some workers, often the committee members, they were a minority.

There were indeed potential or actual incentives for collectivist or entrepreneurial responses. These were, however, partly ideological, involving talk of socialism, worker unity and calls for selfless action; only of long-run relevance, such as the potential for profits from cane farming; or bound up with the substitution of nonmaterial satisfactions, like increased real participation, greater equality and a more just order, for more material returns.

In any case, none of these alternatives was adequately tapped. To be sure, this disequilibrium (between material and social or collective incentives) was exacerbated by the severely depressed conditions in Jamaica and the associated inflation during the years in which the cooperatives were established. While self-denial and sacrifice were, and always had been everyday facts of life for sugar workers, their expectation of cooperative transformation had been that it would reverse, not reinforce, these conditions.

Democracy and Authority

A second conflict affecting the workers and their relationship to the cooperatives was that between democracy and authority. There was a very strong populist--almost anarchist--tendency among the rank and file, leading them to question and often reject any assertion of authority by responsible bodies. Conversely, there was a persistent clamor for direct democracy, that the membership should exercise all decision-making power.

The rank and file were suspicious of and resistant to all representative or higher-level cooperative bodies, even where such bodies had been constituted by the workers themselves. Indeed, the workers had legitimate and longstanding reasons to be suspicious and resentful of "management," but these attitudes were readily transferred to the new worker management. This was reinforced by the fact that in their actions and in the way many members perceived them, the worker leadership was not much differentiated from management, i.e., the staff. What else could the workers think when the committees and chairpersons began to exhort them to work harder, at the same time that these elected leaders seemed to have things easier?

At times the validity of almost any decision of the committee of management would be disputed. At other times, however, the workers' populism was much more calculated to encourage a fuller democratic life within the cooperatives. For example, at Springfield, which was more characterized by this worker populism than Morelands, the rank and file opposed the practice, sanctioned by the rules, whereby the elected committee of management would alone select the cooperative's chairperson from among themselves. The workers argued that this was too important a post to be awarded on any other basis than a general election. Then, again, they also objected to the rule that when a committee member resigned or otherwise lost his/her position in between annual general meetings, a replacement was to be chosen by the remaining committee members, without the necessity of this selection being immediately sanctioned by the general membership.

Unfortunately, the workers' apparent commitment to thoroughgoing democracy was not always in the best interests of the cooperatives. For example, it often impeded operations, such as when the committees feared taking certain decisions, including those which were fully within their authority, without first getting specific authorization at a general meeting. Since such meetings were not regular, because of quorum problems or otherwise, the decisions often ended up being much delayed.

Then, again, while insisting on their right to pass on all important matters, and some less important, the mass of the workers were apparently incapable of implementing this mandate for democracy in a disciplined, responsible and efficient manner. For one thing, the extent and intensity of rank and file participation was low. Hence the general meeting, the main outlet for participation, was inadequate. For example, during the first half of 1978, Springfield called four general meetings. As was its practice, all were specially called to deal with one issue only. In March, there was the problem of arson; in April, the question of where to site a government housing project; then in June, there were two meetings dealing with the discovery of corruption on the part of the assistant manager, a headman and two workers, and their subsequent expulsion. Only the latter meeting achieved a quorum. Morelands, meanwhile, followed its pattern of regular monthly meetings. In every case but one Morelands too failed to make a quorum, and that one was a special situation.

During the first few years of cooperative operations there was clearly a general falloff in participation. In 1975, based on a standardized questionnaire, Stone reported 40 to 45 percent of Morelands members regularly turning out at more important meetings. By 1976, only 31 percent were "consistent participants."[28] In 1978, less than one-quarter were regularly turning out. Stone's 1976 survey covered a number of other cooperative farms as well, including three at Monymusk. In their first year, 1976, all three had higher rates of consistent general meeting participation than Morelands in its second year, averaging 38 percent of the membership or almost the rate reported for Morelands in its first year.[29]

In 1978, both the frequency of general meetings and participation rates were low throughout Monymusk. As at Springfield and Morelands, less than 25 percent were regularly turning out except in special cases. And the tendency was to hold these meetings only sporadically, only when there was some special business or intense member pressure. That there was a falloff in participation is well documented. It was especially striking when compared to the 1975 period when farm by farm organizing at Monymusk was intense. At Springfield, for example, at this time roughly 100 workers, or 50 percent, were regularly coming to general meetings.[30]

Those general meetings that did occur were ineffective. One important factor was the lack of leadership. Neither agendas nor specific resolutions for debate were provided by the committees of management. Partly because of this, discussions tended to be rambling and unfocused. Then, again, the chairpersons often lost control over the meetings. This was due both to their own lack of authority, and to the workers' inexperience with such mechanisms of decision making. Some of the rank and file were totally undisciplined and disruptive. As a result disorganization and chaos often reigned, and democratic decision making was severely restricted. General meetings often became mere outlets for negativism and complaint.

The rank and file's great inexperience with democratic processes was important. There was no real grasp of the process by which differing opinions are freely voiced, widespread discussion and debate take place, and a majority decision is taken which is binding on the organization. For example, there was a widespread feeling that if it were a "real" cooperative there would be much greater unanimity on key issues than was usually the case. The idea that members could disagree but then all accept the majority decision was not understood. Then, again, the rank and file tended to repress their criticisms of the leadership and management personnel when they were present. Thus, their many grievances often did not get translated into public discussion and decision making. There was also only a rudimentary understanding of the formal mechanics of large meetings. For example, there was little experience among the rank and file with putting their thoughts into concrete motions, to be seconded, debated, and then passed or rejected by the body.

The painful contradiction between the rank and file's demands for full democracy and their apparent incapacity to effect it deserves a few further words by way of summary. The cooperatives were indeed structured so as to maximize the potential for democratic decision making, participation and democratic practice. How do we explain the inability of the rank and file to use the existing channels of participation to the fullest? First, there was an absence of leadership, in two senses. As discussed above, the elected leadership tended to take an adversarial approach and was not sensitive to the need to stimulate responsible mass participation. In addition, in general there were no leadership elements among the rank and file. Hence, the workers were unable to utilize the democratic processes constructively. Third, they lacked self-confidence. Fourth, they felt a deep alienation toward their jobs, and increasingly toward the cooperatives. Fifth, in a

number of cases the workers were just acting out what
were in fact anarchist tendencies. In such cases they
were just "raising hell." Alternatively, they were ex-
pressing their resentment toward the fact that "ordinary" workers had been elevated to important positions
of authority. "Chairman?," they would ask with incre-
dulity, "him only irrigator."

This extreme populist perspective affected other
levels of functioning. Within the farm-level committees
of management there was constant pressure to restrict
committee officials from taking any initiatives or en-
gaging in any actions independent of specific committee
mandates. The idea that all authority must emanate from
responsible bodies was often interpreted literally. In
practice this meant that chairpersons and secretaries
were restrained from exercising any authority and discretion, even in terms of implementing committee decisions. Their authority was restricted. Even if they had
to act on some matter not specifically authorized by
the committee, it was expected that they would immediately inform all committee members and/or call a meeting to legitimate the decision. There was no notion of
executive responsibility, no sense of a formula for
meshing democracy and authority.

Culture of Oppression

A "culture of oppression" among the workers[31] also
affected the workers' response to the cooperatives, and
was an important source of their populist attitudes. In
particular, the great difficulty which the committees
of management had in establishing their legitimacy was
based partly on a complex of worker attitudes which at
one and the same time doubted that anybody "like themselves" could really fill such leadership roles; resen-
ted anyone who tried to raise themselves above the
mass; and was severely distrustful of such people. Indeed, a major constraint to the efficient functioning
of the cooperative structure was the low levels of
trust built up over the centuries. The workers did not
have confidence in anyone to manage honestly the affairs of their cooperative societies and farms--all
will steal from them, lie to them, hide things from
them. This attitude developed into an attitudinal paradox: a) because of their low self-concept, they doubted
and did not trust themselves; b) they did not trust
others like themselves (other sugar workers)--"nigger
na good"; one put into a position of power would either
oppress them or steal from them, and probably both; c)
direct democracy therefore was necessary--one's only
protection was being in on every decision; d) but this
required some level of unity, and the low levels of
trust restricted this. This complex of attitudes devel-

oped from a colonial situation in which there were few
people to trust, frequently not even one's fellow slave/
worker. It was carefully nurtured by the colonialists
who saw some political value for themselves in this di-
visive orientation.

This culture of oppression was also reflected in
illiteracy rates approximating 60 to 70 percent, and in
the very low levels of political consciousness and democratic experience. It represented a significant constraint to the entire process. Most of the workers were
"impossible to motivate," and this lack of motivation
was demoralizing to the process of cultural and cooperative education which SWCC embarked on early.[32] The fact
that the period of struggle to establish the cooperatives was relatively short also hindered the process of
education, consciousness-raising and mobilization. The
lack of an ongoing education program after 1976 was also
probably significant.

Some observers have argued that it was essentially
within this group, comprising two-thirds to three-quarters of the workers, that the major problems with the
cooperativization process lay. They did not comprehend
the principles of collective organization and worker
control, and remained uncommitted to the cooperatives.
These were the main victims of cultural oppression.
They represented the main source of resistance and disruption within the work force, the ones not attending
meetings, not supporting majority decisions, and so
on.[33]

The Cooperativization Process and
Worker Attitudes

The pattern of social relations which developed
within the cooperatives, and the implementation process
as a whole, produced dysfunctional attitudes among the
rank and file. In particular, there was a pervasive
attitude among the general membership that "cooperative
just a name," "cooperative just a face card." First,
worker ownership and worker control seemed a sham to
them. Second, the cooperatives were not living up to
their expectations in terms of fulfillment of the
ideals of justice and equality.

Taking the latter first, one of the core arguments
repeatedly emphasized during the 1973-1975 period was
that cooperativization would substantially change
grass-roots realities, ushering in a new period of
greater justice and equality.[34] What the workers experienced during the 1976-1978 period, however, was
that while cooperativization formally transformed ownership, the management structure and the pattern of
social relations, it did not substantially alter the
operating pattern. As a result, the rank and file did

not experience any marked transcendence of existing conflicts and disparities. The "Cooperative System" did not
seem to be functioning for them. This is summarized
below.

One of the major examples of injustice had been the
estate housing system. With the establishment of the
cooperatives, workers for the first time had the authority to decide on the allocation of all existing housing
on the farm compounds. With members of staff no longer,
as before, required to live on the compound, a number of
them gave up their houses. No ordinary rank and file
worker, however, was ever given access to such housing.
In every case--and there were not really many--it was an
elected committee officer or a supervisor (usually a
committee member as well) who was granted the benefit of
the house by the committee of management. By 1978 all
the chairpersons were either residing off their farms
or in such rent-free compound housing, traditionally
reserved for staff.

Meanwhile, at some of the cooperatives, workers'
housing was falling into disrepair. This was the case at
Morelands. Another cooperative even voted to begin
charging workers rental for the dilapidated compound
housing, on the argument that if those members living
off the farm had to pay rent, why shouldn't everybody?
If it had been implemented, this would have caused a
deterioration in the workers' standard of living. In
another case, at Morelands, when an additional "staff
house" became available (with leading committee officers
and supervisors already well housed), it was put up for
rent rather than finding some means of giving the still
ill-housed rank and file workers access to it.[35]

A second area in which there was little change was
the pattern of work allocation. Overseers still played
"favorites," the injustices associated with the task-
rate system remained, and the workers still found themselves with the hardest work at the lowest pay. Women
were treated no differently than before, nor was additional work generated for members of the cooperatives.

In terms of transport, the busha still drove the
jeep; headmen in a number of cases traded their mules
for motor bikes; and the rank and file still generally
walked or rode bicycles.

Fourth, there was no movement toward greater equality of income. Rather, the reverse occurred, with differentials within the work force greater than previously (see Chapter 8). While there were no longer any
capitalists, there was also no surplus to share out.
The few cooperatives that did earn a surplus shared it
out in the manner in which end-of-year bonuses were
traditionally distributed, in proportion to crop earnings.

While the cooperatives were supposed to institutionalize a system of worker ownership and worker con-

trol, this also did not seem to be the reality for many rank and file workers. But then whose cooperative was it? Who other than the workers controlled the cooperatives? There was no clear consensus on this, but there were a number of factors which the workers took into consideration in analyzing their situations.

First, there was the SIA's control of the cooperatives' money. While many workers were not fully aware of this, it was reflected in the attitudes of many staff members who perpetuated the idea of grass-roots powerlessness in the face of alleged government control (an attitude which fit in with the pervasive dependency syndrome). Many rank and file workers took the attitude that the cooperatives were established by the government and it still controlled them. This was reinforced, for example, by the resolution of the loan deposit issue, with the government taking an active role in demanding that this money remain with the cooperatives, and stating that any cooperator who demanded his/her deposit would thereby relinquish his/her place in the cooperative. This, we might add, was quite illegal according to the cooperative rules. It was not a legal basis for forcing any member out of the cooperative.

Second, the continued power of a staff generally thought to be antagonistic to the cooperatives, hostile to the workers, and not responsible to the membership, also contributed to the view that the rank and file were not controlling "their" cooperatives. The staff was seen as an alien force with inordinate power. They retained, or were thought to retain, tight control over decision making and monopolized local finances and bookkeeping. [36] They also were able, in some cooperatives more than others, to control the chairpersons and committees.

Third, the estate and central boards were seen as being divorced from the grass roots, and as having abrogated too much authority to themselves. Many members felt that the chairpersons often made major decisions there, in seeming secrecy and without democratic control.

Fourth, even the farm-level committees often appeared elitist, unilaterally controlling cooperative affairs, sometimes in conjunction with the farm manager, and divorced from democratic control or responsibility.

A final factor which made it difficult for an individual rank and file member to identify with the farm as his or her own was the enormity of the property itself, and the fact of collective ownership. Rural worker-peasant elements were used to identifying five to ten acres as a large property, but here they were faced with 2,000 acres with commensurate financial values. This was difficult for semiliterate individuals to assimilate. This problem was compounded by the absence of a significant education program. Also, the workers

were used to highly individualist forms of property
ownership, even within the marital dyad. But within the
cooperative, ownership was shared by roughly 200 individuals.

All this was critical for the cooperatives' democratic operation. As we have seen, workers felt they
did not control the co-ops since the leaders and staff
were not trusted nor were they expected to act in the
workers' interest. At the same time many also felt that
workers were incapable of rising up to the point where
they could be capable of carrying out farm administrative activities. Since they could never reach this
position, they had to rely on others, but the others
could not be trusted, so in the final analysis they
experienced their situation as hopeless, contributing to
anarchic and negativistic behavior.

NOTES

1. Charles Gide, quoted in International Labour Office, Cooperation (Geneva, ILO, 1956), p. 14.
2. Rodolfo Stavenhagen in Peter Singelmann, "Rural Collectivization and Dependent Capitalism: The Mexican Collective Ejido,"
Latin American Perspectives 5 (Summer 1978), p. 59.
3. Brother Tara, cooperator on Frome Estate, demanding that
members of staff and the estate board of management join in regular work (Workers Time, April 1977, pp. 3-4).
4. To be sure, certain middle-level managers were also op-
pressed, to a degree, by the system. For example, at Monymusk
there were two staff clubs, one for "junior" and one for "senior"
staff, and there was a very clear social division between them.
At Frome, where there was only one staff club, barmen were in-
structed never to serve a junior staff person before a senior member of staff, even if the former had been waiting longer (Brown,
1976).
5. Stone, Social and Economic Studies, 27, p. 2.
6. This designation "black" differs from North American usage.
In the Jamaican context, those of African heritage were also often
distinguished by color, a practice rooted in the slave system and
in the need of the plantocracy to keep the predominantly African
population divided. Traditionally, color was closely correlated
with class. The ruling class was white, the middle class, brown,
and the working class, black. The color-class stratification system is described by Henriques.
7. To be sure, by the 1970s this racist pattern had definitely
begun to change, as men of color began to ascend the social scale
and move into staff positions.
8. This tradition was so strong that the private elementary
school at Monymusk continued in operation after the cooperativization of the estate. From then it began to be directly subsidized
by the workers, through their estate cooperative, even though
few, if any, workers' children attended the school.

9. Levy, Public Opinion, February 24, 1978, p. 12.

10. Stone, Jamaica Sugar Digest, #1 (1975-1976), p. 6.

11. SWCC, "Summary . . . ."

12. Leopold Brown, SWCC Chairperson, in a letter to FMLCo, reprinted in SWCC News, August 1, 1974.

13. Government of Jamaica, Prime Minister's Committee on Co-operative Development on the Frome, Monymusk and Bernard Lodge Estates, "Second Report" (mimeo, n.d.), p. 5.

14. Joe Owens, personal communication.

15. Adapted from Horton, p. 303.

16. Czechoslavak Central Cooperative Council, The Czechoslavak Co-operative Achievement (Prague, 1965), p. 148.

17. Workers Time 1 (February 1976), p. 1.

18. Carl Stone, "Organization and Operation of the Cooperatives," in Report of the Committee Appointed by the Minister of Agriculture, Michael Shaw, Chairman, "The Rescue and Development of the Sugar Cooperatives" (mimeo, April 1978). At Morelands only 10 percent of the workers felt staff was pulling its weight. The Morelands workers were especially critical of their farm manager, whom they compared very unfavorably, in terms of his agronomic ability, with their previous manager. In retrospect, the latter looked good, though they had rejected him in 1974. Still, in 1978, there was no move to replace, or even publicly criticize, the farm manager.

19. Horton has reported similar class and authority conflicts between workers and managerial staff within the Peruvian sugar co-operatives. But there was a much greater incidence of managerial staff turnover in the Peruvian case. One cooperative there had six managers over a five-year period (Horton, p. 303). No doubt in Jamaica the generally poor qualifications of most farm managerial staff restricted their mobility.

20. Mohamed Ali Soliman, "Role of Cooperatives in Land Reform," Development 21 (1979), p. 9.

21. Mao Zedong, "Report on an Investigation of the Peasant Movement in Hunan" (March 1927), Selected Works, Vol. I, p. 24.

22. In Peru, the policy of establishing democratically managed rural communities composed of middle and poor peasants resulted in a similar dynamic. Most comuneros, peasant members of the communities, were poor and lower-class. With leadership, administrative and technical resources thus scarce, power tended to centralize around the individual or individuals who did have these resources. As a result, major decision making was monopolized by a few, participation was low, factional disputes proliferated and labor mobilization faltered (Norman Long and David Winder, "From Peasant Community to Production Cooperative: An Analysis of Recent Government Policy in Peru," Journal of Development Studies 12 [1975]).

The literature on participation contains frequent citations of a similar pattern. Social and economic advantages tend to translate into greater participatory activity. They tend to do so because they confer greater material, psychological and intellectual resources and the motivation to participate. These psychological resources include greater sense of efficacy, greater commitment to participate, often correlated with social stratification patterns, as in Jamaica; greater number of previous participatory experiences (Sidney Verba and Goldie Shabad, "Workers' Councils and Political Stratification: The Yugoslav Experience," American Political Science Review 72 [1978]).

23. Being an officer of a cooperative was considered to be voluntary work. Such officers were only meant to be reimbursed for any time lost from their regular work, due to cooperative duties. The cooperative rules stipulated that such posts were to be otherwise unremunerated.

24. Bates, for example, describes how cooperative leaders were able to use their position to reap sizable benefits for themselves, creating major economic disparities between them and the rank and file, with resulting dissatisfaction among the latter. Among other things they openly paid themselves much higher salaries and used cooperatives' fixed capital for private gain. When there was no work in this building cooperative, the leaders were still paid a salary, but the rank and file were not (Robert H. Bates, Rural Responses to Industrialization: A Study of Village Zambia [New Haven: Yale University Press, 1976], pp. 130-136).

25. Peter Dorner and Don Kanel, Group Farming Issues and Prospects: A Summary of International Experience (New York: Research and Training Network, Agricultural Development Council, 1975), p. 7.

26. Stone, Jamaica Sugar Digest 2 (1976), p. 8.

27. Stone, "Organization and Operation . . . ."

28. Stone, Jamaica Sugar Digest, 1976, p. 1.

29. Stone, "Socio-Political Aspects . . . ," p. 20.

30. Based on reports contained in the minutes of these meetings, Springfield Co-op files.

31. Stone, "Socio-Political Aspects . . . ," p. 3.

32. Joe Owens interview.

33. W. Sean Barlow, "The Sugar Cooperative Movement in Jamaica: A Case Study and General Evaluation," unpublished independent research study, Government Department, Wesleyan University, April 1978.

34. For a good description of this perspective, see Workers Time, "Worker Education Supplement," March 1976.

35. A major exception to this pattern occurred under the government's Sugar Industry Housing Scheme. New housing was built and made accessible to workers. This program, however, was completely separate from the cooperatives.

36. The 10 percent bonus paid to members of staff in 1978, despite the dire financial situation, substantiated the view that the staff retained considerable power. It also suggested to the workers that they were not being told the truth about the co-ops' finances. If things were so bad, how could so much money be found to pay the staff a bonus?

8
Economic Outcomes
at the Grass Roots:
The Workers

The conflicts which developed within the cooperatives were in no small measure due to economic factors.
On the one hand, the workers suffered both a decline in
their real incomes and an increase in the maldistribu-
tion of income within the cooperatives; on the other
hand, the economic performance of the cooperative enterprises was disappointing. These issues are taken up in
this and the following chapters.

PRECOOPERATIVE ECONOMIC CONDITIONS FOR
THE WORKERS

Cooperativization in Jamaica was rooted in deeply
felt political needs to implement a new system of economic and social justice. Sugar workers, along with
banana workers and other unskilled agricultural laborers, were traditionally among the most exploited and
downtrodden of all Jamaicans. As late as 1974, for
example, conditions in Vere still reflected this pattern
of severe social and economic malaise. And it was un-
changing. Little progress had been made in the previous
thirty, even sixty, years.
Consider housing. Almost three-quarters of the
households in the Monymusk area, averaging 4 1/2 persons
per household, were squeezed into one-room or two-room
accommodations. Two-thirds were without electricity; 90
percent without running water (into the house). [1] At
Morelands farm, out of fifty workers and their families
living on the compound, thirteen had one-room in a barracks and twenty-seven had a two-room house. At Springfield farm, with fifty-three families on the compound,
thirty-one had one room in a barracks, six had one room
in a two-room house, while thirteen had two rooms,
either in a barracks or a house. [2]
The employment situation was also depressing. Almost two-thirds of those over 14 were either unemployed
or not in the labor force (and often not in school

139

either). Formal unemployment was 22 percent. Of those working, few were working full weeks; the average was 23 hours worked in the week preceding the survey (during the harvest period).[3]

Up to the 1970s, wages followed a similar pattern. They were both relatively and absolutely low (Table 8.1). Sanderson and Porter actually underestimate the disparities since most sugar workers were task, not daily-paid, workers and, in addition, were only seasonally employed. Estate work, especially cane cutting, was also among the most onerous of all jobs. This helps explain the otherwise paradoxical labor shortages on the estates through the 1960s and into the 1970s.[4]

This social and economic malaise affecting Vere did not differ substantially from other estate and banana plantation areas. In one respect, however, it did stand out, reflecting perhaps the impotence of the political process in the colonial and even post-independence periods. Vere for over twenty years had been the home constituency of successive leaders of the Jamaica Labour Party, the governing party for two-thirds of this time (albeit within the colonial framework until 1962).

A number of factors help explain this pattern of absolute and relative impoverishment. First, large pools of labor were drawn to and established in Vere after 1940 (Chapter 2). The estates "hired" or registered more workers than they actually needed, though providing all with at least occasional work. This produced a large reservoir of unemployed human capital which acted to keep wage rates low. In addition, many workers were provided with company housing and small garden plots, while others had plots off the estate. This facilitated the maintenance of low wages, even below what was necessary to maintain the workers and their families, because they could supplement their wages by subsistence production. This situation benefited foreign capital, the major employer of agricultural labor, in two ways. It helped maintain high profit rates, while facilitating lower export prices, with those exports earmarked for the metropolitan countries.

Second, until the 1940s there was a very low level of worker organization in Jamaica. This did change dramatically after 1938, with sugar and banana workers in the vanguard of the nascent union movement. However, especially after 1950, field workers in the sugar industry did not significantly benefit from this representation (Chapter 2).

Third, low labor productivity tended to reduce the level of returns available to the workers.[5] But even when productivity increased considerably over the years, the productivity gains were not shared with the workers. Sugar workers did not share in the technical progress which occurred in their industry because of their relatively weak political position. Rather, the surplus that

TABLE 8.1
Comparative Wage Structure of Jamaican Industry, 1969[a]

Job Description	Sugar Estates	Banana Industry	Construction	Government Agricultural Operations	Bauxite Companies - Agricultural Operations	Bauxite & Alumina Industry	General Manufacturing
Daily paid workers (male)	$1.08-1.50	$0.65-1.08	$2.36	$1.85-2.00	$1.43-3.00	$6.64-6.80	$1.20-7.20
Tractor drivers	$1.65-3.59	$1.96-2.88	$6.88	$3.33	$2.16-4.56	$11.12-13.60	$2.40-7.36
Mechanics	$1.48-3.50	$3.28-8.38	$3.93-6.40	$2.90-4.00	$3.84	$9.36-12.96	$1.92-12.00

Source: Sanderson and Porter, Exhibit F.

[a]Per 8-hour day.

was generated was utilized in an unproductive manner. It was mostly repatriated by the foreign capitalists. In this case, the labor power of Jamaican sugar workers was literally plundered by foreign capital.

COOPERATIVES AND WORKER INCOMES

The Manley government was of course aware of this socioeconomic situation when it came into office in 1972. The prime minister himself had been chief sugar organizer for the National Workers Union beginning in 1953, later becoming Island Supervisor. He had a deep emotional attachment to sugar workers. At the same time, the government had declared its commitment to easing poverty and inequality nationwide. So the attempt to direct policy outputs at ameliorating material conditions among sugar workers was not surprising.

From the beginning economic outcomes for sugar workers figured prominently in the development of a cooperativization policy. The interministerial planning committee which produced the original proposal for the development of the government's cane lands at Frome, Monymusk and Bernard Lodge dealt explicitly with the question of increasing economic returns for sugar workers. It proposed $1,500 per year as a satisfactory income, and estimated that 30-35 acres per worker would yield that amount. [6]

Cooperativization was not the only aspect of government strategy and policy, nor the only factor, which directly affected sugar worker incomes and living standards after 1972. It was, however, an important part of that strategy and did have an income component to it. Cooperativization could have resulted in a redistribution of income toward the work force through a number of potential mechanisms. These mechanisms included: a) appropriation of the surplus otherwise accruing to the foreign ownership; b) the assumption of managerial functions by cooperators, releasing additional surplus for distribution; c) an increase in the percentage of total work done by members of the cooperative; d) increasing production through more efficient management and/or greater work incentives and labor intensity; e) diversification—the creation of sideline activities or other cash crops, especially during the "dead season"; and f) wage increases granted by the cooperatives.

While the cooperatives project did not explicitly incorporate or commit itself to any or all of these mechanisms, assumptions made at one time or another about the co-ops, by workers, organizers, politicians, planners or observers, did extend to all of them.

The possibility of the cooperatives acting to increase sugar worker wage rates was largely preempted by the industrywide collective bargaining agreement signed

in December 1974. Sugar workers on the twelve estates
then operating won significant rate increases. [7] Task
rates increased 50 percent, cutting rates 100 percent,
and day labor and supervisory rates increased on average
about 125 percent. In other words, prior to any cooperative commencing operations, a wage package was negotiated which significantly increased worker incomes,
more than doubling them in some cases. In this situation, even with the best of intentions and conditions,
it would have been difficult for the cooperatives to
increase incomes further, in the short run.

Morelands cooperative began operations in 1975.
In that year, the average gross income of the worker-
members almost doubled, but this was wholly or almost
wholly a result of the previous December's islandwide
wage increase (Table 8.2). Attempting to adjust 1974
incomes by 1975 wage rates, so that a more adequate
comparison of pre- and postcooperative incomes is possible, yields a 5.8 percent average real increase in
1975, the first year of the cooperative's operations.
There was a further increase in 1976, followed by a decline the following year. [8]

Springfield cooperative began operations in 1976.
Between 1975 and 1977, average gross income actually
registered a slight decline (Table 8.2). Combining the
figures for both Morelands and Springfield, between
1975 and 1977 average gross income increased by 1.2
percent, from $2,212 to $2,238. In general, we can con-
clude that for Monymusk cooperativization did not significantly affect average gross worker income during
its first few years.

The differences observed between the two farm cooperatives are significant and call for some explanation. Contributing most to this divergence was the
large disparity in cutters' gross income (Tables 8.5
and 8.6). Two factors help explain this. First, a much
greater percentage of the Springfield cutting gang
lived in the hills outside Vere, and worked only during
the crop season. In 1975, Morelands' cutters averaged
almost four more weeks of work per year than those at
Springfield. This would be equivalent to an additional
$100/year, assuming the additional weeks occurred dur-
ing the out-of-crop season. Second, the Morelands cutting gang cut more cane, doing all the reaping at their
farm, while at Springfield outside gangs were also
hired. [9] This same factor increased the earnings of certain categories of general laborers at Morelands, in
particular the cane scrappers. But still this does not
adequately explain the observed differences. [10]

Undeniably a major achievement of the cooperatives
was just this stability in earnings. It is remarkable
that the declines registered in 1977 were not more severe. Given the sharp drop in acreage and tonnage
reaped and the abandonment of fields, layoffs and

TABLE 8.2
Average Gross Incomes, Morelands and Springfield
1974-1977 (current dollars)[a]

Year	Average Gross Worker Income at Morelands	Average Gross Worker Income at Springfield
1974[b]	$1,233	$ 974
1975	2,363	2,061
1976	2,442	2,079
1977	2,420	2,055

[a]Average gross income was computed from individual gross income figures obtained from the National Insurance Scheme (NIS) records of each co-op member for each year. Records were available for practically the whole co-op work force.

[b]Adjusted income figures for 1974, computed on the basis of 1975 task rates, were: Morelands - $2,234; Springfield - $1,743. These are only approximations, and are not totally reliable.

reduced incomes would have been almost inevitable under the previous or any major alternative tenure pattern (Table 8.3). The workers clearly had the resources to defend their earnings base. At Springfield, for example, the cutting gang demanded that outside contractors be excluded from the reaping. Against the resistance of the staff they won. At Morelands, during the out-of-crop period there was tremendous agitation for work, reinforced by the workers' awareness that there were numerous fields and drains needing to be weeded, along with other tasks. The cooperatives, as democratic organizations supposed to serve the needs of their members, did tend, though not without resistance, to move in this direction. This remarkable achievement of sustaining workers' incomes was not without its costs, though, as the overall financial situation only worsened. And unfortunately, few workers appeared to be conscious of how much their cooperatives did benefit them in this regard.

The absolute level of gross earnings is also noteworthy. By the mid-1970s, the cooperative workers were among the highest paid agricultural laborers in Jamaica. For example, 1977 average gross income of sugar workers at a large private cane farm in Vere was only $1,092, or one-half the level of cooperators doing the same work.[11] Only about one-quarter of all workers in Jamaica grossed over $40 per week in 1976, but over half of

TABLE 8.3

Change in Acreages and Tons Reaped Compared to Change
in Average Gross Incomes, Morelands and Springfield, 1976-1977

	Morelands			Springfield		
	1976	1977	% Change	1976	1977	% Change
Acres reaped	1,899	1,612	-15.1	2,088	1,694	-18.9
Tons reaped	52,942	33,029	-37.6	63,815	42,003	-34.2
Average gross income	$2,442	$2,420	- 0.9	$2,079	$2,055	- 1.2
Laborers	$2,021	$2,122	+ 5.0	$1,652	$1,560	- 5.6
Cutters	$2,470	$2,423	- 1.9	$1,981	$1,979	- 0.1
Irrigators	$2,625	$2,521	- 4.0	$2,558	$2,452	- 4.1
Supervisors	$3,999	$4,015	+ 0.4	$3,288	$3,663	+11.4

Source: Production figures are based on farm records.
Income figures are based on NIS returns for each year. Workers were placed
into job categories based on the author's observations.

TABLE 8.4
Percentage Distribution of Employed Labor Force
by Income Group, 1976

Weekly Income	Total Employed Labor Force [a,b]	Workers in Agriculture, Forestry, Fishing and Mining [a]	Workers at Morelands and Springfield
No income	6.9%	13.4%	---
Under $10	15.9	57.2	1.7%
$10-$19.99	19.4 ⎤		9.8
$20-$29.99	19.9	24.5	14.0
$30-$30.99	11.4 ⎬		17.6
$40-$49.99	6.8 ⎦		23.2
$90-$99.99	14.4	2.8	33.3
$100 and over	5.4	2.1	0.3
	100.1	100.0	99.9

Source: Department of Statistics, The Labour Force,
1976 (Kingston, 1977); Morelands and Springfield figures
based on NIS returns for 1976.

[a]Percentages for the total labor force and for the
agricultural sector are based on the average of April
and October labor force surveys, and so add up to over
100 percent in the one case.

[b]About 23 percent of the employed labor force made
no reports as to income.

the Morelands and Springfield cooperators did (Table 8.4)
   The material situation of the workers and hence
their attitude toward the cooperatives, was affected by
factors outside of the control of the cooperative movement. Specifically, both increased taxes and inflation
sharply eroded real disposable income between 1975 and
1977.

At the end of 1977, the rural consumer price index was 20.3 percent above the level two years earlier.[12] Average real income thus declined 19 percent during this period. Inflation during 1978, especially following the imposition of an IMF austerity and stabilization package in May, was 51 percent, completely nullifying the 20 percent wage hike won by all sugar workers that year. The ravages of inflation, eating into their wage pack- ets, made things seem even worse to the workers than when they were "two shilling a day" workers. At least then prices were also lower and more stable. At least that is how they perceived it. The experience of rapidly rising prices, especially in 1978, was a destabilizing factor affecting implementation of the cooperatives pro- ject.

At the same time disposable income was also being cut into through increased taxes. In particular, in 1976 the National Housing Trust, committed to financing and building houses for workers, began operations. It was financed by a 5 percent tax on workers' wages, 3 percent paid by employers and 2 percent charged directly to wor- kers' gross wages. Those workers who actually began to move into new government-built housing faced an even more drastic decline in their disposable income, albeit with the benefits associated with having new homes. Mortgage payments, totaling 20 percent of their annual earnings, were deducted by the government from their wages.

An additional factor, again independent of the op- erations of the cooperatives, though not the cooperati- vization process, also affected cooperators' incomes. Members of the pilot cooperatives in 1975, and all other cooperators in 1976, received substantial severance awards from the government, which were then loaned back to the cooperatives. These loan deposits drew 8 percent interest, or 2 percent higher than the normal rate for savings deposits in the banking system. Morelands wor- kers chose to deposit 60 percent of their severance with their cooperative; all the rest deposited 50 percent.

INCOME DIFFERENTIATION WITHIN THE WORK FORCE

Table 8.5 and 8.6 provide data on average income between 1974 and 1977 within broad job categories for each farm. The most striking thing here was the tendency toward increasing inequality within the work force. At Springfield, supervisors, the highest paid category within the work force (non-staff), earned on average only 1.6 times the average income of general cultivation workers in 1974. By 1977, this disparity had stretched out to 2.4 times. At Morelands we see the same trend, but less marked, from 1.5 times to 1.9 times.

Before 1975, income differentials within the work

TABLE 8.5
Average Gross Income of Springfield Workers,
by Job Category, 1974-1977

Year	Laborers	Cutters	Irrigators	Supervisors
1974	$ 821 ($1,371)	$ 888 ($1,759)	$1,312 ($1,967)	$1,321 ($2,972)
1975	1,690	2,084	2,274	3,070
1976	1,652	1,981	2,558	3,288
1977	1,560	1,979	2,452	3,663

Source: NIS returns for each year. The author placed
the workers into job categories on the basis of his
observations while at the farm. The figures in paren-
theses for 1974 are the adjusted incomes, on the basis
of 1975 rate increases, estimated as above, Table 8.2.

TABLE 8.6
Average Gross Income of Morelands Workers,
by Job Category, 1974-1977

Year	Laborers	Cutters	Irrigators	Supervisors
1974	$1,031 ($1,722)	$1,244 ($2,488)	$1,430 ($2,145)	$1,491 ($3,355)
1975	2,016	2,515	2,464	3,897
1976	2,021	2,470	2,625	3,999
1977	2,122	2,423	2,521	4,015

Source: NIS returns for each year. The author placed
the workers into job categories on the basis of his
observations while at the farm. The figures in paren-
theses for 1974 are the adjusted incomes, on the basis
of 1975 rate increases, estimated as above, Table 8.2.

force were not very marked. Though on average the supervisors or headmen were the highest paid workers, many
daily paid supervisors still earned less than other workers, for example, some irrigators. The lowest paid workers still earned on average about two-thirds (Springfield, 62 percent; Morelands, 69 percent) what supervisors earned. There were much greater disparities between staff and workers, especially senior staff, than
within the work force. This was manifest not only in
terms of remuneration but also housing, educational opportunities and recreational facilities.

Within only a few years, however, the situation
changed dramatically, with supervisory personnel splitting off from the general work force. A number of factors help explain this.

First, the three-year contract signed in late 1974
increased wage rates by greater percentages for skilled
and supervisory personnel than for other workers (Table
8.7).

Second, in 1975 after the pilot got going, the
Morelands committee of management decided unilaterally
to raise the rate of pay for supervisors, and no other
workers. Then, in 1976, shortly after all the other
farms at Monymusk became cooperatives, the estate board
also voted to increase supervisors' rates on all those
farms. Later, in 1978, there was a "regularization" of
supervisory rates, in effect, a further slight increase.

Third, there was a tendency to increase the number
of weekly paid rather than daily paid supervisors. This
was partly related to the fact that under the cooperatives all the farm chairpersons, whatever their capacity
prior to the establishment of the cooperatives, became
classified as headmen, drawing weekly salaries of between $80 and $120.

Fourth, committees on all the farms tended to be
disproportionately composed of supervisors, and sometimes dominated by them. Supervisors used their position
and influence to ensure the maintenance and growth of
their incomes.

As a result of these forces, average annual earnings of supervisors at both Morelands and Springfield
nearly tripled between 1974 and 1977, increasing by 180
percent at Springfield and 170 percent at Morelands.
Consequently, as outlined above, income differentials
between work groups in the cooperatives widened. At
Springfield, the lowest only averaged 43 percent of the
supervisors' incomes, and at Morelands 53 percent. Another aspect of this was that in 1977, a year of generally lower incomes, average incomes of the supervisory
group actually continued to increase.

The new stratification within the work force was
epitomized more than anything by the chairpersons. In
all cases they became formally part of the supervisory
group, though few held supervisory positions prior to

TABLE 8.7
Sampling of Rate Changes, 1975

Category	Rate under Old Contract	New Rate, as of Jan. 1, 1975	% Increase
cutting cane	$1/ton	$2/ton	100
all other task rates	vary	vary	50
laborer – males	$2.59/day	$5.30/day	105
scrapping	$2.61/day	$6.13/day	135
headman (daily paid)	$2.74/day	$6.29/day	130
herbicide supervisor	$3.00/day	$6.60/day	120
cutting headman	$3.08/day	$6.69/day	117
loading supervisor	$3.69/day	$7.43/day	101
waybill headman	$2.74/day	$6.29/day	130

Source: Official Monymusk rate schedules, dated January 1, 1974 and January 1, 1975, Monymusk files.

cooperativization. In reality, they formed a new "job" category, that of the chairperson. This was in effect sanctioned in January 1976 when the Monymusk estate board (composed mostly of the chairpersons) passed a resolution stating that chairpersons should be reimbursed for the work they did as chairpersons. This was wholly inconsistent with the cooperative rules. A corollary to this was that in 1978 the Springfield Cooperative secretary was being paid for his work in taking the minutes at committee meetings. Again this was against all cooperative rules.

At any rate, by 1977 the chairpersons were averaging $5,778 in gross income, or over three times the average general cultivation worker's income. In this, and other ways, chairpersons were objectively converging with staff, though not in all respects. The process of convergence gave every indication of continuing.

In general, then, the mass of sugar workers experienced a decline in real income during the initial period of project implementation. This was not a reflection on the cooperatives--structural change at the grass roots did not cause the decline. On the other

hand, if the cooperatives had fulfilled their potential
--toward greater equality, more sideline and productive
out-of-crop activities--the picture could have been different. How much different, given the drought and other
political and social constraints to the cooperativization program, is debatable.

More concretely though, cooperativization did have
two major positive contributions in this regard. First,
as already pointed out, the new structure of social relations protected workers' incomes when conditions deteriorated in 1977. Second, the severance payments provided a major boost to gross incomes, not only in the
year of payment but in subsequent years because of the
accumulation of interest on the loan deposits.

However, while sugar workers' incomes declined in
real terms, incomes of a subset of these workers did
not. In this and other respects, chairpersons, secretaries, other committee members, and supervisors have to
be differentiated from the mass of grass-roots workers.
These positions came to be interlocked to a great extent. Supervisors were disproportionately represented
on the committees, especially in the official positions
of chairperson and secretary. And to justify their
weekly "pay," all chairpersons became headmen if they
were not already such. Secretaries too tended to be or
to become supervisors. This relatively small group at
each farm, and on the estate board, used their positions
to influence the distribution of benefits available
through the cooperatives. In particular, the pattern of
income distribution within the cooperatives became
skewed in a way it never had before, and this was reflected in the reactions of the rank and file to the
cooperatives.

NOTES

1. SWCC, "Economic and Social Survey."
2. SWCC, "Population Statistics for Monymusk Workers Compounds" (mimeo, May 1973).
3. SWCC, "Economic and Social Survey."
4. For the 1965 crop, thirteen of sixteen estates reported
shortages of cutters, ranging from 7.5 to 39 percent of the total
cutting force required (and excluding two estates in exceptional
circumstances and reporting even higher shortages). Half of the
estates were deficient in loading personnel, too, ranging between
14 and 33 percent of their total requirements in this category
(Mordecai Report).
5. According to one government estimate in the 1970s, productivity in the agricultural sector was one-quarter that prevailing
in other sectors (Government of Jamaica, Green Paper on Agricultural Development [Kingston, 1973], p. 15).
6. Ministry of Agriculture, "Development of Frome/Monymusk/

Bernard Lodge Lands," p. 3.

7. The All Island Jamaica Cane Farmers Association negotiated separately for its members, which included all cane farmers apart from the estates. For many years sugar workers on cane farms received lower wages for most tasks; their annual earnings in the 1970s were still less than those of estate workers, and they were far less protected by the unions. In 1976, the cooperatives formally became members of the AIJCFA, but workers still insisted on being considered part of the estate sector in labor-management matters.

8. Between 1975 and 1977, there were no significant exogenous influences on gross incomes, since task rates remained stable in most instances.

9. But in 1977 this was not the case, with the Springfield gang cutting virtually all the cane. Still, the interfarm disparities remained.

10. Other possible explanations, which could not be confirmed, were corruption at Morelands and/or a tendency for Morelands' supervisors to offer higher rates for certain tasks.

11. Based on the NIS returns for workers employed at Old Yarmouth Farms Ltd., Race Course, Vere.

12. Jamaica, Department of Statistics, Statistical Yearbook of Jamaica, 1977 (Kingston: Government Printer, 1978).

9
Economic Outcomes
at the Grass Roots:
The Farms

Having assessed the socioeconomic impact of the cooperatives on the work force, we now turn to a discussion of agricultural performance. An important goal in reforming the sugar industry was to reverse its decade-long decline--to increase production, productivity and financial viability. It was hoped that the cooperatives would be able to: a) increase labor productivity through a better use of resources and the provision of enhanced material and moral incentives for the work force; b) increase production, not only through productivity gains, but also as a result of a new partnership between government technocrats and the cooperatives; c) improve the cost and profit picture through greater managerial efficiency, volunteer labor inputs, reduced class conflict and increased productivity; and d) increase the stability of the industry, as workers would have a greater incentive to stay with, or even to enter, the sugar industry.

The cooperatives faced the monumental task, however, of needing to establish viable economic units out of submarginal operations, while at the same time effecting an historic social transformation. These twin tasks greatly increased the complexity and difficulty of the implementation process.

BACKGROUND

When the sugar workers took over cane farming operations at Frome, Monymusk and Bernard Lodge, these estates had been in decline for ten years, as had the industry as a whole. Production at Monymusk in 1973 was the lowest in over twenty years (Figures 9.1 and 9.2). For each of the years between 1969 and 1973, the cane: sugar recovery ratio was higher than it had been in any previous year since 1938.[1] Not surprisingly, between 1967 and 1972 (excluding 1971, for which figures were unavailable), cane farming operations at Monymusk lost

154

FIGURE 9.1
Monymusk Estate, Cane Production, 1940-1975

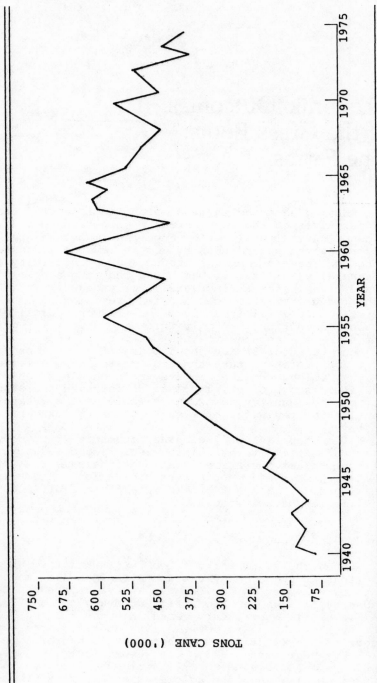

Source: Monymusk Estate, cultivation records.

155

FIGURE 9.2
Monymusk Estate, Cane Yields, 1940-1975

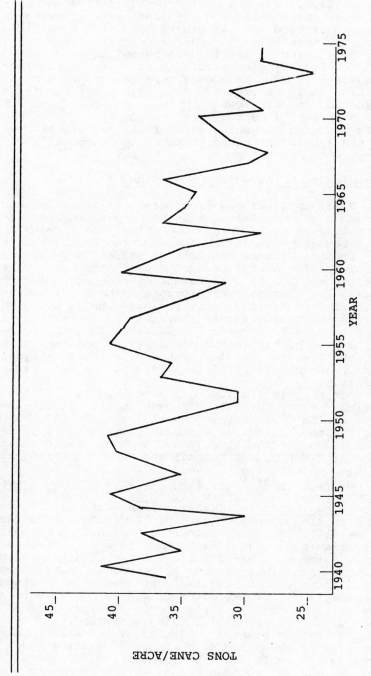

Source: Monymusk Estate, cultivation records.

$5.1 million, an average of over $1 million per year.[2]

Both Springfield and Morelands were affected by, and participated in, the general decline. Cane yields at Morelands were below 29 tons/acre in the two years immediately prior to its transformation to a worker cooperative. Sugar yields were similarly low. At Springfield an average of 28.1 tons cane/acre was reaped annually in the five years before 1976.[3] In both cases the figures reflected historic lows.

A number of factors were responsible for the poor performance at Monymusk. Each of the factors also affected the subsequent performance of the cooperatives.

Extension of Cultivation to Marginal Areas

Jamaican sugar manufacturers traditionally tended to emphasize the maximization of cane throughput, even where this resulted in pushing their cane farming operations beyond the point of optimum production. This was the practice because the bulk of value added occurred in the processing operations and because economies were derived from capacity utilization of the processing facilities. The manufacturers focused on maximizing cane throughput rather than farm revenues. Hence there was a tendency on the integrated estates (factory-farms) to plant cane on lands normally marginal for that crop. At Monymusk in particular production was continued on lands subject to saline conditions and/or water shortages. These practices resulted in losses on the cane farming operation.

For example, following the construction of the new central factory in 1949, Monymusk doubled its acreage in cane, adding 9,000 acres between 1949 and 1960. The land used for this expansion was mainly in bush, or ruinate. In addition, in the late 1950s, a considerable amount of land was taken out of bananas and tree crop production and planted with sugar cane.

But this additional land put into cane to a large extent proved to be incapable in an economic sense of supporting that crop. This is shown quite clearly in a field-by-field study of cane yields at Morelands farm (Table 9.1). The sharp drop in yields during ratooning is particularly significant. Cane is a crop that is generally ratooned; that is, the cut cane stalk is allowed to grow again. This is done to overcome the high costs of replanting. Ratooning can continue, in some cases, for over twenty crops, although replanting is generally advised by the fifth or sixth crop. Ultimately this depends on the actual yields being generated.

The data presented in Table 9.1 illustrate the non-viability of these fields for cane production. Even on first ratoon, only eight of the thirty fields could yield on average the minimum of thirty tons/acre

TABLE 9.1
Cane Yields of the John Cuffie, Two Sisters, Good Hope and
Cotton Walk Sections of Morelands Farm[a]
1961-1974

Cane Class	Number of Field-Crops[b]	Average Tons Cane per Acre Reaped	Average Tons Cane per Acre Reaped by Large Private Cane Farm, 1970-1974
Plant cane	85	36.6	42.8
First ratoon	86	27.2	40.3
Second ratoon	79	23.1	39.4
Third ratoon	54	22.4	31.4
Fourth ratoon and over	42	25.3	34.1

Source: Monymusk Estate cane cultivation records; Jamaica, Sugar Industry
Research Institute; Old Yarmouth Estates, Ltd., farm records.

[a]Each section was composed of a number of discrete fields, 30 fields
altogether, totaling 469 acres, or approximately one-quarter of the entire
cane cultivation at Morelands.

[b]Number of crops in which a field was planted in the particular cane
class during the period. With 30 fields and 14 years the maximum number
of field-crops was 420. Some fields were not always reaped.

generally considered as the breakeven point. By second ratoon, only one field of the thirty averaged over thirty tons/acre. The contrast with Old Yarmouth Estates, an efficient private cane farm in the area, is stark. The thirty fields considered here, brought into production after 1949 and representing one-quarter of Morelands' acreage in cane during this period, were too unproductive. An inordinate amount of uneconomic replanting was needed to maintain yield levels. And the yields of even the newly planted cane remained disturbingly low.[4]

As late as 1978, most of these four sections of Morelands farm were still in production. By then, however, they were part of Morelands cooperative, which no longer shared in any profits earned from the processing operation.

Morelands was not the only cooperative saddled with nonviable cane fields. In 1974 the Frome Monymusk Land Company estimated that 2,000 acres of its land ought to be phased out of cane in the short run.[5] Two years later WISCo's managing director estimated that up to 4,000 acres, mainly at Monymusk (but also at Frome), were not yielding and could not yield the minimum necessary for reliable profits.[6] Most of this land was taken over and utilized by the cooperatives.

The cooperatives in effect continued the practice of maximizing throughput rather than farm revenues. This practice continued until the drought (see below) forced the cooperatives to take large portions of their land out of cane. However, those lands taken out of cane remained idle, and the Monymusk cooperatives found themselves in the embarrassing and unproductive position of being among the largest owners of idle land in Jamaica.

Excess Labor

The second factor which historically contributed to poor performance results at Monymusk was the pattern of low labor productivity and high unit costs which developed. The problem of excess labor in the cane fields was initially a management ploy to keep down the price of labor. With unionization, however, management's problems began to mount. The practice of registering workers and assigning them to specific farms, which began after 1960, reduced flexibility and froze surplus labor problems.

One management response was to mechanize certain field operations, in particular in-field loading and haulage. This occurred during the late 1950s and early 1960s and resulted in considerable redundancy.

Still, the excess labor problem remained, and Monymusk was known throughout the industry for its excessive number of workers. As production declined in the 1960s

and early 1970s, labor productivity declined as well.
Between 1964 and 1975, while the field labor force at
Monymusk (harvest, cultivation and tractor and transport
workers) contracted by 17 percent (500 workers), labor
productivity dropped by 18 percent.[7] Then in 1975 the
situation worsened as certain wage rates, including the
basic rate for cutting cane, doubled and others increased by 50 percent. Workers were also guaranteed at
least three days work per week in the out-of-crop
period. The problem was not only at the field level, but
also in management. The importance attached to bureaucratization and labor control resulted in excessively
high administrative overheads.[8]

Further rationalization of the labor force was constrained by the high cost of paying severance to workers, ooposition to layoffs from the workers, unions and
government, and the rising unemployment in the cane
region.[9]

This was the situation confronting the cooperatives
as they took over Monymusk Estate, with FMLCo arguing
that as many as 50 percent of the field workers could
feasibly be displaced.[10]

Poor Quality Irrigation Water

Irrigation, using both rivers and deep wells,
figured prominently in cane production at Monymusk. During the 1960s, Vere in fact had the greatest concentration of wells in Jamaica.[11] This source of irrigation,
however, was plagued by a major problem. As a technical
study group stated in 1961:

> The volume of water that passes daily underneath
> the plains is estimated to be 100,000 cubic yards
> per hour. Of this quantity approximately 50,000
> cubic yards are now being drawn off by wells and
> any further drilling should be advisedly done with
> great caution as there is risk of lowering the
> water table which would allow (by sea pressure) the
> water in lower Vere to become saline and bring
> disaster to the sugar industry in that area. There
> were signs of such evidence in 1957, when due to
> insufficient rainfall the water shed failed to ade-
> quately recharge the underground source, the saline
> contents rose in some of the wells.[12]

Despite this and other reports of increasing salinity
during the 1960s, drilling of new wells continued. In
1975 it was reported that 10 percent of the cane land in
Vere was already saline and that over 50 percent of all
the land in cane was subject to saline intrusions during
drought periods, with a substantial negative effect on
yields.[13] Such a serious drought did occur in 1976

(Table 9.2).

The drought not only increased the saline content of the water used for irrigation but, by lowering the water table, also increased the amount of power needed for pumping. This, coupled with the rapid escalation of energy costs, resulted in large increases in irrigation costs for the cooperatives.[14] It also pointed up the fact that most of the fields needed significant reblocking to increase the efficiency of water utilization, something that WISCo had delayed doing for years. The 1977 and 1978 crops were especially hard hit by this cost and water quality problem.

Institutionalization of Inefficient Operating Practices

Over the years, especially during the 1960s, a number of inefficient and costly agricultural practices developed at Monymusk. For example, there was an excessive amount of harvesting done on weekends, at premium-time rates. Originally initiated to regularize and maximize the throughput of cane, this practice of weekend harvesting was eagerly extended by the workers who engaged in numerous ploys to ensure that cane would have to be cut on weekends. These included absenteeism and "go-slows" on Thursdays and Fridays, and even, on occasion, the illicit burning of a field prior to the

TABLE 9.2
Average Annual Rainfall,
Springfield and Morelands Farms,
1971-1977

| Year | Average Annual Rainfall (inches) [a] | |
	Morelands	Springfield
1971	29.89	30.78
1972	25.71	28.53
1973	37.49	45.43
1974	28.71	32.56
1975	23.87	24.90
1976	8.11	7.75
1977	27.24	33.00

Source: Monymusk Estate reports prepared for the Sugar Industry Research Institute.

[a]Between 1942 and 1970 average annual rainfall at Monymusk Estate was 40.49 inches.

weekend.

For a time, too, the loading and transport of cane involved a night, as well as a day, shift. This was instituted by WISCo to provide a steady flow of cane to the factory. Again, the practice of night loading proved financially beneficial to workers in the tractor and transport department, although productivity was low and costs to the estate were high.

A final example of inefficient operating practices instituted under WISCo at Monymusk was the system for reaping fields. Overseers and cutters would first survey the field to be cut and estimate its yield in tons. Often an interlude of bargaining ensued with each side arguing the validity of its estimate. If no agreement could be reached, a "wildcat" strike by the cutters or a "lock-out" by management was not unknown.[15] Once an agreement had been reached, the cutters would then be paid by the chain for the area cut.[16] The system thus got its colloquial name, "chainrage," as opposed to its alternate, "tonnrage," with the cutters paid strictly by the tons cut. If the total tonnage cut was in fact less than the estimate, the reapers would still be paid as agreed. WISCo was the only cane farming operation to use this practice.[17] It was finally eliminated at Monymusk after the cooperatives took over, as was the practice of weekend reaping. Night loading had ceased slightly earlier.

Inefficiency and Losses Incurred by the Tractor and Transport Department

Another factor which impeded the efficient operation of Monymusk during the late 1960s and early 1970s was the poor performance of its tractor and transport department. It was responsible for all cane loading, haulage and mechanical cultivation operations, as well as for the maintenance of all the estate's vehicles.

One of the more notable features of tractor and transport's operations during this period was the 33 percent increase in its in-crop work force, despite little increase in mechanization and a decline in production during these years.[18] In 1978 an evaluation of the operations of this department concluded that most of this additional labor force was essentially redundant, unnecessary to efficient operations.[19]

After the estate was broken into eight farm-cooperatives, the tractor and transport unit was retained as a centrally managed service department, reorganized as a cooperative in its own right. Unfortunately it retained the inefficiencies of the pre-cooperative period.

MONYMUSK AND THE VIABILITY QUESTION

The deep-seated agroeconomic problems at Monymusk meant that the new cooperative farms had very poor prospects for viability in the short run. However, this was not completely recognized by the workers or others involved in the cooperativization process until after they actually began operations. As late as mid-1975, for example, there were still illusions about the future viability of the cooperatives. For example, it was then being stated that there were "good indications" that the pilots could achieve self-reliance by 1978.[20] SWCC News generally carried a similarly optimistic line. To an extent, SWCC was indeed unaware of the true picture. This was mainly because FMLCo had been systematically denying SWCC any financial information. It was not until late 1975, as the Prime Minister's Committee on Co-operative Development continued meeting on the problems of implementing its decisions, that a closer look was taken at the viability of the cooperatives. Only then did aspects of the true picture begin to be revealed.[21]

After the cooperatives formally took over WISCo's cane farming operations from FMLCo in 1976, the gloomy economic picture was clarified further. The USWCC financial controller, with long experience in the sugar industry, wrote in mid-1976:

> It would appear that, given the present financial structure, Monymusk can never become a viable enterprise, for, by the time the requirements for profits have been met, the borrowings with the resultant finance charges, have reached such proportions that they can never be absorbed by the cash generated from operating profits and depreciation.[22]

Table 9.3 depicts his forecast of the operating picture at Monymusk. Even in the best possible case, Monymusk would still be operating at a loss by 1980 according to this prediction. In actuality a much worse situation developed.

The situation at Monymusk was fundamentally much more unstable than that at either Frome or Bernard Lodge. In fact, based on his analysis, the financial controller recommended that it be treated as a "special case." Of course, the financial and viability projections of all the cooperative farms at the three estates were affected not only by the economically marginal operations that they took over, but also by the splitting of what had traditionally been integrated factory-farm operations. No longer did the farming division have access to the value added provided by processing, international marketing and the other linked operations of the previous owners, multinationals Tate and Lyle

TABLE 9.3
Operating Forecast, Monymusk, 1976

| | Financial Year | | | | |
	1976	1977	1978	1979	1980
Production - tons cane ('000)	--	480	496	527	534
Operating loss/ (profit)($'000)	2,672	3,140	1,216	(14)	(724)
Interest payments ($'000)	176	531	841	1,032	1,116
Net loss/(profit) ($'000)	2,848	3,671	2,057	1,018	392

Source: Blakeley; Sugar Industry Authority, p. 3B.17.

and United Fruit Company. And, of course, the situation at Monymusk was greatly worsened by the drought which was experienced almost immediately, especially affecting the 1977 and 1978 crops.

PERFORMANCE

Morelands

The Morelands cooperative took over farm operations in time to begin reaping the 1975 crop. The planting and cultivation of this crop, however, occurred prior to the formal initiation of the cooperative. Basic production statistics, with 1974 comparisons, follow.[23]

	1974	1975	% Improvement
Production (tons cane)	51,920	58,968	13.6
Tons cane/acre	28.52	31.67	11.0
Tons sugar (from cane)	5,295	6,094	15.1
Tons sugar/acre	2.91	3.27	12.4
Tons cane/ton sugar	9.81	9.68	1.3

In general the cooperative registered increases of more than 10 percent. While cane yields were still low by historical standards, the quality was good.[24] Hence it took less cane to produce one ton of sugar in 1975 than any year since 1965.

Morelands' 1975 performance compared very favorably with that of the rest of Monymusk Estate (Table 9.4),

which retained its traditional production structure
(despite the replacement of WISCo by FMLCo in 1974).

The cooperative's financial results for 1975 reflected the positive agronomic performance. A $70,000
surplus was earned, amounting to approximately $400 per
member. After the statutory allocation to the reserve
fund, the surplus was in fact distributed to all members as a bonus.

Morelands' exceptional performance during its
first year as a cooperative requires further discussion.
First, the educational and technical assistance resources available to Morelands in 1975 were significant.
A cooperative education officer, attached to FMLCo,
worked intensively with the Morelands membership and
leadership during this time. In addition, FMLCo provided considerable management assistance. Clearly FMLCo
had a substantial interest in ensuring the success of
Morelands and the other pilot cooperatives--not only to
reinforce its own bureaucratic position, but also to
undermine SWCC. It will be recalled that while SWCC
busied itself preparing the other farms and sugar workers for eventual cooperativization, FMLCo tried to
establish the pilots as a separate association under its
control. After 1976, with FMLCo no longer in the picture, the government failed to provide adequate technical assistance to the cooperatives then being established. Similarly, as trouble developed in the educational program, it was never fully implemented for the
other cooperatives (until 1980).

Another aspect of the Morelands situation was the
relatively high level of consciousness of the workers.
Morelands was situated in Lionel Town, the center of
SWCC's organizing efforts. Morelands' workers were among
the early leaders in the cooperative movement; SWCC's
first chairperson was a foreman from Morelands. He
later became the first chairperson of the Morelands

TABLE 9.4
Percent Change in Key Production Statistics,
Morelands Farm and Monymusk Estate,
1974-1975

	Morelands Farm	Monymusk Estate
Production	13.6% increase	decrease
Tons cane/acre	11.0% increase	1.0% increase
Tons sugar/acre	12.4% increase	3.8% increase

Source: Monymusk Estate agricultural records.

cooperative.

But possibly most significant, in terms of Morelands' financial performance in 1975, was that the cost
of certain services provided to Morelands by the estate
were absorbed by FMLCo. Hence operating costs were arti-
ficially low.[25] In addition, Morelands apparently received an unlimited quota at the factory.[26] Normally,
the factory gives each large cane supplier a daily
quota, thus regulating the flow of cane from the farms
to the factory. Without quotas, Morelands was able to be
more flexible with its reaping schedule and, in particular, was able to reap a greater percentage of the cane
when its sugar content was highest.

Moreland's production performance subsequent to
1975 was extremely poor (Table 9.5). In 1976 production
dropped back down to 1974 levels, despite an increase
in production for the estate as a whole. Significant
declines in all production indices were registered,
with total production and yields dropping to the lowest
levels on record. Then, in 1977, the full brunt of the
previous year's drought was felt. The depths to which
production sank in 1977 were unimaginable before the
event. Yields dropped below those of the most inefficient farmer. Almost 300 acres had to be abandoned, due
to the severity of the drought and its effects on water
quality. While there was some recovery the following two
years, 1979 production levels were still quite low.

The financial picture was affected further by the
following factors. First, the discovery of cane smut
disease in Jamaica forced Morelands to undertake a
heavy replanting program. During 1978-1979, one thousand
acres were replanted with smut-resistant strains. This
was over half of Morelands' cultivated acreage and represented an enormous financial burden. Second, because
of inflation and because farm workers were also cooper-

TABLE 9.5
Cane Production, Morelands,
1976-1979 and 1970-1974

	1976-1979 Average	1970-1974 Average
Production (tons cane)	43,584	59,772
Tons cane/acre	27.47	31.62
Tons sugar/acre	2.57	2.97

Source: Compiled from Monymusk Estate records.

ative members, cost reduction strategies, as a response
to the lowered production levels, were severely constrained. In particular, there was pressure to maintain
members' income levels. Finally, a vicious circle phenomenon developed. The financial scissors caused primarily by production declines on the one hand and cost
increases, on the other, forced the cooperatives to cut
back on certain inputs and activities. For example, the
cultivation of the crop lagged and fertilizer usage
dropped. This of course harmed production more.

Not surprisingly, with all this happening and with
the decline in production as well, serious losses were
incurred during these years. These totaled $1.8 million
for the four years (1976-1979), or about $10,000 per
member.

Springfield

Springfield cooperative, like Morelands, performed
well in its first year of operations, 1976, as illus-
trated below:

	1975	1976	% Improvement
Production (tons cane)	59,462	63,815	7.3
Tons cane/acre	29.50	30.56	3.6
Tons sugar	6,224	6,537	5.0
Tons sugar/acre	3.09	3.13	1.3
Tons cane/tons sugar	9.55	9.76	decline

Springfield, one of the better managed farms, with fewer
water problems, did better in 1976 than most of the
other Monymusk cooperatives. Nonetheless, in 1976, as in
subsequent years, all the Monymusk farms suffered financial losses. Springfield's net loss that year was
$224,000.

Springfield's 1977 crop, like that of every
other cane farm in the region, was decimated by the
drought (Table 9.6). While yields improved in 1978,
fewer acres were reaped than even the previous year when
in fact hundreds of acres had to be abandoned as not
worth reaping. The 515 acres of standover cane in 1978,
which had to be left over for reaping during the 1979
crop at lower yields, represented a loss of more than
13,000 tons of cane.[27]

There were two major reasons for this excessive
standover cane in 1978. First, a dispute between the
farm and the cane cutters resulted in cane being left
uncut. The cooperative members opposed the practice of
bringing in outside cutting gangs to help reap the crop,
feeling that they should get the work. The manager
argued that there was too much standing cane for the
members to reap efficiently.

Second, the inefficiency of the tractor and trans-

TABLE 9.6
Springfield Cooperative Production Data,
1976-1979

	1976	1977	1978	1979
Production	63,815	42,003	50,288	56,259
Acres reaped	2,088	1,694	1.509	1.822
Tons cane/acre	30.56	24.80	33.33	30.87
Tons sugar	2,537	3,557	4,489	5,471
Tons sugar/acre	3.13	2.10	2.97	3.00
Tons cane/ton sugar	9.76	11.80	11.20	10.28

Source: Monymusk Estate records.

port service cooperative meant that there were not
enough vehicles and they were not organized efficiently
enough to take up the whole crop during the optimal processing time. This affected Springfield more than most
of the cooperatives, for example, Morelands, since it
was located farther from the factory.

Although Springfield's production performance in
1979 was better, it was still hurt by having 200 acres
of standover cane. There were a number of other problems as well. The severe internal situation of the tractor and transport service cooperative, involving management problems, excessive mechanical breakdowns due
to poor maintenance, and lack of spare parts, hampered
Springfield's performance. In addition, the start of
the crop at Springfield was delayed by the dispute over
severance payments. Finally, Springfield, like the
other cooperatives, was the victim of poor cash flow.
This meant that the crop could not be adequately cared
for; for example, either fertilizer was not available
or only available at the wrong times.

Regardless of its relatively good production performance (compared to other cooperatives), Springfield's
financial picture was bleak. Between 1976-1978 the cooperative lost $1.7 million or the equivalent of almost
$10,000 for each of its members.

A Comparison

The cooperatives' performance during their first
years of operation was not good. However, the numerous
environmental factors which affected operations, in particular the drought, make it very difficult to assess

the independent influence of the cooperative restructuring itself. Would the farms have done better or worse between 1975 and 1979 if cooperatives were not established? Or would their performance have been relatively unchanged? While hardly definitive, we have attempted a brief comparison of the performance of the cooperatives with that of a large private cane farm.

Old Yarmouth Farms Ltd. was a private cane farm of 1,100 acres in the same Vere region as the Monymusk cooperatives. In addition to cane, it maintained about eighty head of beef cattle as well as a few race horses. It was considered to be well-managed; its managing director was also chairman of the Vere Cane Farmers Association.

While also affected by the drought in 1976-1977, Old Yarmouth did not have the same serious saline water problems as did most of the cooperatives. This was mainly because it was situated farther inland.[28] In certain other respects it was also better off than the cooperatives. First, it regularly delivered cane to both sugar factories in the area, unlike the cooperatives which were tied to the Monymusk factory alone. This increased Old Yarmouth's flexibility. If one factory was backed up, Old Yarmouth could deliver its cane to the other factory, rather than having to wait and risk the possibility of the cane growing stale.[29]

Second, all its tractor and haulage work was performed using equipment owned and operated by Old Yarmouth itself. It did not have to rely on outside contractors or a separate tractor and transport department as did the cooperatives. Hence, this facet of its operations was always handled more efficiently than on the cooperatives. In particular, Old Yarmouth never had to leave standover cane to be cut during the subsequent crop.

Third, Old Yarmouth's size was within what is considered to be the optimal range for cane farming operations in Jamaica (500-1,000 acres). Farms of a larger size, like the cooperatives, were considered to suffer from diseconomies of scale, such as management.[30]

Finally, its labor costs were much lower than those of the cooperatives. In 1977, for example, Old Yarmouth paid $5.44 in labor costs for each ton of cane, compared to $8.81 at Springfield and $12.60 at Morelands. This reflected the lower wage rates paid at Old Yarmouth and its more efficient use of labor.[31]

Table 9.7 presents a summary of Old Yarmouth's production performance between 1974 and 1979. Two things stand out from these figures. First, average yields at Old Yarmouth were far higher than those at Monymusk. Prior to the drought they were normally between 35 and 39 tons/acre compared to around 30 tons/acre for Morelands and Springfield. Second, all the acreage ready for reaping _was_ reaped, compared to the case at More-

TABLE 9.7
Old Yarmouth Farms Ltd., Production Data,
1974-1979

	1974	1975	1976	1977	1978	1979
Production (tons cane)	32,646	34,046	32,764	29,695	30,548	27,027
Acres reaped	841	875	884	894	894	893
Tons cane/ acre	39.18	39.18	37.14	33.23	34.18	30.27

Source: Compiled from Old Yarmouth Farms Ltd.,
records.

lands and Springfield where in 1979, for example, 270
acres of cane were left standing.

We have attempted two sorts of comparisons. Table
9.8 provides comparative data showing how the three
farms fared during the actual drought year, in comparison to their previous performance. While there is no
difference in terms of cane quality, Old Yarmouth
clearly "weathered" the drought better than the cooperatives. Among other factors, both Morelands and Springfield had to abandon part of their crops, while Old Yarmouth did not; Morelands had a more difficult salinity
problem; and Old Yarmouth clearly had better quality
land, on average, to begin with.

Table 9.9 takes a slightly longer view, comparing
the precooperative, predrought performance with post-
drought production for all three farms. Here it appears
that Morelands and Springfield were rebounding better
from the drought experience. While actual production was
still down for all three farms, yields were up at the
cooperatives but were continuing to decline at Old Yarmouth.

This comparison is limited. Many factors affect
production and yields. However, it does suggest that the
basic production experience of the cooperatives during
their difficult early years of existence was roughly
comparable to efficient private cane farms in the same
region.

SUMMARY

The agricultural performance of Morelands and
Springfield cooperatives during their first few years of
operation was poor. During this period they were buf-

TABLE 9.8
Relative Effect of the Drought on Production Levels and Yields, Morelands, Springfield and Old Yarmouth Farms

	TONS CANE			TONS CANE/ACRE			TONS CANE/TON SUGAR		
	1975-76 Average	1977	Decline	1975-76 Average	1977	Decline	1975-76 Average	1977	Decline
Morelands	55,955	33,029	41.0%	29.78	20.34	31.7%	10.21	11.82	15.8%
Springfield	61,631	42,003	31.9%	30.03	24.78	17.5%	10.18	11.76	15.5%
Old Yarmouth	33,405	29,695	11.1%	38.16	33.23	12.9%	10.18	11.77	15.6%

Source: Morelands, Springfield, Old Yarmouth farm records.

TABLE 9.9
Production and Yields, Morelands, Springfield and Old Yarmouth Farms, 1974-1975 and 1978-1979

	TONS CANE			TONS CANE/ACRE		
	1974-1975 Average	1978-1979 Average	% Change	1974-1975 Average	1978-1979 Average	% Change
Morelands	55,444	44,183	20.3	30.10	30.76	2.2
Springfield	59,462[a]	53,274	10.4	29.22	32.09	9.8
Old Yarmouth	33,346	28,788	13.7	39.18	32.23	17.7

Source: Morelands, Springfield, Old Yarmouth Farm records

[a]1975 only; 1974 figures on production are not equivalent, since additional acreage was planted that year. This acreage was not handed over to the cooperative in 1976.

feted by many factors. These included: a) low rainfall
levels generally, and a serious drought in 1976; b)
scarcity of spare parts and other inputs, such as fertilizer, due to Jamaica's acute foreign exchange crisis;
c) the need to cut back on certain agricultural operations, such as manual weeding, due to the cooperatives'
financial problems; d) the degradation of the water supply due to saline conditions; and e) inefficiencies in
haulage operations.

In addition, the agrarian reform process itself engendered certain difficulties and conflicts. A number of
staff members were fired or left, while others exhibited
extremely negative attitudes. Some members were disen-
chanted with the cooperatives, while others tried to
gain advantages for themselves. The cooperative management structure was clearly new and in a period of transition and development. Finally, the political storm
centered around the cooperatives also affected
performance at the grass roots.

The poor performance of the cooperatives is not
surprising; it resulted from the effects of all of these
factors and the fundamentally unstable and unprofitable
situation which the cooperatives inherited. What is surprising, however, is that none of these factors were
seriously considered in the rush to condemn the cooperatives. What is also surprising is that there was precious little in the way of material support, assistance
or sensitivity from many of those involved in policy
implementation. The reasons for this become apparent
when we look, as we have, at the political and administrative context in which the cooperativization process
unfolded.

NOTES

1. Monymusk Estate, cultivation records. The sugar recovery
ratio is the amount of cane needed to produce one ton of sugar. It
is a measure of cane quality and processing efficiency. The less
cane needed per ton of sugar, the better.

2. Stone, "An Appraisal of the Co-operative Process in the
Jamaican Sugar Industry," p. 3.

3. Monymusk Estate, cultivation records.

4. In bad years, the overall results would be disastrous. For
example, in 1973, not one of 73 fields, totaling over 1,000 acres
and over half of Morelands' total acreage, could yield over 30 tons
cane/acre. In fact, there were 355 acres which could not produce
even 20 tons cane/acre (Dan Mulvey, "Memorandum," SWCC, mimeo,
June 1974).

5. FMLCo, "Operational Plans," p. 6.

6. Frank Tomlinson, "Overmanning Can Bring Losses to Sugar
Cooperatives," letter to the editor, Jamaica Daily Gleaner, April 1,
1976. Minimum yields were considered to be an average of three tons

of sugar per acre over a normal replanting and ratooning cycle, or roughly 30 tons of cane per acre, with a cane:sugar recovery ratio of 10:1.

7. Farm records, Monymusk cultivation office; Gordon.

8. Blakeley; Mordecai Report.

9. FLMCo, "Operation Plans," p. 4.

10. Ibid.

11. Jamaica, Sugar Industry Welfare Labour Board, "Vere Impact Study" (mimeo, November 1961), p. 5.

12. Ibid., p. 4.

13. L. Ramdial, "The Effect of Saline Water on Two Sugarcane Varieties" (Mandeville: Sugar Industry Institute, mimeo, 1975).

14. The financial situation became so serious that the government was forced to establish a special irrigation subsidy program for cane farmers in Vere.

15. For an example of such a strike, and management's use of "scabs," see James Phillips, chapter 6.

16. That is, given the agreed estimate of how much a field would yield in tons, this was averaged out by the number of rows and chains cut.

17. Interview with Noel Lyon, managing director, FMLCo, August 4, 1977.

18. Monymusk Estate records; Gordon, p. 15.

19. Sam Lawrence, "Diagnostic Report--Monymusk Tractor and Transport Cooperative" (Kingston, mimeo, 1978).

20. Fr. Tony Byrne and Fr. Jim Schecher, "Progress Report on Social Action Centre Development Programme" (SAC, June 1975), p. 5.

21. Jamaica, Prime Minister's Committee on Co-operative Development on Frome, Monymusk and Bernard Lodge Estates, "Report of the Trelawny Beach Meeting" (mimeo, 1975).

22. Blakeley, p. 5.

23. 1974 figures were computed from the annual Sugar Industry Research Institute (SIRI) Cane Yield Survey; 1975 figures were taken from official farm records. Note that the smaller amount of cane needed to produce each ton of sugar in 1975 compared to 1974 represented an increase in productivity or cane quality.

24. Between 1965 and 1972, cane yields at Morelands averaged 33.9 tons of cane per acre. Prior to the 1960s, they were even higher.

25. SIA, p. 38.

26. Ric Mentus, "Interview with Ronald Thwaites" [a USWCC attorney], Jamaica Daily News, March 28, 1976.

27. Having standover cane results in lower revenues and higher unit costs, as the cane must be cared for over a longer period of time than normal.

28. In this respect it was more like Springfield than Morelands.

29. Cane which has been burnt to facilitate reaping, as was common in Jamaica, needs to be processed within forty-eight hours. Subsequent to that it grows progressively staler and its sugar content declines.

30. E. A. Simms, Sugarcane Production Cost in Jamaica (Mandeville: Sugar Industry Research Institute, 1977).

31. The sugar worker unions negotiated separate contracts with the cane farmers and with the factory-farms or estates. Traditionally it was assumed that the estates were more profitable and could afford greater labor costs; hence workers on cane farms were paid according to lower pay scales. (Old Yarmouth, Springfield and Morelands wage data based on National Insurance records.)

10
The Political Economy
of Grass-Roots Reform:
Summary and Conclusion

By the 1970s, the dialectic of history had opened Jamaica up to the forces of reform and revolution. Ten years of political independence had neither facilitated national liberation nor initiated a process of development. On the contrary, it resulted in a deepening of the contradictions associated with underdevelopment. By 1972, bourgeois political and economic authority in Jamaica found itself in crisis.

Nowhere was this more true than in agriculture, and in particular within the sugar sector. Foreign interests were still dominant, land was severely maldistributed, and canefield laborers suffered intense socioeconomic deprivation. The sugar industry, moreover, had clearly lost its previous economic dynamism. On all counts it was performing well below the levels of the 1960s. These economic and social factors made change a priority.

In addition, the balance of political forces had begun to tip away from the landed sugar elite. This was perhaps most manifest when Tate and Lyle, which had clearly dominated the sugar industry since the 1940s, disposed of its large cane properties in the late 1960s. Tate and Lyle's sale of Frome and Monymusk Estates to the JLP government signaled a shift in power within the industry, even though the company retained its processing operations. The United Fruit Company followed shortly with the sale of Bernard Lodge Estate. The shift was reinforced in 1972 when the PNP, running a populist campaign, was swept into office. The PNP was more nationalist than the JLP; was closer to elements within the middle class which had their own grievances against the foreign sugar elite; was headed by a longtime union protagonist; expressed a commitment to change favoring the "small man"; and foresaw a potential political windfall from initiatives in the cane belt.

Conditions in Jamaica in the 1970s, thus, were favorable to reform, especially a reform targeted at the sugar estates. In sugar, as elsewhere in the society,

change appeared to be both necessary and possible. It
became the mission of Michael Manley and the People's
National Party to translate this necessity and possibility into reality.

Within a few years, their efforts resulted in the
establishment of twenty-three self-managed sugar cooperatives, three secondary-level estate cooperatives, and
one tertiary-level cooperative. This cooperative structure replaced one in which control rested in just a few
hands, those of the foreign owners and top managers,
with the workers an exploited majority.

Although it was limited to the three sugar estates,
the cooperativization program became the most significant initiative in land reform during the Manley regime
and probably in the entire history of Jamaica. The establishment of the sugar cooperatives: a) extended control of over 40,000 acres of prime cane lands to members
of the working class; b) sought a fundamental transformation of social and production relations in the rural
areas; c) provided the impetus for a militant, organized
political mobilization of workers; d) provided what was
considered by some to be a precedent and a model for the
possible reform of the entire plantation system, including the factories; and e) was an innovative experiment
in socialism and worker participation.

The sugar worker cooperatives were one aspect of
the substantial, if unplanned, transformation of the
entire Jamaican sugar industry which occurred during the
1970s. In 1970, fifteen estates processed all the sugar
cane produced in Jamaica; half of this cane was grown on
their own lands. Ownership of these estates, or factory-
farms, was predominantly in foreign hands. The powerful
Sugar Manufacturers Association was also controlled by
this same foreign group. The remaining 50 percent of the
cane was grown on private cane farms, with approximately
350 farms providing two-thirds of this total.

By 1978 only twelve of the factory-farms were still
in operation. Seven of these were owned by the government's National Sugar Company; the five others were
owned by local enterpreneurs. Those owned by the government made up 75 percent of total industry capacity. In
eight years, the dominant foreign interest in sugar
manufacturing had been eliminated and the Sugar Manufacturers Association was only a token of what it used to
be. The Sugar Industry Authority, a governmental statutory body, now wielded substantial authority and control
over the industry as a whole. Meanwhile, the twenty-
three sugar worker cooperatives were producing roughly
one-third of the cane processed in Jamaica.

This transformation of the sugar industry along
nationalist, statist and democratic lines was more extensive than that affecting any other sector except possibly public utilities. This was not altogether surprising. The plantation system symbolized all that was

objectionable in Jamaica's colonial and neo-colonial
past; hence, it was a prime target of the nationalist,
reform-minded government.

The state's increased involvement in major sectors
of the economy--trade, tourism, bauxite, the public services and the sugar factories--was an important step
consistent with socialist principles. But the cooperativization of the cane lands pointed toward far more
fundamental changes in social relations. The sugar cooperativization program, in particular, came to epitomize
the government's stated socialist ideals. "You must understand," Manley stated to members of the cooperatives
in 1975, "that you are becoming the pioneers of socialism."[1]

These ideals, the methods utilized, and the democratic socialist perspective underlying it all epitomized a democratic reformist approach to overcoming underdevelopment. The ideals were consistent with the aspirations of many Third World nations for social and
economic change. They were consistent as well with the
dominant themes of the 1970s which focused on the rural
poor, participation, distribution, new organizational
patterns, and development as distinguishable from growth.
In many senses, in fact, the Jamaican development effort
during this period epitomized the development thinking
of the 1970s. It was not accidental that Prime Minister
Manley became a world figure during this period. More
than any other leader, except perhaps Julius Nyerere,
Manley came to represent this perspective. Manley not
only expounded this perspective, but also led his government to try to implement it in terms of Jamaica's
domestic development policy and its foreign relations.
His regime became a symbol--a test case of this reformist development policy and of its implications for
North-South relations.

The Jamaican experience with its program of reform
is thus of considerable importance for those concerned
with the development process. The social and economic
disarray within Jamaica, and within the sugar cooperatives by the late 1970s, makes the task of analysis even
more pertinent. What can we learn from this case, the
Jamaican attempt to transform foreign-controlled, hierarchical sugar estates to self-managed worker cooperatives? What happens when a government of reform ini-
tiates a policy aimed at restructuring agrarian social
relations in the context of a wider process of change?

MACROPOLITICS AND REFORM

The People's National Party was formed in 1938 during a period of political and social ferment in Jamaica,
and immediately became the main anti-colonial political
force. Some of its early leaders were influenced by

Fabianism and British socialist politics, and during the
1940s a radical wing with ties to the trade union movement developed within the party. When the left was
purged in the early 1950s, the social democratic tendency was greatly weakened. This led to a twenty-year
period in which the political line of the PNP was generally indistinguishable from its more conservative JLP
rival.

By the 1970s, the PNP was rooted primarily within
the middle strata, with ties as well to liberal capitalist elites and with a base in the trade union movement.
Its lack of support from rural workers, small farmers
and the urban unemployed reflected its contradictory
attitude toward these groups. It was the PNP, for example, that supported the initial moves to mechanize the
sugar industry in the late 1950s and early 1960s, even
though this meant throwing thousands out of work. The
party nonetheless retained a socially liberal outlook,
the legacy of its social democratic roots. Many party
members were committed to the need to assist the poor
and downgraded through paternalist social reforms.

In the 1970s these reformist inclinations were
strengthened and the social democratic traditions revived. This reflected the advent of a new, reform-
minded, party leader, Michael Manley; the growing influence within the party at the same time of younger, more
left-leaning professionals; a growing recognition within
the society that the growth-oriented development policies of the 1950s and 1960s, policies on which both
major parties had initially agreed, had failed; and the
success in 1972 of a populist, reform-oriented, election
campaign strategy.

While these factors strengthened nationalist and
reformist tendencies within the PNP, prior to 1974 the
party which had won the general election, and the government which had taken power could still best be characterized as "liberal bourgeois." A decidedly moderate,
liberal capitalist tendency prevailed, though not without discordant notes. The government's program at this
time was only mildly reformist.

This orientation was reflected in the government's
initial approach to the disposition of the Frome, Monymusk and Bernard Lodge Estates. On the one hand reorganization along cooperative lines was favored from
the beginning. Cooperatives were viewed as a way of
benefiting those who would not otherwise have access to
such agricultural resources; as a means of gaining a
political foothold in the cane belt, which, especially
around the Monymusk area, was typically JLP territory;
and as a convenient mechanism for symbolizing the reformist or populist inclinations of the post-1970 PNP.

Other aspects of the initial cooperative planning and implementation, however, suggested a more conservative political and administrative orientation. These early plans called for an individual leasehold rather than a collective farm structure; envisioned a very slow phasing-in process; proposed a centralized model of management with administrative control in the hands of the government, rather than a self-management approach; benefited only the upper stratum of the work force rather than the mass of workers; hoped to create a new middle stratum of farmers in the cane belt; and put administration of the project in the hands of a statutory body which was run by very conservative personnel.

These contradictions were of course not lost on the sugar workers. Although they initially had been stimulated by the government's pronouncements on the benefits of cooperativization, the workers quickly lost faith, recognizing the limitations of the government's professed commitment both to themselves and to the program. Their skepticism was shared by Social Action Centre organizers and it was reinforced by the thinking prevalent within radical circles at the time. Here the Manley government was seen as a mere tool of a foreign and local capitalist elite. The workers' response, supported by SAC, was to organize and exert continual pressure on the government.

During 1974 and 1975, the fundamental parameters of the cooperativization policy with respect to its design and administration were changed. First, a new managing director and a completely new board of directors, including three workers, were named to FMLCo. Second, the original structure proposed for the cooperatives was fundamentally altered. The need for a collective structure for farm production was accepted, replacing the initial idea of having one cooperative linking small individual leaseholds. The new arrangement also restricted membership to registered field workers. Third, rather than phasing in the establishment of the cooperatives over a number of years, the government agreed in 1975 to alter its timetable. As a result, seventeen cooperative farms began operations in 1976 after only one year of experimentation with the three pilots.[2] Finally, FMLCo's original plan for the state to exert considerable control over the cooperatives was scrapped. A decentralized model, with the workers controlling the cooperatives, was accepted.

These radical changes were mainly the result of two factors. SWCC's organization and influence were crucial in orienting the cooperativization process more toward the needs and interests of the agro-proletariat and away from other strata. SWCC was a direct outgrowth of the workers' struggles for land and decent housing. It was firmly committed to representing the workers' interest. SAC, which contributed leadership and organizational resources to SWCC, extended this perspective, adding a more explicitly socialist orientation.

The sugar worker movement led by SWCC was militant and committed to establishing the cooperatives and to increasing the political representation of the workers. Most important, it sought to attain these democratic-socialist goals through aggressive means. SWCC sought to lead the workers themselves to sweep aside the plantation system, believing that only through worker mobilization could such reforms be initiated and successfully implemented. Only through "struggle" with "anti-worker," "anti-cooperative," and "anti-socialist" forces in the society and in the government could the workers understand and rise above their dependent and subordinate roles. SWCC attempted to educate the workers not only about the cooperatives, but also about their political history and their contemporary class situation.[3]

The second factor which contributed to the radicalization of the cooperativization policy and which reinforced SWCC's activity at the grass roots, was the political dynamic at the national level. In 1974, the PNP began to diverge from the "liberal" or "bourgeois reformist" orientations which had characterized it since the late 1940s. In class terms, the bourgeoisie and its ideology began to lose its dominant position, although the leadership of the party remained essentially middle-class.[4] The PNP attempted to form a more "popular-based" multiclass coalition, still incorporating elements of the bourgeoisie, but in a more subordinate position. It was at this time that the PNP adopted democratic socialism as its formal ideology. The attempt to transform social relations in the cane belt in a radical way via self-managed worker cooperatives fit well with this perspective.

The politics of reform in Jamaica after 1974 was founded on the fundamental principle of democratic socialism, that the state could reconcile basic social conflicts essentially by changing the patterns of economic distribution and political power built into existing production relations. In this way more benefits and greater social and economic participation could be ensured for many of those traditioanlly excluded. Hence, a greater parity between the capitalist elite and society as a whole would be achieved, and the trend toward rural and urban marginalization would be reversed. The basic economic framework in Jamaica was to be the "mixed economy."[5]

In effect, this was a second phase in the post-1972 development of Jamaican political economy (Table 10.1). Identifying these phases, and their underlying political-economic realities, is crucial to understanding the ongoing cooperativization process. National political trends were both reflected in and reinforced by grass-roots developments. The process of change at the local

TABLE 10.1
Jamaican Political Development,
1972-1977

Period	Political Characterization
1972-1974	bourgeois liberalism
1974-1977	democratic reform

level was linked to macropolitical realities in complex
and fundamental ways.[6]

Between 1974 and 1976, the logic of the government's initial acceptance of the benefits of the cooperatives, its political needs, SWCC's activity and organization, and national political trends, all combined to
push the cooperativization reform further in a more
radical direction. At the same time, though, the policy
moved further away from the orientations of many who
held office in the government and the PNP. Many of those
who supported the policy of cooperativization became increasingly uncomfortable with, and opposed to, the innovative implementation process favored by SWCC. They wanted to forestall active involvement of the clientele,
opposed their mobilization, and favored a greater degree
of state control of the process. These views not only
clashed strongly with those of the PNP left and SWCC,
but at the other extreme they tended to blend with those
of groups which opposed both the reforms and the government itself. This internal conflict within the PNP was
readily exploited by these opposition groups. As a result, serious constraints were imposed on the establishment of the cooperatives.

In effect, a middle-class party of reform had over-
stepped itself. The reform process gradually began to
extend itself beyond the regime's political base. Without a willingness to risk mobilizing new support sectors, the regime rapidly used up its "line of credit"
with the groups within the society that made up its
foundation. It thus found itself with neither the political nor the administrative resources necessary to
carry forward the reform process to a successful conclusion.

The conflict and the opposition engendered by the
radicalization of the cooperativization process in the
mid-1970s, even and especially within the government and
governing party, had its roots in three contradictions
built into the political dynamic of the second period.

First, there were institutional contradictions. The
dynamics which accelerated the implementation of the
cooperativization policy imbued it with a decidedly

working-class perspective and helped to move national
political trends and rhetoric to the left, but they were
not firmly rooted in fundamental changes in power relationships either within the PNP or within the government. The political base essential for sustained radical
change was, hence, both weak and inconsistent. This was
especially so in view of the mounting opposition within
the broader society to the reforms.

Only after the 1976 election was there more than a
token leftist presence in the cabinet, though even then
it was limited. Both the PNP parliamentary group and
the cabinet retained a generally moderate stance
throughout the 1972-1980 period. Decision making within
the PNP was strongly influenced by a group of bourgeois
farmers and professionals. This was especially the case
after the leftist general secretary was removed in 1977,
following internal divisions and pressure from the right
wing of the party. The trade union wing of the party
was also under the influence of a politically conservative leadership.

Thus, rather than being solidly based within the
ruling party, the reforms came to depend for support on
a coalition including some younger elements within the
PNP and radical forces outside the party. As the latter
became more involved, traditional elements within the
PNP became even more antagonistic and sought to weaken
that influence. The movement for reform thus had a weak
base, despite the PNP's substantial parliamentary majority and despite the reform's apparent support from
lower-class strata. Most parliamentarians and many in
the party were lukewarm supporters, at best, and potential political support among the masses remained largely
unmobilized.

The orientation of the national communication media
was another important institutional constraint to the
development of reformist policies. The two most widely
circulated daily newspapers, both published by the same
company, took the lead in opposing the government with a
virulent campaign to discredit any of its "socialist"
tendencies. This helped weaken support for grass-roots
reform in general, and the cooperatives in particular.
The government sought to balance this opposition by providing financial assistance to another daily newspaper
and by increasing its presentations and influence over
the national radio and television networks. But it was
never completely successful in counteracting this powerful opponent.

The second major contradiction derived from the
reality of Jamaica's economic situation. Inevitably
there was a conflict between the drive to establish new
patterns of mobilization and distribution, which
siphoned off scarce political and economic resources,
and the country's need for large-scale productive investments and an immediate increase in production and

exports. The poor performance of the cooperative farms
heightened this tension.

For example, while the regime felt from the very
beginning that the cooperatives were an important long-
term investment which could help to ensure the survival
and viability of the sugar industry, it had to contend
with pressures to increase production in the short run.
These pressures included the demands of the factories
for maximum cane throughput, the economy's need for
foreign exchange, the government's expressed commitment
to bring the industry back to an annual production of
450,000 tons of sugar, and its political need to show
rapid improvements in the society. The impact of these
pressures was reflected, for example, in the government's insistence that marginal lands should be kept in
cane rather than used to diversify the production mix.

The acute economic problems Jamaica experienced in
the post-1975 period exacerbated this tension and imposed substantial constraints and pressures on the implementation process. There were fewer resources for implementation, including money for subsidies and for hiring staff to assist the cooperatives. There was increased pressure on the whole sugar industry to produce
more cane as quickly as possible to help decrease the
foreign exchange gap. This became particularly acute
during 1976 when earnings from both bauxite exports and
tourism declined.

In addition, the country's economic difficulties
increased the domestic influence and power of international aid agencies such as the IMF and the World
Bank. Between 1977 and 1980, Jamaica agreed to accept
an economic stabilization program which was demanded by
the IMF. The conditions of the austerity package further
restricted the government's options with respect to the
cooperatives as did the terms of its agreement with the
World Bank for financial aid for rehabilitation of the
Frome and Monymusk factories.[7] Of course, the agreement
with the IMF was itself the result of the intense political struggles which were taking place within the
PNP, the government and the society as a whole, as well
as in the international arena. It also reflected, in
part, the relative strength of the moderate, pro-
capitalist wing.

Economic realities at the local level--realities
which the government did not struggle against, or even
for the most part acknowledge--were also an important
factor constraining the process of social transformation. First, the workers took over cane farms which had
been part of integrated farm-factory operations. Because the bulk of the value added within such an operation, as in the industry as a whole, occurred in the
processing operations, and because efficiencies required fullest possible utilization of the capacity of
the processing facilities, the managers of these opera-

tions emphasized the maximization of cane throughput.
In practice this meant planting cane on lands normally
marginal for that crop. While this benefited the enterprise taken as a whole, it pushed the cane farming
operation beyond the point of optimum production. That
is, the price of the cane being produced was less than
its cost of production. This became a problem for the
cooperatives because the reform split the factory-farm
complexes, giving the workers control only over the
farms, with the government taking over the factories.
At Monymusk, between 2,000 and 3,000 acres of cane land
(out of 20,000) were in fact marginal, incapable in an
economic sense of supporting that crop. But the government, now controlling the factory and seeking to maximize its own sugar production, resisted efforts to deac-
tivate or diversify these marginal areas.

A second constraint on the economic viability of
the cooperatives was the high ratio of labor costs to
productivity which they inherited. According to one
estimate, excess labor totaled as much as 50 percent of
the existing work force. This situation was made even
worse in 1975 when most task rates doubled and others
increased 50 percent, without any matching increase in
production. In addition the cooperatives inherited an
assortment of longstanding, but inefficient, operating
practices.

The deep-seated agroeconomic problems at Monymusk
meant that the new cooperative farms had very poor prospects for economic viability at least in the short run.
This was not completely recognized by the workers, however, until after they actually began operations. To
make matters worse, the cooperatives at Monymusk suffered a severe drought in 1976, and their financial
situation reached crisis proportions.

The poor economic performance of the farms effectively diminished the resources available to the cooperatives. Most important, it weakened the legitimacy of
the reform process, and it denied the cooperative farms
the economic wherewithal to carry forward other tasks
more actively, like diversification or education. Their
economic problems to a large degree were certainly determined by conditions which no enterprise could control. But other problems were founded in politics. For
example, the decision to include all registered workers
as members in the cooperatives, entrenching existing
labor surplus inefficiencies in the very structure of
the organizations, was a political decision by the government, as was the insistence that cane be produced,
even on marginal, uneconomic lands.

The third contradiction enveloping the reform process, and the cooperatives in particular, was inter-
related with those previously mentioned. While the PNP's
democratic socialism was not meant as a fundamental
attack against the whole capitalist or neo-colonial

order in Jamaica, in practice capitalism was undercut.[8]
First, the policies of redistribution and the new state
activism limited the possibilities for capital accumulation in the short run. This was especially the case as
the state began to compete with the private entrepre-
neurs and to take over certain activities. Second, the
increasing grass-roots mobilization which developed,
partly as a response to governmental initiatives,
threatened capitalism. This was a threat both in practice, for example, through the land takeovers which
occurred, and in terms of the political potential of
such a mobilization. Third, political attacks on the
"21 families," while not meant to condemn the entire
capitalist class, in practice were viewed as an attack
by the class as a whole. Finally, though this was not
the PNP's intent, Jamaica's growing ties with the
socialist countries and the nonaligned movement, and its
role in the debate calling for a New International Economic Order, were viewed as a fundamental attack on the
Western world, especially by the United States.

     As a result of these factors, the regime was faced
with opposition from very powerful local and foreign
capitalist interests, a reaction which occurred primarily between 1976 and 1980. An anti-socialist campaign
was thus waged in the economy, in the media, and on the
verandas. Its aim was to split the PNP and to erode the
legitimacy of the socialist orientations. It effectively
reinforced the class orientations of those who pre-
dominated within the PNP and government.

LOCAL-LEVEL POLITICAL ECONOMY AND REFORM

     The Jamaican case shows the existence of substan-
tial grass-roots resources available for mobilization
and reform, just as it shows the difficulties inherent
in such mobilization and the fragility of the resources
involved.
     Political, economic and social reality at the local
level represented both resources and constraints for the
cooperativization process. The ability to tap these resources and neutralize the constraints in the context of
the cooperative reform was significantly affected by
political conflict at the national level, as well as by
administrative impediments. The demobilization of the
workers' movement after 1976 effectively stifled all
efforts to effect a permanent alteration of the class
structure at the local level. The absence of administrative linkages served to isolate the cooperatives even
more from other potential sources of support.[9] This.
represented one of the major constraints on the cooperativization program: the government's failure --indeed
its unwillingness--to tap the large reservoir of resources and political will which existed at the local

level, and which could have been oriented to social
transformation of the plantation system. The stagnation
of the cooperativization program was in no small way a
result of this failure.

Sugar workers represented a large reservoir of opposition to the plantation system, especially the injustice, inequality and oppression which were entrenched
within it. The oppressive work relations, the low economic returns, the poor living conditions they were forced
to bear, the insecurity and the lack of democracy were
all significant issues for the sugar workers. The potential for tapping this resource was exhibited during the
1973-1975 period of worker mobilization. Certainly what
occurred in Vere in those years was the most significant
episode of grass-roots mobilization in modern Jamaican
history. And it produced results, proving for a time to
be a more formidable force than the state bureaucracy
or the more conservative elements within the government.

In a technical, as well as political, sense SWCC
was important to this reform process. SWCC's sensitivity
to local needs and interests, as well as its educational
work among the workers, filled a need the government
neglected. The government had neither the commitment nor
the resources to reach its sugar worker clientele as
SWCC did. In addition, SWCC's efforts to maintain its
independence made it a more legitimate intermediary with
most JLP-affiliated workers than any PNP or governmental
agency could have been

The process of demobilization from 1976 on effectively constrained the cooperativization process by
weakening the organization which had largely made that
process possible. For example, without SAC's active in-
involvement, the workers heading the cooperatives were
left more or less on their own, before they had had a
chance to fully develop their resources for leadership;
before they had any real experience of farm management;
before the leadership potential of other workers, who
may have been more capable or more representative, even
had a chance to surface.[10] To the degree that identifying
and developing such a local leadership is a primary organizing task, the cooperative movement was thus set
back.

While the need and commitment of the sugar workers
to change the plantation system could be used to generate substantial resources, the same workers also exhibited certain traits which acted as constraints to the
cooperativization process. They were largely illiterate,
poor and occupied very low status positions in the
Jamaican social order. They had almost no experience in
substantive democracy, where people join together as
equals to make key decisions about their lives or the
lives of their communities or associations. Many of the
cooperators at Monymusk had little or no experience as
owners of farms or as shopkeepers to fall back on. They

possessed little. Finally, in sociopsychological terms,
they were used to taking orders, not giving them; they
were constantly denigrating themselves and others like
themselves; they felt little hope in the future; and
they were prone to expect paternal-dependency relationships vis-a-vis those of a higher class and lighter
color.

While there was substantial support for the co-ops
within the progressive movement in Jamaica, on the whole
other significant resource potentials were largely unmobilized. In a number of ways, the working class did
not support the sugar worker movement. In the first
place, a schism developed between the field workers who
became members of the cooperatives and the workers in
the sugar factories who did not. There had always been
socioeconomic disparities between the two groups; yet
their objective interests were similar and they were
part of one bargaining unit. With the formation of the
cooperatives, the interests of the field workers began
to diverge from those of the factory workers. The field
workers in effect became cane farmers demanding efficient and reliable service from the factory. Although
they remained part of the union, the cooperative leadership began to oppose strike actions in the factory.
Divisions were exacerbated both by the fact that cooperatives were not established in the factories, and by the
severance payments which were awarded to field workers
but were never available to factory workers, even after
the government took over the factories. In fact, to be
sure, most cooperators continued to see themselves as
workers, not farmers.

Second, personal and ideological differences developed at the grass roots between SWCC and the workers'
unions, involving both the NWU and the BITU. This conflict weakened SWCC locally as well as nationally; in
particular, the NWU leadership lobbied with the government against SWCC, and especially its organizers from
SAC. SWCC was seen as a threat, as an organizational
force which had the potential to disrupt the unions'
traditional ties to the workers. The conservative local
and national union leaders affiliated with the NWU were
particularly aghast at SWCC's socialist orientations.

At the local, as well as national level the actual
performance of the cooperatives affected their potential
for resource mobilization. Apart from its socioeconomic
impact on the workers (see below), the performance of
the farm enterprises represented a source of material
resources and an important factor affecting the legitimacy of the process. Poor performance thus diminished
the resources available to the cooperativization process. Their economic problems were certainly determined
to a large degree by conditions which no enterprise
could control. But other problems, as mentioned above,
were founded in politics.

188

Overall, the structural and operational charac-
teristics of the plantation system resisted change,
with important implications. In a sense, this is not
surprising. There were over 300 years of tradition and
continuity embedded in the system of plantation production. Morelands farm, for example, had been farmed in
the same way for at least 200 years. More important,
those who benefited from that system were firmly established within it. Most of the overseers had been with
their farms for at least twenty years; during this time
they had internalized the system's oppressive patterns.
For the most part, these overseers remained in their
positions during the transition to cooperatives, retaining much arbitrary power. Even the workers exhibited ambiguous attitudes toward the plantation system, mixing
hostility with feelings of dependency.

One important area in which traditional plantation
patterns hardly changed at all despite the transformation of the farms into cooperatives was the labor process. In the first place the task-rate system remained
intact, and the actual allocation of work remained in
the hands of the overseers and foremen. The workers
continued to perceive this labor process as hierarchical
and oppressive. Second, income inequalities were largely
reproduced within the cooperatives. There was no narrow-
ing of the gap in incomes between workers and staff, although a small select group of workers, supervisors and
elected leaders, saw their incomes reach a par with
staff levels. While this was a change from the precooperative pattern, it was viewed negatively by most of
the rank and file workers who were excluded. In addition, real wages declined substantially during the first
few years of the cooperative experience. The workers
did not understand that their incomes would certainly
have fared much worse under any alternative arrangement;
they did not understand the protection afforded by
their new relationship to the production process. As
far as they were concerned, the establishment of the
cooperatives had led neither to any improvement in
their incomes nor to their receiving any disbursements
out of profit.

There were other areas in which expected changes
did not occur or were minimal. In most cases the workers did the same jobs under the cooperative structure
as they always had. There were practically no opportunities for upgrading. Most strikingly, until 1979, there
was little in the way of worker education, despite the
fact that this was desired by the workers and had been
defined as an explicit function of the cooperatives.
Also, there were no efforts to diversify the activities
of the enterprises. They were still totally immersed in
cane, even though over a thousand acres were lying idle
at Monymusk because at least some of the land unsuited
for profitable production of cane was removed therefrom.

Hence, despite the apparently radical transformation from plantation enterprise to cooperative enterprise, in a broader sense there was no substantial shift
in the social relations of production. In practice, the
changes were in many instances more formal than substantive. As a result, continuity was more salient than
change for many workers. This could not help but affect
the cooperativization process.

At the local level, the status quo was most
strongly supported by the middle class, including medium
to large cane farmers, small business people and members
of the estate staff. These elements represented the same
class which at the national level turned most strongly
against the PNP after 1974.

Prior to 1976, the overseers and other estate staff
persons were the most active local-level opposition to
SWCC and the cooperatives. The staff organized among
themselves, intimidated workers, spread rumors, lobbied
strongly at the national level, and worked closely with
FMLCo in its anti-SWCC efforts.

After 1976, once the cooperatives were in operation, opposition took other forms. One of the most demoralizing aspects of this opposition was the staff members' continued verbal assaults on the cooperatives,
their new employers. They lost little time in propagat-
ing the view that the workers were unprepared and un-
qualified for worker control. As opinion leaders in the
community, they were able to spread their views easily
and this indeed became the dominant perspective in the
area. Such a view was also accepted by most government
bureaucrats at the national level.

Staff opposition was also expressed through their
apathetic participation in the affairs of the worker
cooperatives. Whether by design or by incompetence,
they impeded the democratic processes within the cooperatives. They did not attend meetings, provided few and
inadequate reports, and made no efforts to help to diversify production.

ADMINISTRATIVE PROCESS AND REFORM

The cooperativization reform was an innovative
agrarian policy which diverged substantially from the
established practice in the agricultural sector. In this
respect, the implementation of the cooperativization
policy differed from the other major component of the
PNP's agrarian reform program, its land-lease project.
The program provided supplemental plots of land to small
farmers. It was closely patterned on a private tenancy
program run by one of the bauxite companies in Jamaica.
It also incorporated aspects of previous attempts at
land settlement dating back to the nineteenth century.
In contrast, the cooperatives program had no historical

model to build on.

The innovative, nonincremental nature of the cooperatives program was manifest in a number of ways. In the first place, apart from the mid-nineteenth century replacement of wage slavery for chattel slavery--the political-economic significance of which can be questioned--the pattern of social relations in the cane belt had never been significantly altered. The concept of sugar workers taking control of the cane lands was a very radical notion. It was also a significant departure from the scheme previously proposed by the JLP of selling the estate lands in lots of 100 to 500 acres to individual farmers. Furthermore, the proposed structure for the cooperatives themselves was innovative. There was only one functioning producer cooperative in all of Jamaica at the time. It had only twenty members and was over twenty years old. A few other collective farms had been tried but failed. Almost all of the agricultural cooperatives in existence in 1974 were limited to one function--marketing. In general, cooperatives had had a checkered history in Jamaica, with many people, including many sugar workers, believing that Jamaicans "can't cooperate."

There was also a substantial degree of innovation at the grass roots. The role played by SWCC in the policy process diverged from standard bureaucratic expectations and experiences. While other rural interest groups, such as the Cane Farmers Association and the Jamaica Agricultural Society, were involved in agricultural policy making, they had lost touch over the years with their grass-roots membership. By the 1970s, both the CFA and the JAS were, in fact, controlled by larger farmers whose main skill was manipulating their grass-roots constituencies; they effectively ignored their formal responsibilities of representing and being answerable to the membership, the majority of whom were small farmers. As a result, both organizations had become conservative and bureaucratized, with a pragmatic leadership interested only in incremental change. Government officials and political elites had developed well-structured and mutually beneficial relationships with these leaders. SWCC, on the other hand, was a new and different entity. Between 1974 and 1976, at least, it was militant, leftist, tenacious, committed to its worker-membership and insistent on playing an active and ongoing role in the implementation process.

SWCC's power and perspective were reflected in the decentralized administrative structure which was established. After 1976, SWCC became the agency responsible for implementing the cooperatives program at the grass roots. That is, the local policy delivery system was a nongovernmental organization. Decentralization of authority was itself innovative in the Jamaican context; but decentralization of authority to a private entity

(really semi-private, since cooperatives were regulated
by the state) was practically unheard of for such an
important governmental policy.

The sugar workers were expected to play entirely
new roles as cooperative members and farm owners; those
who for years had been at the bottom of the social
structure, were suddenly given the opportunity and the
mandate to participate in ways normally monopolized by
other strata. They were given formal authority over
those who had previously dominated them socially and
psychologically. The reversal of roles intrinsic to the
cooperatives further required the overseers and other
members of staff to interact with the sugar workers in
ways hitherto unimaginable. Finally, there was little
apparent consideration of the fact that those who had
never known economic freedom might have difficulty in
wielding their new freedom responsibly and wisely. It
was assumed, it seemed, that rural proletarians could
almost overnight be transformed into a petty bourgeoisie.

The political-administrative leadership within the
government proved incapable of, or unwilling to, deal
with the discontinuuities intrinsic to the policy process. The apparatus established to deal with the reform
was not consistent with the needs or logic of cooperativization. On the one hand, no group within the cooperative leadership structure had either sufficient
authority or resources to carry the difficult process
forward, especially following the removal of SAC's
influence. SAC had the organizational experience, the
sensitivity to the workers and their needs, and the
commitment to grass-roots mobilization and reform which
were necessary to implement the cooperatives successfully. However, SAC was largely removed from the policy
arena during the post-1975 demobilization. At the same
time, the linkage between the local policy delivery
system and national political and administrative
authorities was poorly articulated. Hence there were no
adequate channels for stimulating or ensuring compliance at the local level with national directives or
needs; neither was there a flow of administrative resources to the fields. The normal policy hierarchy was
not working, resulting in a degree of organizational
disarray.

In effect, the traditional production structure
had been discarded, but it was not replaced by an administratively viable alternative. Neither the government nor the grass roots generated and provided the
necessary resources to carry out the implementation of
the new cooperative structures.

Vertical linkages did not develop for a number of
reasons. First, neither the Kingston-based administrative elites nor the political leadership knew how to
relate to this new cooperative "animal" they had helped

to create. None of the major administrative agencies involved with the cooperatives had had any experience
dealing with "soft technologies," ones dealing with the
social dimension of development--community development,
grass-roots mobilization, social and attitudinal changes.[11] The lack of exposure and sensitivity to the
special administrative needs entailed in "soft-techno-
logy" options never appeared to be a matter of concern.
Even the Cooperative Department officers, who were more
used to filling the necessary roles, failed to attend
to the special needs of the sugar worker cooperatives.
They saw working with the management committees on farm
management matters as their main job. Certainly this was
important. But this left some of the more problematic
organizational matters, especially the relations between
the mass of sugar workers, the committees and the staff,
virtually unattended. The Cooperative Department was not
provided any additional resources with which to deal
with the sugar worker cooperatives.

Linkages broke down for political reasons as well.
As discussed in Chapters 3 and 4, FMLCo expended considerable effort to compete with and weaken SWCC. This
produced a tension between SWCC and the bureaucracy. It
was heightened by the administrators' apparent support
for an administrative pattern more centralist and hierarchical than that to which SWCC was committed. To be
sure, SWCC's populist tendencies created an inhospitable
environment for strong, governmental involvement with
the cooperatives, at least prior to 1976.

This disagreement was reflected, for example, in
the conflict over a worker education program. Wanting
to gain control over the cooperatives to ensure SAC's
isolation, the minister of agriculture refused to allow
USWCC to accept a large grant for its education program
from the Inter-American Foundation.[12] His ministry, however, made no move to fill the gap. As a result, there
was no viable education program until 1979, when a
similar grant from the IAF was finally approved. But
this was rather too late to help the sugar workers
grapple with the substantially new and different kinds
of participation intrinsic to the process of making the
cooperatives effective.

Vertical linkages also were hampered by the complexity of the cooperative structure. There were three
levels--the farm cooperatives at the base, the estate
cooperative linking these primary cooperatives, and the
Kingston-based central coordinating body. And there was
the government attempting to ensure efficiency and compliance with its needs throughout the cooperative structure. At best this worked in a cumbersome manner. Difficulties were encountered communicating within the co-
op structure and between it and the government, and in
establishing a sense of strong cooperative identity
among the workers.

First, grass-roots cooperative members did not have
a clear understanding of the nature of the higher-level
cooperative bodies, such as the estate boards of management and the central board, and were given little substantive information of their activities and decisions.
There were no established channels through which the estate cooperative could communicate effectively with its
members. The chairperson from each farm cooperative sat
on the estate board as a formal representative of that
farm; but only rarely did he/she make formal reports to
constituents about activities and decisions at the
estate level. The chairperson would occasionally inform
his/her committee of management about important matters
affecting the farm, but this rarely filtered out to the
general membership. The ordinary members got information, if at all, by word of mouth, and usually in a mis-
leading or erroneous form.

Information flowed, if at all, from the estate
board to the estate chief executive to the farm managers
to their staff and finally to the workers. From the perspective of the worker-members, this flow through the
staff was the way information had always traveled on the
estate. Maintenance of these communication patterns
under the cooperative restructuring tended to reproduce
preexisting social relations and to camouflage the fact
that the decisions were being made by the workers' own
representatives. And, of course, the power of the cooperatives' general membership was therefore curtailed.

USWCC was even more cut off from the grass roots.
Although it distributed a short newsletter for a while,
this was canceled for financial reasons. As a result
this central-level worker body had even less salience
for the average cooperator than his or her estate cooperative.

The functioning of the three-tiered cooperative
structure was also affected by "acute localitis."[13]
Directives from both the central and estate cooperatives were frequently ignored at the farm level. There
were few resources to ensure compliance, especially in
view of the relatively low levels of legitimacy and
salience which those bodies had for most staff and cooperative members at the farm level. Hence, accounta-
bility was weakened. Interaction between the government
and the cooperatives was thus made more difficult because the cooperative leaders had trouble ensuring that
they were in fact speaking for the whole of the cooperatives.

Finally, the development of vertical linkages was
hindered by the plurality of administrative hierarchies
which were involved with the cooperativization policy.
The Sugar Industry Authority, the Ministry of Agriculture and the Department of Cooperatives all had a substantial role to play with regard to the cooperatives.
The Sugar Industry Research Institute (nominally part

of SIA) was also involved. Their roles continually over-
lapped, but there was no effective mechanism for in-
tegrating their efforts.

Why were there these anomalies in the implementation process? Why was the administrative strain so
great? Clearly, the policy process seemed to have extended beyond the administrative capacity. The bureaucracy was neither politically nor technically prepared
to carry out the cooperativization process. It is important to remember that the technocrats' original proposal
of a multipurpose cooperative with individual leaseholds
was more in line with traditional roles and expectations
than the collective farm model, incorporating all workers, which was finally adopted. Likewise, the orientation toward bureaucratic control characteristic of FMLCo
was standard operating procedure, in contrast with
SWCC's emphasis on worker control. Similarly, the government's pilot approach and expressed intention to
phase in the other cooperatives over a period of years
was more gradual and manageable than what was finally
agreed to in 1975.

The radicalization of the policy under pressure
from SWCC, and in the context of the democratic reformist trends of 1974-1976, was not associated with any
consciousness that the administrative institutions and
mechanisms themselves needed to be reoriented.[14] To the
contrary, those administrative mechanisms frequently
were allowed to operate at cross purposes with the cooperativization process. This was more than just a
failure to recognize the particular administrative needs
of the cooperatives; that could have been excused on
the grounds of inexperience. It was, in fact, a political resistance to fulfilling those needs in ways consistent with the process of agrarian reform. Moreover,
it was also a misconception of the cooperativization
process. There was, in general, too narrow a focus on
technical and economic aspects of the cooperatives
and too great a disregard of political and social factors which continued to be important subsequent to the
actual organization of the cooperative farms.

If the state was not to be "smashed," at least it
could have been altered to make it more consistent with
the reform process. This did not occur, and it had an
enormous effect on the entire process.

CONCLUSION

The policies adopted in Jamaica between 1972 and
1980 were an attempt to respond to the crisis of underdevelopment in which Jamaica found itself. Michael
Manley's problem was how could Jamaica transcend the
economic and social contradictions which permeated the
society. His solution was the path of democratic reform.

His failure was nowhere more manifest than in the 1980
election, which canceled, at least for some years, his
program of "power for the people" and progressive
change.

A program of democratic reform is typically both
ambitious and necessary. It is ambitious in terms of
its sweeping commitment to broadly-based social and economic reform and the reintegration of the mass of the
population into the social fabric. It is necessary in
terms of the growing debilitation of underdevelopment
with which it is meant to cope.

Carrying out such goals, however, requires more
than will and good intentions. It requires the mobilization of political support and resources across a
broad spectrum of the society. Here, the democratic reformist must face three fundamental problems. First,
the reformist program is inherently conflictual. The
status quo must be disrupted, but the status quo has its
supporters and beneficiaries. These opponents are powerful, all the more so if, as in the Jamaican case, they
coalesce under the "anti-socialist" banner.

Second, the possibilities for opposition and disruption are multiplied within an open, pluralist political system. Here, organization, resources and access
often count the most. And these are the areas in which
elite interests, both domestic and foreign, typically
thrive. The democratic reformer seeks to play the political game by rules that ultimately favor the opponents of change unless very active, persistent, and
well-directed mobilization of the majority occurs.

Third, the political composition of the reformist
coalition typically is skewed toward domination by
middle-class interests. This certainly was the case in
Jamaica. In order to mobilize the requisite political
support among small farmers, agricultural workers,
working-class individuals, and lumpen elements--and in
a democratic society this has to be done rapidly and
usually with actions visibly beneficial to these op-
pressed classes--the middle class must look beyond its
immediate class interest and traditional class ties. In
addition, reform may place this stratum in opposition
to powerful foreign powers.

In such a situation, the choices before the reformist leadership can truly appear to reflect a "no-
win" politics:

> If the country holds to its determination to work
> for a more just society, with all that this en-
> tails in terms of serious policies, it may find
> that the incremental inflows arising from private
> foreign investment do not materialize. In this
> event, it will find economic growth to be incon-
> sistent with the maintenance of an open society.
> If it is committed to such a society, it may face

a political catastrophe.

On the other hand, if it dismantles the assault upon injustice, it will doubtless recover a 'good' reputation as a locus for foreign investment. The incremental flows may resume, but at an internal price of social betrayal including a return to the path of growing social inequality. Once again, the likely outcome in an open society, is political catastrophe.[15]

Such a regime would only move to the left if some or all of the following conditions are fulfilled: a) a relatively strong left political movement exists within society (as in Chile in the 1960s); b) there are some traditions of state intervention in the economy; c) liberal foreign policy orientations prevail in the United States, as in the late 1930s; d) the world system encompasses modes of political-economic support for Third World countries alternative to those presented by the multinational corporations and conservative developed countries; and e) mass organizations exist and are mobilized for structural change.

With the above conditions largely unfulfilled in the Jamaican case, a radical path could not be taken very far. Internal problems within the regime also blocked a reformist path. The regime was left in the late 1970s with reformist rhetoric and a reformist program on paper, but without the power to pursue the substance of reform. In such a situation of immobilization, Manley's electoral defeat in 1980 was perhaps inevitable.

This has been a study of the process by which a political economy deals with the problem of reform. This "problem," as I have said, devolves from the need to confront a number of political and economic demands simultaneously. There is: a) the necessity of reforming neo-colonial and exploitative structures, so as to redistribute resources and power; b) the need to ensure that the process of capital accumulation proceeds and that economic growth ensues; c) the need for mobilization of political resources, which must necessarily include some form of mass mobilization; and d) the need for maintenance, if not expansion, of a democratic political process. Each of these demands must be confronted. And all must be confronted at one and the same time. This is the crux of the problem of reform.

In the Jamaica case, the regime successfully confronted only the last, and then only partially. I have argued that the political dynamism and reformist momentum of the 1974-1976 period was, in effect, only superficial. Its foundation remained a middle-class party, a conservative administration and an unmobilized agricultural working class. I have tried to show how the reform process was constrained at the macro- and microlevels by these factors, and how opposition forces both contributed to and expanded their own political base on the basis of these constraints.

Perhaps without the presence of an articulated left element in the country's politics, of militant mass organizations, of a history of radical state activism, and of a sympathetic international system, nothing more could have been expected. Indeed, this may be the most hopeful conclusion. For the historical dialectic continues into the 1980s, but now with a strengthened left, more experience with cooperatives and other forms of socialist development, and a history of grass-roots mobilization.

NOTES

1. Michael Manley, speech to sugar cooperatives.

2. The government and SWCC were subsequently criticized for speeding up the process in this way. SWCC's argument was that the workers were ready then, momentum needed to be maintained and any delay risked the future reversal of the reform with the workers not getting the land. In fact, while a tremendous burden was placed on implementation, there would have been economic and other problems regardless. With hindsight we can say that in the post-1975 period the government indeed would have been likely to halt the cooperative movement. In effect SWCC was right. (See Chapters 4 and 6).

3. Hinton provides a fascinating view of a similar dynamic during the early years of the Chinese agrarian reform (William Hinton, Fanshen [New York: Monthly Review Press, 1966]).

4. This conception has also been used to characterize the Peronist regime in Argentina (Mario Eduardo Firmenich, "Firmenich: A Political Analysis," NACLA's Latin America and Empire Report 11 [January 1977]).

5. Similarly, Peruvian reformers in the early 1970s tried to develop a system that was "neither capitalist nor socialist."

6. For a different view of post-1972 Jamaican political economy, and for a much more detailed and definitive discussion of events during this period, see Evelyne Huber Stephens and John D. Stephens, "Democratic Socialism in Dependent Capitalism: An Analysis of the Manley Government in Jamaica," Politics and Society 12 (1983) and Evelyne Huber Stephens and John D. Stephens, Democratic Socialism in Jamaica: The Political Movement and Social Transformation in Dependent Capitalism (forthcoming, 1985).

7. IBRD, "Sugar Rehabilitation . . . ."

8. The essentially pragmatic perspective of the democratic socialist program is clear, for example, in the PNP's major statement of its program (People's National Party, Democratic Socialism--The Jamaican Model [Kingston: PNP, December 1974]).

9. Whether such administrative linkages serve as a basis of support or not of course depends on their nature as well as their existence.

10. See Chapter 6 for a discussion of SAC's ouster and the demobilization of the workers' movement.

11. These approaches contrast with the "hard" technologies utilized, for example, in a school building program, a rural electrification project, or a rural market program. For these projects procedures can be routinized and flexibility is less essential. Hence, both bureaucratic discretion and local-level interaction can be minimized. Whereas "soft" development projects attempt to use people to effect complex institutional change, the "hard" technology approach emphasizes the use of money and capital to build things; also, the former usually proceed without an established knowledge base while the latter frequently utilize established methodologies. Finally, the effects of "soft" projects are harder to measure as they often clash with bureaucratic tendencies, and are harder to implement. For a good discussion of the administrative constraints to implementing participatory rural development strategies, and the need for bureaucratic reorientation, see David C. Korten and Norman T. Uphoff, Bureaucratic Reorientation for Participatory Rural Development (Washington: National Association of Schools of Public Affairs and Administration, Working Paper Number 1, 1981).

12. The Inter-American Foundation had been impressed with SAC's earlier work in establishing an education program for the sugar workers. The proposal from USWCC incorporated a significant role for SAC.

13. John D. Montgomery, "The Populist Front in Rural Development: or Shall We Eliminate the Bureaucrats and Get on with the Job," Public Administration Review 39 (January/February 1979). He writes: "The weaknesses of an extreme localism are as debilitating as the pathologies of an unrestrained bureaucracy" (p. 59).

14. "So far, too, little attention has been given to dealing with bureaucratic structures as variables to be modified and managed in support of particular kinds of policy outcomes, such as poverty alleviation. Yet it has become evident that assisting disadvantaged groups requires procedures and approaches on the part of the assisting agencies which differ considerably from the usual norms of the typical public agency" (Korten and Uphoff, p. 2).

15. Michael Manley, address to the Board of Governors of the Inter-American Development Bank, May 1979, quoted in Girvan, Bernal and Hughes, p. 147.

Abbreviations

AIJCFA (or CFA)	All Island Jamaica Cane Farmers Association
BITU	Bustamante Industrial Trade Union
FMLCo	Frome Monymusk Land Company
IAF	Inter-American Foundation
IMF	International Monetary Fund
JAS	Jamaica Agriculture Society
JLP	Jamaica Labour Party
MWCCFA	Monymusk Workers Cooperative Cane Farmers Association
NSC	National Sugar Company
NWU	National Workers Union
PNP	People's National Party
SAC	Social Action Centre
SIA	Sugar Industry Authority
SIRI	Sugar Industry Research Institute
SMA	Sugar Manufacturers Association
SWCC	Sugar Workers Coordinating Council
USWCC	United Sugar Workers Cooperative Council

Selected Bibliography

SOURCES ON JAMAICA

Abbott, George C. "The West Indian Sugar Industry, with Some Long Term Projections of Supply to 1975." Social and Economic Studies 13:1, March 1964.
Ahiram, E. "Income Distribution in Jamaica, 1958." Social and Economic Studies 13:3, September 1964.
Barlow, W. Sean. "The Sugar Co-operative Movement in Jamaica: A Case Study and General Evaluation." Unpublished independent research study. Middletown: Government Department, Wesleyan University, April 1978.
Barraclough, Solon. "Land Reform Consultation in Jamaica." FAO Memorandum, unpublished. January 23, 1974.
Beachey, R. W. The British West Indies Sugar Industry in the Late 19th Century. Oxford: Basil Blackwell, 1957.
Beckford, George L. Persistent Poverty. New York: Oxford University Press, 1972.
_____. "Plantations, Peasants and Proletariat in the West Indies." Socialism! 1:3, Kingston, September 1974.
Belinfanti, A. U. "Sugar Cane Cooperatives at Frome, Monymusk and Bernard Lodge." Unpublished memorandum submitted to the Jamaican Cabinet, April 2, 1976.
Best, Lloyd. "Outlines of a Model of Pure Plantation Economy." Social and Economic Studies 17, March-December 1968.
Blakeley, J. M. "The Viability of USWCC." Unpublished report, May 1976.
Bloomfield, C. A. "The Functions and Activities of the Sugar Manufacturers' Association (of Jamaica) Ltd." The Jamaica Association of Sugar Technologists Journal, Proceedings for the Year 1967, Vol. XXVIII.
Brewster, Havelock. "Jamaica's Life or Death--The Sugar

Industry." New World Pamphlet, No. 4, Kingston, December 1967.

_____. "The Social Economy of Sugar." New World Quarterly 5:1-2, Kingston, 1969.

Broom, Leonard. "The Social Differentiation of Jamaica." American Sociological Review 19:2, April 1954.

Brown, Matthias. "The Sugar Cooperatives in Jamaica (A Cooperator's Views)." Paper presented at the First West Indies Sugar Technologists' Conference, Kingston, November 1976.

Burnett, Alvin, et al. "Plan for Development of Frome, Monymusk, and Bernard Lodge Lands." Report prepared by an Inter-agency Government of Jamaica team, mimeo, December 10, 1972.

Byrne, Fr. Tony, and Fr. Jim Schecher. "Progress Report on Social Action Centre Development Programme." Mimeo, Kingston: Social Action Centre, June 1975.

Carnegie, James. Some Aspects of Jamaica's Politics, 1918-1938. Kingston: Institute of Jamaica, 1973.

Caribbean Food and Nutrition Institute. "Nutritional Status of Young Children in the English-Speaking Caribbean." Kingston, September 1977.

Chase, R. Darwin. A Report on the Co-operative Movement in Jamaica. Kingston: Ministry of Agriculture, 1971.

Chen-Young, Paul. "The Economic-Political Dilemma in Jamaica." Economic Report-Jamaica, I, August 1975.

Chin, Lester A.D. "Development of the Bernard Lodge Sugar Factory." Typescript. Kingston, September 1974.

Cohen, Yehudi A. "The Social Organization of a Selected Community in Jamaica." Social and Economic Studies 2:4, March 1954.

Craton, Michael, and James Walvin. A Jamaican Plantation--The History of Worthy Park, 1670-1970. Toronto: University of Toronto Press, 1970.

Cumper, George. "Labour Demand and Supply in the Jamaican Sugar Industry, 1830-1950." Social and Economic Studies 2:4, March 1954.

_____. "A Modern Jamaican Sugar Estate." Social and Economic Studies 3:2. September 1954.

Curtin, Philip D. Two Jamaicas-The Role of Ideas in a Tropical Colony, 1830-1865. New York: Atheneum, 1970.

Davison, R. B. "Labour Shortage and Productivity in the Jamaican Sugar Industry." Kingston: Institute of Social and Economic Research, 1966.

Donaldson, Noel. "The West Indies Sugar Company-Where From, Where To." Jamaica Sugar Digest. Kingston, May-August 1976.

Eastwood, David. "Irrigation Water Quality." Jamaica Sugar Digest. May-June 1976.

Eaton, George E. Alexander Bustamante and Modern Jamaica. Kingston: Kingston Publishers, 1975.

Edwards, D. T. "Agricultural Development in Jamaica, 1943-1961." In G. L. Beckford, ed., Proceedings of the 3rd West Indian Agricultural Economics Conference. Kingston, 1968.

Edwards, David. An Economic Study of Small Farming in Jamaica. Kingston: Institute of Social and Economic Research, 1961.

Eisner, Gisela. Jamaica 1830-1930: A Study in Economic Growth. Manchester: Manchester University Press, 1961.

EPICA Task Force, Jamaica. Caribbean Challenge: A People's Primer. Washington: The Task Force, 1979.

Eyre, Alan. "Land and Population in the Sugar Belt of Jamaica." Kingston: Department of Geography, University of the West Indies, n.d.

Forsythe, Dennis. "Race, Colour and Class in the British West Indies." Mimeo. Department of Sociology, University of the West Indies, n.d.

Foster, Philips, and Peter Creyke. The Structure of Plantation Agriculture in Jamaica. College Park, Maryland: University of Maryland, Agriculture Economics Experiment Station, Miscellaneous Publication 623, 1968.

Frome, Monymusk Land Company Ltd. "Operational Plans." Draft, August 1974.

_____, Staff Association. "Position Paper on the Development of Cooperatives." Presented to the Prime Minister's Committee on Co-operative Development, 1975.

Girvan, Norman. Foreign Capital and Economic Underdevelopment in Jamaica. Kingston: Institute of Social and Economic Research, 1971.

Girvan, Norman, Richard Bernal, and Wesley Hughes. "The IMF and the Third World: The Case of Jamaica, 1974-80." Development Dialogue, 1980:2

Gonsalves, Ralph. "The Rodney Affair and Its Aftermath." Department of Government, University of the West Indies, October 1975.

_____. "The Trade Union Movement in Jamaica: Its Growth and Some Resultant Problems." In Carl Stone and Aggrey Brown, eds., Essays on Power and Change in Jamaica.Kingston: Department of Government, University of the West Indies, 1976.

Gordon, Derek. "Housing and Population in South Clarendon." Sugar Industry Housing Ltd., Technical Report No. 1, n.d. (ca. 1975).

Greenslade, R.W. "Discussion Paper-Finance USWCC." Kingston, April 25, 1978. Paper presented at Seminar on the Co-operatives, Mandeville, Jamaica, April 27, 1978.

Hall, Douglas. Free Jamaica 1838-1865: An Economic History. New Haven: Yale University Press, 1959.

Harbridge House, Inc. Blueprint for the Future: A Long-Range Plan for the Jamaican Sugar Industry.

Prepared for the Sugar Manufacturers' Association (of Jamaica) Ltd., Boston, 1971.

Hart, Richard. Forward to Freedom. Kingston: People's Educational Organization, October 1952.

_____. The Origin and Development of the People of Jamaica. Montreal: International Caribbean Service Bureau, 1974.

Harvard Business School. "The Frome Monymusk Land Co. Ltd.- Case Study." 1975.

Henriques, Fernando. Family and Colour in Jamaica. London: MacGibbon and Kee, 1968.

Higgins, Winston. "The Bernard Lodge Sugar Workers Co-operatives." USWCC, 1977.

_____. "Bernard Lodge, Frome and Monymusk Pilot Project Design and Operations." Mimeo, n.d.

_____. "Frome/Monymusk/Bernard Lodge Development Project." Frome Monymusk Land Company, 1973.

International Bank for Reconstruction and Development. "Current Economic Situation and Prospects of Jamaica." Report No. 967a-JM, 1976.

_____. "Staff Appraisal Report--Sugar Rehabilitation Project, Jamaica." Report No. 1732a-JM, January 19, 1978.

Jamaica, The Commission of Enquiry on the Sugar Industry of Jamaica, 1959-1960, H. Carl Goldenberg, Chairman. Report of the Commission of Enquiry on the Sugar Industry of Jamaica. Kingston, 1960. Cited as Goldenberg.

Jamaica, Cooperative Development Centre. "Agricultural Co-operatives in Jamaica." Kingston, 1978.

Jamaica, Department of Cooperatives. "The Development of Cooperatives on Sugar Cane Lands." Discussion paper presented to the Prime Minister's Committee on Co-operative Development, May 5, 1975.

_____. "Sugar Cane Cooperatives." Report prepared for the Planning Group Subcommittee of the Prime Minister's Committee on Co-operative Development, May 12, 1975.

Jamaica, Department of Labour. "Trade Unionism in Jamaica, 1918-1946." Kingston, n.d.

Jamaica, Department of Statistics, Agricultural Census Unit. Census of Agriculture, 1968-69.

_____. Census Report, 1943. Kingston.

_____. Census Report, 1960. Kingston

_____. "Sample Survey of Sugar and General Workers, 1956." Kingston, 1957.

Jamaica. "Green Paper on Agricultural Development." Kingston, 1973.

Jamaica, House of Representatives. Ministry Paper No. 13. "Report on Purchase of WISCo Lands by the Government." June 15, 1971.

Jamaica, Labour Department. Report on an Economic Survey among Field Workers in the Sugar Industry, November 1944. Kingston, 1946.

Jamaica, Ministry of Agriculture. Agriculture Sector Survey, Sugar Industry Review. Kingston, 1974.
_____. "Development of Frome/Monymusk/Bernard Lodge Lands." Kingston, 1972.
Jamaica, Prime Minister's Committee on Co-operative Development on the Frome, Monymusk and Bernard Lodge Estates. "Report." May 21, 1975.
_____. "Second Report." N.d.
_____. "Report of the Trelawny Beach Meeting." 1975.
Jamaica, Sugar Industry Authority. The Sugar Industry Rehabilitation Programme. Prepared by Minster Agriculture (England). Draft, July 1976.
Jamaica, Sugar Industry Commission, Robert B. Barker, Chairman. Report of the Sugar Industry Commission, 1944-45. Kingston, 1945.
Jamaica, Sugar Industry Enquiry Commission, John Mordecai, Chairman. Report of the Sugar Industry Enquiry Commission, 1966. Kingston, October 1967. Cited as Mordecai.
Jamaica, Sugar Industry Research Institute. (Formerly Sugar Research Department, Sugar Manufacturers' Association.) Annual Report. Mandeville, Jamaica, various years.
Jamaica. Sugar Industry Welfare Labour Board. "Vere Impact Programme." November 1961.
Jefferson, Owen. The Post-War Economic Development of Jamaica. Kingston: Institute of Social and Economic Research, 1972.
Lawrence, Sam. "Diagnostic Report--Monymusk Tractor and Transport Cooperative." Mimeo. Kingston, 1978.
Le Franc, E.R.M. "The Co-operative Movement in Jamaica: An Exercise in Social Control." Social and Economic Studies 27, March 1978.
Levy, Horace. "Report on the Social Action Centre Programme among Sugar Workers in Westmoreland, Clarendon and St. Catherine." Kingston: Social Action Centre, June 1974.
_____. "What's Wrong with the Sugar Co-ops." Public Opinion, Kingston, February 24, March 6, and March 13, 1978.
Lewis, Rupert. "Black Nationalism in Jamaica in Recent Years." In Carl Stone and Aggrey Brown, eds., Essays on Power and Change in Jamaica. Kingston: Jamaica Publishing House, 1977.
Lindsay, Louis. "Colonialism and the Myth of Resource Insufficiency in Jamaica." Kingston: Institute of Social and Economic Research, 1974.
_____. "The Myth of Independence: Middle Class Politics and Non-mobilization in Jamaica." Working Paper No. 6. Kingston: Institute of Social and Economic Research, 1975.
Lyon, Noel A. "Managing Director's Report on the Frome Monymusk Land Company Ltd., August 1974-December 1974." Kingston: Frome Monymusk Land Co.,

December 10, 1974.

Manley, Michael. The Politics of Change-A Jamaican Testament. London: Andre Deutsch Ltd., 1974.

_____. A Voice at the Workplace-Reflections on Colonialism and the Jamaican Worker. London: Andre Deutsch Ltd., 1975.

Marshall, W. K. "Aspects of the Development of the Peasantry." Caribbean Quarterly 18:1, March 1972.

Marshall, Woodville K. "Notes on Peasant Development in the West Indies since 1838." Social and Economic Studies 17:3, September 1968.

Mentus, Ric. "Interview with Richard Fletcher." Daily News, March 7, 1976.

_____. "Interview with Carl Stone." Daily News, February 15, 1976.

_____. "Interview with Ronnie Thwaites." Daily News, March 28, 1976.

Miller, Claude. "A Review of Our Political Line." Socialism! 3:8 and 3:9. Kingston: Workers Party of Jamaica, August-September 1976.

Mulvey, Dan. "Memorandum." Sugar Workers Coordinating Council, June 5, 1974.

Munroe, Trevor. "The Marxist 'Left' in Jamaica, 1940-1950." Working Paper No. 15. Kingston: Institute of Social and Economic Research, 1977.

_____. "The New Political Situation." Socialism! 1:6. Kingston: Workers Party of Jamaica, December 1974.

_____. The Politics of Constitutional Decolonization, Jamaica, 1944-1962. Kingston: Institute of Social and Economic Research, 1972.

Munroe, Trevor, and Don Robotham. Struggles of the Jamaican People. Kingston: Workers Liberation League, 1977.

New World Group Pamphlet No. 5. "King Sugar and the New World-Story of the Great Sugar Debate." Kingston, June 1968.

Owens, Joseph. "Report on Community Development Project at Monymusk, Lionel Town, 1 March 1974-31 August 1974." Kingston: Social Action Centre, August 31, 1974.

_____. "Report on Housing and Employment Survey of the Monymusk Estate Area." Kingston: SWCC, 1974.

_____. "Suggestions Towards a Plan for Subdivision of Monymusk Estate into Cooperative Farms." Mimeo. September 1973.

_____. "Who Should Control the Government-Owned Sugar Estates?" Mimeo. N.d., ca. 1972-1973.

Parnell, E. "Sugar Cane Cooperatives Operating on Lands Leased from the Frome Monymusk Land Company Ltd." Mimeo. February 19, 1975.

Parnell, Edgar. "Sugar Worker Co-operatives-An Emergency Report." Presented to the Registrar of Co-operatives, July 1976.

Patterson, Orlando. "Social Aspects of the Sugar Indus-
    try." New World Quarterly 5:1-2. Kingston, 1969.
People's National Party. "Action Programme for Farmers."
    Kingston, 1947.
_____. "A Plan for Progress, 1948-49." Kingston,
    n.d.
_____. "PNP, A Plan for Today--1940." Kingston, n.d.
_____. "PNP Election Leaflet Number 1." Kingston,
    1949.
_____. "PNP, What Can Be Done One Day." Kingston,
    n.d., ca. 1940.
_____. "Programme for Action Now." Statement of
    Policy issued by the PNP Annual Conference, August
    12, 1945.
Phelps, O. W. "The Rise of the Labour Movement in
    Jamaica." Social and Economic Studies 9:4, Decem-
    ber 1960.
Phillips, James J. Fe Wi Land a Come: Choice and Change
    on a Jamaican Sugar Plantation. Ph.D. thesis, Brown
    University, June 1976.
Phillips, Peter. "Jamaican Elites: 1938 to Present." In
    Carl Stone and Aggrey Brown, eds., Essays on Power
    and Change in Jamaica. Kingston: Jamaica Publishing
    House, 1977.
Ramdial, L. "The Effect of Saline Water on Two Sugarcane
    Varieties." Mandeville, Jamaica: Sugar Industry
    Research Institute, 1975. Mimeo.
Reid, Stanley. "An Introductory Approach to the Concen-
    tration of Power in the Jamaican Corporate Economy
    and Notes on Its Origin." In Carl Stone and Aggrey
    Brown, eds., Essays on Power and Change in Jamaica.
    Kingston: Jamaica Publishing House, 1977.
Roberts, Wesley A. The Jamaican Plantocracy: A Study of
    Their Economic Interests, 1866-1914. Ph.D. thesis,
    University of Guelph, 1972.
Robertson, Paul D. "Political Behaviour at the Grass
    Roots Level: A Study of Electoral and Party Poli-
    tics in Jamaica." M. Sc. thesis, University of the
    West Indies, 1971.
Sanderson and Porter, Inc. Jamaica Sugar. Jamaican Sugar
    Industry Survey, Phase One, prepared for United
    Nations Industrial Development Organization, New
    York, 1971.
Sangster, Ian. Sugar and Jamaica. London: Thomas Nelson
    & Sons, 1973.
Schecher, Jim. "Report on Co-op Member Education Pro-
    gramme Carried Out by Social Action Centre in Con-
    junction with USWCC Member Services Department."
    Mimeo. Kingston: SAC, 1976.
Senior, Olive. The Message Is Change. Kingston: Kingston
    Publishers, Ltd., 1972.
Shaw, Michael, Chairman. "The Rescue and Development of
    the Sugar Cooperatives." Report of the Committee
    Appointed by the Minister of Agriculture, Michael

Shaw, Chairman, April 1978.

Shillingford, John Davison. Financial Potential and Welfare Implications of Sugar Cane Harvest Mechanization on Jamaican Plantations. Ph.D. thesis, Cornell University, 1974.

Simms, E. A. "Sugarcane Production Cost in Jamaica." 1976 Crop Year Survey. Mandeville, Jamaica: SIRI, September 1977.

Smith, M. G. "The Plural Framework of Jamaican Society." British Journal of Sociology 12:3, 1961.

_____. A Report on Labour Supply in Rural Jamaica. Kingston: Government Printer, 1956.

Stephens, Evelyne Huber and John D. Stephens. "Democratic Socialism in Dependent Capitalism: An Analysis of the Manley Government in Jamaica." Politics and Society 12:3, 1983.

_____. Democratic Socialism in Jamaica: The Political Movement and Social Transformation in Dependent Capitalism. Princeton: Princeton Univ. Press, 1985.

Stone, Carl. "An Appraisal of the Co-operative Process in the Jamaican Sugar Industry." Social and Economic Studies 27:1, March 1978.

_____. "Class, Community and Leadership on a Jamaican Sugar Plantation." Economic Development and Cultural Change 24:4, July 1976.

_____. Class, Race and Political Behaviour in Urban Jamaica. Kingston: Institute of Social and Economic Research, 1973.

_____. Electoral Behaviour and Public Opinion in Jamaica. Kingston: Institute of Social and Economic Research, 1974.

_____. "The Morelands Sugar Co-operative." Jamaica Sugar Digest 1975:2, 1976:1, 1976:2.

_____. "Organization and Operation of the Cooperatives." Mimeo, March 1978.

_____. "Political Aspects of Postwar Agricultural Policies in Jamaica (1945-1976)." Social and Economic Studies 23:2, June 1974.

_____. "Regional and Community Voting Patterns in Jamaica (1959-1976)." Mimeo, n.d.

_____. "Socio-Political Aspects of the Sugar Co-operatives." Kingston: Department of Government, University of the West Indies, May 1976.

_____. "Statement to Workers." Mimeo. November 28, 1975.

Sugar Workers Coordinating Council. "Economic and Social Survey." Mimeo. 1974. See Owens, 1974.

_____. Landroom. Monthly bulletin of Westmoreland branch, 1974-1975.

_____. "Minutes of the October 25th Meeting with the Minister of Agriculture." Mimeo, n.d.

_____. "Organization of Workers' Management Committees at Frome, Monymusk and Bernard Lodge." Mimeo presented to Frome Monymusk Land Company. June 1974.

_____. "Population Statistics for Monymusk Workers' Compounds." Mimeo. May 1973.

_____. "Position Paper on Cooperative Development." Presented to the Prime Minister's Committee on Cooperative Development, April 15, 1975.

_____. "Propositions Concerning Workers' Committees." December 3, 1974.

_____. "The Role and Function of the Workers' Committees of Management." Mimeo. October 1974.

_____. "Rules and Functions for Workers' Committees of Management." Mimeo. October 1974.

_____. "Summary of Meeting with Mr. Winston Higgins, Cooperative Officer of the Frome Monymusk Land Company." Mimeo, June 3, 1973.

Tekse, Kalman. "Internal Migration in Jamaica." Kingston: Jamaica Department of Statistics, April 1967.

Thomas, Clive. "Diversification and the Burden of Sugar to Jamaica." New World Quarterly 5:1-2, Kingston, 1968.

Tomlinson, Frank. "Overmanning Can Bring Losses to Sugar Cooperatives." Letter to the editor, Daily Gleaner, April 1, 1976.

United Sugar Workers Cooperative Council. "Education for the Sugar Worker Co-ops." Transcript of radio broadcast, Spring 1978.

_____. "Urgent Petition to the Prime Minister Concerning Sugar Workers Cooperatives." Mimeo. March 2, 1976.

West Indies Sugar Company Ltd. Annual Report. London, various years.

_____. "Plan for Future Success." Mimeo. August 1972.

_____. "WISCo in Jamaica." London, n.d., ca. 1964.

_____. WISCo News. Monthly in-house journal.

SOURCES ON TOPICS OTHER THAN JAMAICA

Adelman, Irma, and Cynthia Taft Morris. "Performance Criteria for Evaluating Economic Development Potential: An Operational Approach." Quarterly Journal of Economics, May 1968.

Alavi, Hamza. "The State in Post Colonial Societies: Pakistan and Bangladesh." In Kathleen Gough and Hari Sharma, eds., Imperialism and Revolution in South Asia. New York: Monthly Review Press, 1973.

Arrighi, Giovanni, and John Saul. "Socialism and Economic Development in Tropical Africa." Journal of Modern African Studies 6:2, 1968.

Baran, Paul A. The Political Economy of Growth. New York: Monthly Review Press, 1957.

Barkai, H. "The Kibbutz: An Experiment in Microsocialism." In Jaroslav Vanek, Self-Management. Baltimore: Penguin, 1975.

Barraclough, Solon L. "Agricultural Policy and Land Re-
    form." Journal of Political Economy 78:4, July-
    August 1970, supplement.
_____. "Politics First." Ceres, September-October
    1974.
Barraclough, Solon, and Arthur Domike. "Agrarian Struc-
    ture in Seven Latin American Countries." Land Eco-
    nomics 42:4, November 1966.
Baviskar, B.S. "Cooperative Sugar Factories in Maharash-
    tra: A Brief Overview." LTC Newsletter, No. 51,
    January-March 1976.
Blumberg, P. "Alienation and Participation: Conclu-
    sions." In Jaroslav Vanek, ed., Self-Management:
    Economic Liberation of Man. Baltimore: Penguin,
    1975.
Brinkerhoff, Derick W. "Inside Public Bureaucracy: Em-
    powering Managers to Empower Clients." Rural Devel-
    opment Participation Review 1:1, Summer 1979, Rural
    Development Committee, Cornell University.
Brutents, K. The Liberation Struggle of the Asian and
    African Peoples at the Present Stage and Revolu-
    tionary Democracy. Moscow: Novosti Press Agency
    Publishing House, 1977.
_____. National Liberation Revolutions Today. 2
    volumes. Moscow: Progress Publishers, 1977.
Carroll, Thomas F. "Peasant Cooperation in Latin Amer-
    ica." In United Nations Institute for Social De-
    velopment (UNRISD), A Review of Rural Cooperation
    in Developing Areas--Rural Institutions and Planned
    Change. Vol. 1. Geneva: UNRISD, 1969.
Cleaves, Peter S. "Implementation Amidst Scarcity and
    Apathy: Political Power and Policy Design." In
    Merilee S. Grindle, ed., Politics and Policy Imple-
    mentation in the Third World. Princeton: Princeton
    University Press, 1980.
Cliffe, Lionel. "Traditional Ujamaa and Modern Producer
    Cooperatives in Tanzania." In Carl Gosta Widstrand,
    ed., Co-operatives and Rural Development in East
    Africa. New York: Africana Publishing Co., 1970.
Clower, Robert. Growth without Development. Evanston,
    Ill.: Northwestern University Press, 1966.
Cockcroft, James D. "Last Rites for the Reformist Model
    in Latin America." In James D. Cockcroft, Andre
    Gunder Frank, and Dale L. Johnson, Dependence and
    Underdevelopment: Latin America's Political Eco-
    nomy. Garden City, N.Y.: Doubleday and Co., 1972.
Cohen, John M. and Norman T. Uphoff. Rural Development
    Participation: Concepts and Measures for Project
    Design, Implementation and Evaluation. Rural
    Development Monograph No. 2. Ithaca, N.Y.: Rural
    Development Committee, Center for International
    Studies, Cornell University, 1977.
Cornelius, Wayne. "Nation-Building, Participation and
    Distribution: The Politics of Social Reform under

Cardenas." In Gabriel Almond et al., eds., Crisis, Choice and Change. Boston: Little, Brown, 1973.

Dorner, Peter. Land Reform and Economic Development. Baltimore: Penguin, 1972.

Dorner, Peter, and Don Kanel. "Group Farming Issues and Prospects: A Summary of International Experience." New York: Agricultural Development Council, 1975.

Esman, Milton J. "Development Administration and Constituency Organization." Public Administration Review 38:2, March/April 1978.

Feder, Ernest. "Counterreform." In Rodolfo Stavenhagen, ed., Agrarian Problems and Peasant Movements in Latin America. Garden City, N.Y.: Doubleday and Co., 1970.

_____. "Six Plausible Theses about the Peasants' Perspectives in the Developing World." Development and Change 6, 1973-74.

Felete, Ferenc, Earl O. Heady, and Bob Holdren. Economics of Cooperative Farming. Leyden and Budapest: A. W. Sijthoff and Akademiai Kiado, 1976.

Feldman, David. "The Economics of Ideology: Some Problems of Achieving Rural Socialism in Tanzania." In Colin Leys, ed., Politics and Change in Developing Countries. Cambridge: Cambridge University Press, 1969.

Feldman, Rayah. "Rural Social Differentiation and Political Goals in Tanzania." In Ivar Oxaal et al., eds., Beyond the Sociology of Development. London: Routledge and Kegan Paul, 1975.

Fitzgerald, E.V.K. "Peru: The Political Economy of an Intermediate Regime." Journal of Latin American Studies 8:1, May 1970.

Fortmann, Louise. "Pitfalls in Implementing Participation: An African Example." Rural Development Participation Review 1:1, Summer 1979.

Frank, Andre Gunder. Capitalism and Underdevelopment in Latin America: Historical Studies of Chile and Brazil. New York: Monthly Review Press, 1967.

_____. Lumpenbourgeoisie: Lumpendevelopment. New York: Monthly Review Press, 1972.

Frankel, Francine R. India's Green Revolution-Economic Gains and Political Costs. Princeton: Princeton University Press, 1971.

Freebairn, Donald K. "The Dichotomy of Prosperity and Poverty in Mexican Agriculture." Land Economics 45, February 1969.

Galeski, Boguslaw. "The Prospects for Collective Farming." LTC No. 95. Madison, Wisc.: Land Tenure Center, October 1973.

_____. "Types of Collective Farm in Poland." In Peter Worsley, ed., Two Blades of Grass. Manchester: Manchester University Press, 1971.

Goulet, Denis. "Political Will: The Key to Guinea-Bissau's Alternative Development Strategy."

212

International Development Review 19:4, 1977.

Griffin Keith. _The Political Economy of Agrarian Change_. Cambridge: Harvard University Press, 1974.

Grindle, Merilee S. "The Implementor: Political Constraints on Rural Development in Mexico." In Merilee S. Grindle, ed., _Politics and Policy Implementation in the Third World_. Princeton: Princeton University Press, 1980.

Harik, Iliya. _The Political Mobilization of Peasants: A Study of an Egyptian Community_. Bloomington: Indiana University Press, 1974.

Hinton, William. _Fanshen_. New York: Monthly Review Press, 1966.

Horton, Douglas Earl. _Haciendas and Cooperatives: A Study of Estate Organization, Land Reform and New Reform Enterprises in Peru_. Ithaca, N.Y.: Latin American Studies Program, Cornell University, 1976.

Ilchman, Warren F. and Norman T. Uphoff. "Beyond the Economics of Labor-Intensive Development: Politics and Administration." _Public Policy_ 22, Spring 1974.

_____. _The Political Economy of Change_. Berkeley: University of California Press, 1971.

International Bank for Reconstruction and Development. _Rural Development_. Washington: IBRD, 1975.

International Labor Office. _Employment, Growth and Basic Needs: A One-World Problem_. New York: Praeger, 1977.

Korten, David C., and Norman T. Uphoff. _Bureaucratic Reorientation for Participatory Rural Development_. Washington: National Association of Schools of Public Affairs and Administration, Working Paper No. 1, 1981.

Lamb, Geoff. _Peasant Politics: Conflict and Development in Murang'a_. New York: St. Martin's Press, 1974.

Lehmann, David. "Agrarian Reform in Chile, 1965-1972: An Essay in Contradictions." In David Lehmann, ed., _Peasants, Landlords, and Governments: Agrarian Reform in the Third World_. New York: Holmes & Meier Publishers, 1974.

_____. "Political Incorporation vs. Political Stability: The Case of the Chilean Agrarian Reform, 1965-1970." _Journal of Development Studies_ 7:4, July 1971.

Leys, Colin. _Underdevelopment in Kenya_. London: Heineman, 1975.

Lipsky, Michael. "Standing the Study of Public Policy Implementation on Its Head." In Walter Dean Burnham and Martha Wagner Weinberg, eds., _American Politics and Public Policy_. Cambridge: MIT Press, 1978.

Long, Norman, and David Winder. "From Peasant Community to Production Co-operative: An Analysis of Recent Government Policy in Peru." _Journal of Development Studies_ 12:1, October 1975.

McClintock, Cynthia. "Reform Governments and Policy

Implementation: Lessons from Peru." In Merilee
Grindle, ed., Politics and Policy Implementation
in the Third World. Princeton: Princeton University Press, 1980.

Migdal, Joel S. Peasants, Politics, and Revolution.
Princeton: Princeton University Press, 1975.

Montgomery, John D. "Allocation of Authority in Land
Reform Programs: A Comparative Study of Adminis-
trative Processes and Outputs." Administrative
Science Quarterly 17:1, March 1972.

_____. "The Populist Front in Rural Development:
or Shall We Eliminate the Bureaucrats and Get On
with the Job?" Public Administration Review 39:1,
January/February 1979.

Moore, Barrington, Jr. Social Origins of Dictatorship
and Democracy. Boston: Beacon, 1966.

Owens, Edgar, and Robert Shaw. Development Recon-
sidered-Bridging the Gap between Government and
People. Toronto and London: D. C. Heath & Co.,
1972.

Petras, James. Critical Perspectives on Imperialism and
Social Class in the Third World. New York: Monthly
Review Press, 1978.

Quick, Stephen A. "The Paradox of Popularity: 'Ideological' Program Implementation in Zambia." In
Merilee Grindle, ed., Politics and Policy Implementation in the Third World. Princeton: Princeton
University Press, 1980.

Roca, Santiago. "The Peruvian Sugar Cooperatives: Some
Fundamental Economic Problems, 1968-1972."
Economic Analysis and Workers' Management 9:1-2,
Belgrade, 1975.

Rochester, Anna. Lenin on the Agrarian Question. New
York: International Publishers, 1942.

Saul, John S. "The State in Post-Colonial Societies:
Tanzania." In Ralph Miliband and J. Saville, eds.,
Socialist Register, 1974.

Seers, Dudley. "The Meaning of Development." International Development Review 19:2, 1977.

_____. "The New Meaning of Development." Interna-
tional Development Review 19:3, 1977.

Sharpe, Kenneth Evan. Peasant Politics: Struggle in a
Dominican Village. Baltimore: Johns Hopkins University Press, 1977.

Singelmann, Peter. "Campesino Movements and Class Conflict in Latin America: The Functions of Exchange
and Power." Journal of Inter-American Studies and
World Affairs 16:1, February 1974.

_____. "Rural Collectivization and Dependent Capi-
talism: The Mexican Collective Ejido." Latin
American Perspectives 5:3, Issue 18, Summer 1978.

Soliman, Mohamed Ali. "Role of Cooperatives in Land
Reform." Development 21, 1979.

Stavenhagen, Rodolfo. "Collective Agriculture and

Capitalism in Mexico: A Way Out or a Dead End?" _Latin American Perspectives_ 2:2, Summer 1975.

Steenland, Kyle. _Agrarian Reform under Allende_. Albuquerque: University of New Mexico Press, 1977.

Stuart, Robert C. _The Collective Farm in Soviet Agriculture_. Lexington, Mass.: D. C. Heath, 1972.

Tai, Hung-chao. _Land Reform and Politics: A Comparative Analysis_. Berkeley: University of California Press, 1974.

Tarrow, Sidney. _From Center to Periphery: Alternative Models of National-Local Policy Impact and an Application to France and Italy_. Western Societies Program Occasional Paper No. 4, Ithaca, N.Y.: Western Societies Program, Center for International Studies, Cornell University, 1976.

Ulyanovsky, R. _Socialism and the Newly Independent Countries_. Moscow: Progress Publishers, 1974.

Uphoff, Norman T., and Milton J. Esman. _Local Organization for Rural Development in Asia_. Ithaca, N.Y.: Rural Development Committee, Center for International Studies, Cornell University, 1974.

Vanek, Jaroslav. _The Participatory Economy_. Ithaca, N. Y.: Cornell University Press, 1971.

_____. "The Worker-Managed Enterprise as an Institution." In Jaroslav Vanek, ed., _Self-Management_. Baltimore: Penguin, 1975.

Verba, Sidney, and Goldie Shabad. "Workers' Councils and Political Stratification: The Yugoslav Experience." _American Political Science Review_ 72:1, March 1978.

Wallerstein, I. "The State and Social Transformation: Will and Possibility." _Politics and Society_ 1, 1971.

Wignaraja, Poona. "A New Strategy for Development." _International Development Review_ 18:3, 1976.

Worsley, Peter, ed. _Two Blades of Grass: Rural Cooperatives in Agricultural Modernization_. Manchester: Manchester University Press, 1971.

Zemelman, Hugo. "The Political Problems of Transition: From the Assumption of Political Power to Revolutionary Power." In Federico Gil et al., eds., _Chile at the Turning Point_. Philadelphia: Institute for the Study of Human Issues, 1979.

Index